Shortcuts to Hit Songwriting

126 Proven Techniques for Writing Songs That Sell

ROBIN FREDERICK

TAXI MUSIC BOOKS™
Los Angeles, California

Published by:
TAXI Music Books, a division of MicroMini Media, Inc.
5010 Parkway Calabasas #200
Calabasas, CA 91302

Visit TAXI Music Books at:
www.songwritingbooks.com.

TAXI Music Books
Publisher: Michael Laskow
Executive Editor: Robin Frederick

Taxi Music Books and Taxi Books are trademarks of
MicroMini Media, Inc.

MicroMiniMedia

Cover Design by LeeAnn Nelson for Nelson Design
Page Design by Lynn Snyder for Crest Graphic Design

Acknowledgments

I owe a deep debt of gratitude to Michael Laskow who believed this book should be written and was willing to back up that belief by publishing it! To Andrea Brauer and Carolyn Rae Cole, thank you for helping to make this book and TAXI Music Books a reality. Thanks to Ronny S. Schiff for her knowledge and patience, and to Rachel Laskow and Bethany Rubin for their eagle-eyed proofreading. To LeeAnn Nelson of Nelson Design and Joyce L'Heureux and Lynn Snyder of Crest Graphic Design, my deep appreciation for contributing to the look and readability of this book.

I am grateful to the talented songwriters it has been my privilege to coach and the members of TAXI who have taught me to look at songs in new ways and who amaze me with the beauty of their emotions and willingness to take the risk of revealing them in lyrics and melodies. They continually remind me why I love songwriting and how important *every* song is.

As I worked on this book and studied the hit songs referred to in its pages, my respect for the writers of those hit songs grew immeasurably. I want to express my gratitude to *all* of the songwriters who create the melodies and lyrics that enrich our lives so much.

This book is dedicated to my sisters, Marcia and Carla, who love art and music. We've spent many glorious hours talking about it, living it, and sharing it. I could never have written this book without them.

Robin Frederick
Santa Monica, CA
July, 2008

About the Author

Over her twenty-five-year career in the music industry, Robin Frederick has written and produced hundreds of songs for television, record albums, musical theatre, and audio products. Her songs have aired on the Disney Channel and PBS stations and have been recorded by artists as diverse as Whoopi Goldberg, Mickey Mouse, and Nick Drake. As Director of A&R and Production for a division of Rhino Records, Robin oversaw the creation of more than sixty albums. She has served on the board of the Recording Academy (the GRAMMY organization) and is past president of Los Angeles Women in Music.

Through her work as a music jounalist in magazines, album notes, and online, Robin has shared her insights into songwriting with hundreds of thousands of readers. She currently oversees the screeners on TAXI's A&R Team, offering songwriting advice to TAXI's 11,000 members.

Table of Contents

PART THREE: Shortcuts to Hit Song Structure

PART FOUR: Shortcuts to Hit Lyrics

PART FIVE: **Shortcuts to Hit Melodies**

Part Six: Shortcuts to Hit Chords & Grooves

PART SEVEN: Shortcuts to Hit Songs

Foreword

Hit songwriters aren't born. That's a fact. How many songwriting prodigies can you name that have written a hit song before they finished elementary school?

You may have been born *talented*, but the truly great songwriters have added *craft* to their talent to become the most successful people in their field. If you want to be like them, you need to do what *they* did. Learn from the best.

Having been on the creative side of the music business since 1974 as an engineer and producer, then as Founder and Chief Executive Officer of the indie A&R company, TAXI, I've been privy to nearly every songwriting book published in modern times. As a voracious reader, I've read the majority of them.

Jason Blume and John Braheny have penned two of the books I consider to be the classics in this genre, but we haven't seen a *new* classic—a "must own"—in quite some time. The long wait is over.

Robin Frederick's *Shortcuts to Hit Songwriting* is so good, that after reading a draft of the first few chapters, I decided to personally start a publishing company and make Robin's book our flagship title.

Any of the top publishers in our arena would have jumped at the chance to sign a deal with Robin. Why did I risk so much of my money to beat them to the punch?

Because this book solves two huge problems that I believe are the reasons most songwriters never become *hit* songwriters: One, you don't have the time to learn song craft because you live in such a fast-paced world. Two, learning *anything* feels like work.

Shortcuts to Hit Songwriting is a quick-and-easy read because it is so engaging that you'll feel like you're hanging out with your best friend who just happens to *be* a successful songwriter. And it won't feel like work because it gives you something no other book on the subject does nearly as well, if at all. It tells you *why* these priceless tips and techniques are well … priceless!

Other authors may have taught you the "how." Let Robin Frederick be the first to give you the "why." Once you've got those keys to the kingdom, you'll never have to think about *what* contrast is or *why* it matters.

The techniques in this book will become second nature before you finish reading it. You're going to know what the top songwriters in the music business know, and the way Robin gives you those techniques will make them stick with you for the rest of your life.

You can feel good that *your* investment in this book was much smaller than mine, but your ultimate payoff could be huge by comparison. Go write a hit!

Michael Laskow
Founder & CEO, TAXI

Introduction

How to Get the Most From the Shortcuts!

The best way to use this book is to read it *while* you are writing songs. Use the Shortcuts to give you new ideas to try, send you in directions you might not have thought of, and suggest ways to get your songs started, moving forward, *and* completed. Your creativity is a muscle—the more you use it, the stronger it gets! Let the Shortcuts in this book suggest ways to give your creativity a workout.

You can read straight through the entire book, or focus on one aspect of songwriting by working through a section, or pick individual Shortcuts that look like they would be helpful for your songwriting situation. Whatever works best for you.

Experienced songwriter or beginner

If you've already written a few songs—or many songs—then you're in great shape. Most of the Shortcuts have a "Do It Now" box that suggests trying the Shortcut in a song of your own. Don't worry about messing up your song. One of the wonderful things about songwriting is that there's an "Undo Button." If you don't like the results, back up and return to what you wrote originally, then feel free to try something else.

If you've never written a song, that's fine, too. Start with the first few Shortcuts in each section: *Structure, Lyrics, Melody,* and *Chords.* They'll help you create the raw material you need to get going.

Hit song examples

As you read the Shortcuts, listen to the hit songs that are identified as examples. *This is the best way to learn to write hits for today's market.* You can hear the techniques described exactly as they are used in proven hits. In the back of the book on page 265, you'll find a list that includes many of these songs. If you don't already own them, I urge you to buy the songs in your genre and refer to them as you go through the book.

Using a "ghost song"

Several Shortcuts recommend using hit songs as patterns to practice writing new songs of your own. This is an excellent exercise that can help you expand your songwriting skills rapidly! However, remember that the hit song (or "ghost song") is protected by copyright. You can use it to help you practice songwriting techniques, but *be sure you don't use any of the melody or lyric in your own songs.*

See Shortcut 2 for a step-by-step guide to using hit songs as ghost songs.

No "music speak"!

There are no music notes, no treble or bass clefs, no fancy "music speak," and no time signatures in this book. The one and only time you'll see music notation is when it's used to show you what a song is *not*. You do not need to be able to read notes in order to write songs. Rely on your *ears*; listen to the hit songs referred to in the Shortcuts and use the "count to 4" technique in Shortcut 74 to study and learn melody writing skills.

Understanding the "why" of song craft

Don't take my word for it. Listen to the hits. Check things out for yourself!

Don't think you have to do something "just because" there's a rule that says so. Song craft is not a set of arbitrary rules; these concepts were developed from experience. Songwriters have been seeking ways to attract and hold listeners ever since the very first song. The techniques that have proven successful have become part of a body of knowledge, one that can help you communicate your ideas and feelings effectively to your listeners.

The emphasis in this book is on those elements of song craft that are characteristic of today's hit song styles. They are broken out into individual, manageable Shortcuts. This gives you the opportunity to listen to and try out specific techniques, experiencing the results for yourself.

Don't take my word for anything. Go check it out. Listen to the hit songs referred to in the Shortcuts and look for other examples on your own. Of course, there are always going to be exceptions and you'll find them. They don't disprove the effectiveness of the Shortcuts, only that you don't have to use every single one of them to write a song with hit potential. Not every hit song uses every Shortcut but they *all* use some of them!

Songwriter credits vs. recording artist credits

Throughout this book, the hit song examples are referred to by the song title and the name of the artist who recorded the best-known version. It's not my intention to slight the songwriters who wrote these wonderful songs. I just feel this is the best way to identify a song quickly and accurately. The Song List on page 265 includes many of the songs referred to in the book and the names of the songwriters.

For updates and new tips, visit www.RobinFrederick.com.

PART ONE

The Quick Start Manual

For you impatient types who want to jump in

feet first, I applaud you! So, let's get going.

The four Shortcuts in this section will introduce you

to important basic concepts and show you

the quickest way to begin acquiring the skills

you need to write hit songs …

Shortcut #1

Give the Music Industry What It Wants

If you give them what they want, <u>they</u> will want you!

"But," you ask with a puzzled look, "What *does* the industry want?" On the surface, it appears that most industry types don't have a clue what they want. After all, it's well known that A&R folk live by the saying, "It's safer to just say 'no'." But eventually, even *they* have to say yes or they won't be producing results for the label that pays their salary. It's the same for publishers, producers, and artists. So, what makes them say "YES" to a song?

What are they looking for?

Sometimes, we get so close to our own business that we don't see what's obvious, so let me give you an example that isn't music related. Let's say you're running a major airline and you're looking to buy a few airplanes for your fleet. Now, imagine someone arrives at your office and tries to sell you a DC-9. It was a great plane back in 1970 but it's not what you need to compete in today's jumbo jet, pack-'em-in-like-sardines airline business. Would you feel sorry for Joe DC-9 and buy his airplane? Or would you tell him it's not what you're looking for? No doubt about it, if you value your company and your job, you're going to usher him politely out of your office and tell him it's not in the cards. As you shut the door behind him, you hear him mumble under his breath that you're an idiot who just doesn't know what he wants. But, of course, you *do* know what you want—a product that is current, competitive, and meets the needs of today's market. Makes sense, right?

The music industry is no different. It has specific needs. The major record labels have a pipeline through which they promote and sell their artists in the most efficient and competitive way and they need to fill it. The most significant factor in this pipeline is mainstream, commercial radio. The record label's artists must release songs that can get national, mainstream radio airplay. *Got* to have it! If you can deliver that, then believe me, *they* will want *you*. But if you insist on trying to sell them what you think they *should* want, they will keep showing you the door.

The industry wants songs that are current and competitive. The goal: mainstream radio airplay.

How to find out what the music industry wants

Everything you need to know about what the music industry wants is available for FREEEEEE. It's on the radio every day. So …

1. **Listen to the radio**
   Check out the radio stations in your area that play hit songs in a style that interests you. Many large radio stations stream their programs online. Check their Web sites for more information.

2. **Check the radio airplay charts**
   You can see the current radio airplay and music charts online or in music trade magazines. (See "Shortcut Resources" on page 261 for the quickest

way to locate music charts.) Don't drive yourself crazy trying to figure out why each and every song is on a chart. Look for a general, overall sound and identify those songs that embody it. Write down a few titles that sound interesting.

3. Download the hit songs you're interested in

Look for hit songs you like!

When you have a shortlist of songs, go to iTunes or any of the legal download sites on the Internet. Check out the 30-second excerpts and when you hear a song you like, buy it. Remember, it's important to find something you *like*— you don't want to start hating what you do! If you don't hear anything that appeals to you, consider looking through different music styles and radio charts until you find something that attracts you.

4. Study the hits

Once you've found a song you like, spend some time studying it because this, right here, is what the music industry wants:

- Big, memorable, catchy hooks
- Plenty of contrast between song sections
- Lots of forward momentum in the melody and lyrics

Radio needs songs that keep their listeners tuned in.

Why does the industry, especially radio, want these things? *Because listeners respond to them.* Catchy hooks are *memorable*, contrast grabs *attention*, and forward momentum makes the audience feel like they're being swept along on a wave of *pure energy*. And as long as listeners like what they hear, they're going to keep listening … all the way to the commercials at the end. Which is just what radio wants them to do. Radio stations need to sell advertising time; the songs that are the most *useful* to radio are the ones that get listeners to stick around long enough to hear the ads. Record companies need radio airplay in order to sell music so they want to give radio *the kind of songs it can use.* See how this works?

That challenging, elegant, sophisticated song you wrote may be your own favorite—and it may be a good album track for you as an artist—but if it doesn't work well for mainstream radio, it won't attract major record labels and big publishers. *It's not a reflection of how good your song is, just an assessment of its usefulness to radio. Please remember that!*

5. Use the Shortcuts

Now look through your own songs. If they haven't got the kind of forward momentum, attention-getting hooks, and memorability you hear in the songs on the radio, consider writing a couple of new songs or rewriting the ones you have. Use the melodic, structural and lyric Shortcuts in this book. Blend these ideas with your own style to create something that is both uniquely your own *and* keeps listeners involved, interested, and tuned in. You can do it!

Shortcut #2

Use Hit Songs as "Ghost Songs"

The quickest, most effective Shortcut ever!

If you're in a hurry and want to start using the song craft that hit songwriters use *now*, practicing good songwriting skills, and hearing results, then this is the Shortcut for you! The best way to pick up the techniques and tools of writing solid, commercial songwriting in any genre—from mainstream Pop to Country to Rock—is to use an existing, contemporary hit song as a pattern for writing an original song of your own. I call the existing hit a "ghost song" because by the time you're finished writing, it will be invisible. No one will ever know it existed!

Why use a ghost song?

First, because songwriting is a lot like riding a bicycle—it's something you learn by doing. You want to embed the structure and "feel" of hit songs just like you acquire that sense of balance that keeps you upright on a bicycle. The ghost song functions like training wheels on your songwriting bike, providing support while allowing you to focus on one thing at a time—lyrics, melody, chords, or structure.

The second reason to use a ghost song is to make sure that as you practice your songwriting skills, you're not reinforcing old habits. We all have them: those predictable transitions, familiar melodic patterns, and cliché lyrics. Let the ghost song lead you into new discoveries and ideas with proven commercial, contemporary appeal.

Using a ghost song is like collaborating with the best songwriters in the business!

The third reason is to learn specific melody writing techniques in your genre. For example, contemporary Pop songs use a lot of rhythmic twists in their melodies. How do you pick up this technique? By using hit songs with this type of melody as ghost songs! You'll be embedding the feel of this melodic device as you write your own lyrics to the ghost song. Of course you could just learn to play the hit song but that's not nearly as effective as singing those melodies with your own lyrics. You lay claim to the melodic style by hearing it with *your* lyric.

And the last reason: writing a fresh melody and a vivid, insightful lyric while juggling a chord progression and song structure is *a lot* to demand of yourself. Most songwriters end up focusing on one aspect—melody, for example—while letting another, the lyric, lag behind. Unfortunately, when you step back to have a listen, all you hear is the raw, unfinished lyric. You're disappointed; you might even abandon the song. Wouldn't it make more sense to focus on just one facet of songwriting at a time, knowing you'll come back to the others? That's where a ghost song can really come in handy.

9 steps for turning a ghost song into a new song

In this series of steps, I suggest writing the new lyric first. You could do it the other way around, writing a new melody to a ghost song lyric, but I've found this particular sequence of steps works well. The ghost song melody gets embedded while you're working on the lyric, helping you develop an intuitive feel for the melodic devices the song is using. Getting the melody "under your skin" is a big plus.

REMEMBER! The melody and lyrics of the ghost song are protected by copyright. Using them as a pattern for writing a new song is an exercise. *Do not use any portion of a copyrighted song in any work of your own.*

> 1. **Listen to recent hit songs to find one you like.** You can pick a song from the Song List on page 265 or use "Shortcut Resources" on page 261 to help you locate current hits.

> 2. **Select one of these songs to use as a ghost song.** Not all songs work well. You want one with solid song structure and a melody you can sing along with. If you're having trouble with the next few steps, try a different song.

> 3. **Write out the complete lyric of the ghost song while becoming familiar with the melody.**

See Shortcut 21 for more info on song hooks.

> 4. **Locate the "hook."** The hook is the most memorable line in the song, often the first line of the chorus. Now, create a hook lyric of your own that you can comfortably sing to the ghost song melody in the same place. Notice I said "comfortably"; don't drive yourself crazy trying to match the original syllable for syllable. Make your hook lyric phrase something you're interested in writing about, an original idea. This is going to be *your* song.
>
> *Hint:* The hook lyric in a hit song usually, though not always, includes the title of the song. I'm going to suggest that *you always include your title in the hook line* since I want you to develop the rest of your lyric based on it.

> 5. **Next, fill in the rest of the chorus lyric.** If the ghost song repeats its hook phrase, repeat yours in the same place. Use your title/hook phrase as a guide to the lyric content. What questions does it suggest? What problem or solution? What emotions? This is *your* lyric so don't look to the ghost song for ideas on what to say. Read Shortcuts 44 through 53 for help in writing a verse and chorus based on your title.

> 6. **Write a verse lyric to the ghost song melody.** Develop your lyric using the suggestions in Shortcut 46. If you're writing only lyrics, go ahead and complete the song using the ghost song structure and melody as a guide. If you're writing both lyrics and melody, stop after your first verse and chorus lyric is completed and move on to Step 7.

➤ 7. **To start creating a new melody, one that's different from the ghost song, try using the natural melody *that's already embedded in your lyric*.** When we speak, we use many of the same components that make up a song melody—pitch (the highness or lowness of a note), volume, and rhythm. Try speaking the first line of your chorus lyric with plenty of emotion. Listen for the pitch and rhythm in the words, then exaggerate them. Read Shortcut 76 to learn more about this very useful technique.

➤ 8. **Once you've got a melody for your first line, you can use the pattern of repetition and variation you find in the ghost song to continue your melody.** If a melodic phrase repeats in the ghost song, try repeating yours; if it varies, change yours. This is a great way to get a feel for the highly organized melodies of hit songs. Check Shortcut 103 for more ideas on writing a new melody to your ghost song lyric.

➤ 9. **You can use the chord progression of the ghost song for your practice songs or come up with a new progression of your own.** Many songs use similar chord progressions.

(!) *The lyric and melody of the hit song are protected by copyright. This exercise is for practice only.*

When you finish this exercise, you'll have a song with a solid structure and you'll have given your creative muscles a workout, embedded new lyric and melody writing techniques, and practiced "riding the bicycle." The next song you write will reflect this experience!

Do It Now

Follow the steps for turning a ghost song into a new song. Go as far as you can, at least to Step 4. You can return to the song within a day or two and finish the remaining steps.

Hint: Try to approach this exercise with a sense of fun. Turn it into a game. When you're listening to the car radio, make up new chorus lyrics for hit songs, silly ones or serious ones. It's a great way to ease into it.

See "Shortcut Resources" on page 261 for information on where to find current music charts, hit songs, lyrics, and legal downloads.

Shortcut #3

Learn From the Hits!

Don't reinvent the wheel.
Study and learn from recent hit songs.

Check this out: An eccentric rich guy is offering a million dollars to anyone who can weave a basket that will hold water. You decide to go for it. First you try to figure it out on your own. After a few months, all you have to show for it is a lot of soggy basket-weaving material. So you read a few books on basket weaving; you learn a few techniques and your baskets start looking better but they're still not watertight.

Then you get serious. You do more research and locate a tribe whose elders know how to make baskets you could cook soup in! They have earned the million dollars themselves and they are happy to show you how. You travel across the world to study with them and over the course of a year or two you learn the secret of making baskets that hold water.

Go directly to the source to learn your craft! Study today's hit songs.

I have good news for you: It's easier to learn how to write *songs* that hold water than baskets! The "elders" are as close as your iPod or CD collection. If you work hard, you can pick up the skills in a few weeks. My point is this: Go directly to the source to learn your craft. *You'll save yourself a lot of time and frustration if you study those who have been there before you.*

Learn how to listen

To go to the source, to learn from hit songs, you'll need to listen to them a little differently than you would normally. If you want to understand how a hit song creates its magic, you need to know how it affects the listener. Since you can't get inside someone else's reactions, the best thing to do is to watch your own reactions. That's why I always suggest that you work with songs you like. These are the ones that *evoke a response* in you and you're going to be studying that response. The way to learn what works is to maintain an awareness of your own reactions and then ask why you react as you do.

Start listening now

Sit down with one of your favorite hit songs and listen through it just as you usually do but keep some portion of your attention focused on yourself. Notice how you react to the different parts of the song.

- Where does the song have the most emotional intensity for you?
- When did you take in information about the situation?
- Does the song pull you forward, making you want to keep listening?
- What part of the song do you want to hear again?
- After the song is over, what part of it do you remember?

Now, take some time to study how that song creates those effects by analyzing the lyrics, melody, and structure.

➢ **Listen to and analyze lyrics**
A good songwriter introduces information in a way that reveals the situation and characters as the song progresses, keeping the listener involved. Images, action words, and direct statements make it possible to feel what the singer is feeling. Shortcuts 47 through 73 will give you details on how to achieve these effects.

➢ **Look for structure**
A hit song has a clear organization that creates just the right amount of repetition and variation for listeners. There's also a roller coaster effect—energy increases in some places in the song and drops in others, keeping the song from becoming monotonous. Check out Shortcuts 21 through 35 to find out how to create a dynamic, identifiable structure for your song.

➢ **Learn what makes melodies tick**
A strong melody leads you forward into the next line and then the next section of the song. It develops in an organized way that never overwhelms. Hit songs use a mix of repetition and variation to create memorability and a sense of forward momentum. To take any melody apart and learn what makes it tick, you need to be able to *count beats*. Shortcut 74 will explain how to do this. With this simple skill, melodies become an open book for you to read and study.

Learn your craft—a range of skills you can use to produce the effects you want.

Don't reinvent the wheel ... or the song

Often songwriters try to reinvent songwriting, fearing that if they "borrow" from existing hits, they'll lose their individual voice. But, just like basket weaving, what you need to learn is *craft*, a range of techniques and skills you can use to produce the effects you want. Take that craft and use it for your own ends, fill it with your individual message and infuse it with your own distinctive style. Just as no two baskets are identical, no two songs are ever the same. Your song is always an expression of you.

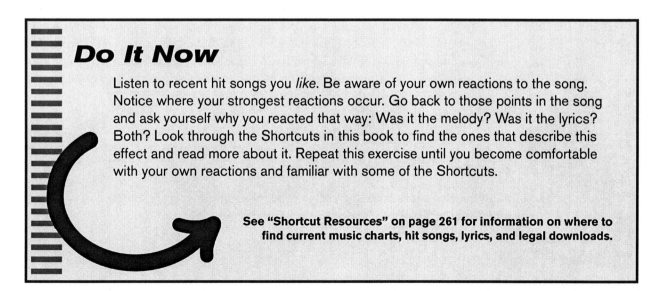

Do It Now

Listen to recent hit songs you *like*. Be aware of your own reactions to the song. Notice where your strongest reactions occur. Go back to those points in the song and ask yourself why you reacted that way: Was it the melody? Was it the lyrics? Both? Look through the Shortcuts in this book to find the ones that describe this effect and read more about it. Repeat this exercise until you become comfortable with your own reactions and familiar with some of the Shortcuts.

See "Shortcut Resources" on page 261 for information on where to find current music charts, hit songs, lyrics, and legal downloads.

Shortcut #4

"Quick Start" Resources

Find what you need to get started ... right now!

To begin studying hit songs and use them as ghost songs for writing practice, you'll need to know where to find recent hits in the genre you're interested in. (Read Shortcut 11 for more on choosing a genre.) This Shortcut will give you enough resources to get you started immediately. To learn more about the resources available to you, see page 261.

The Song List on page 265 includes songs that are used as examples in the book.

1. **Look through the Song List**

   You'll find a list of hit songs sorted by genre in the back of this book on page 265. These songs demonstrate many of the techniques described in the Shortcuts and offer an introduction to the four largest commercial genres: Pop, Rock, Country, and R&B/Soul.

2. **Buy the songs that interest you**

   If you don't already own them, buy a few of the songs on the Song List. You can purchase them with legal Internet download programs like iTunes. Choose songs you like—you'll be spending a lot of time with them.

3. **Find the lyrics**

   It's a good idea to listen to the lyrics in the context of the song so you hear how they work with the melody and structure. If you like to read the lyrics as you listen, you can find them in large compilations called "fake books" or online. As a songwriter, I recommend using the legal Web sites that pay for displaying lyrics. Yahoo! Music (www.music.yahoo.com/lyrics) is easy to search and likely to have all the hits you need.

4. **Find the chords**

   If the song has a straight-ahead, four-chord progression you can probably figure it out by listening. Otherwise, consider buying a fake book or sheet music. Fake books include the lyrics, chords, and lead melody line of dozens, often hundreds of songs. Sheet music can be bought online and downloaded immediately. The Web sites that provide free chords for hit songs are often incorrect and may not have the publisher permissions they need. I leave the decision of whether or not to use those sites up to you.

Do It Now

Go through the Song List on page 265 and buy the songs you're interested in. Then work through Shortcuts 2 and 3 using those songs.

PART TWO

Lay the Shortcuts Groundwork

To do your best work as a songwriter, make certain

you're prepared for the demands of the job.

Whether it's organizing your resources,

picking up new skills, or creating a workspace,

be sure you have everything you need

to do the job right …

Shortcut #5

What Is a Hit Song?
You Might Be Surprised

Know what you're aiming for so you can hit your target.

The answer to the question "What is a hit song?" might seem obvious: 1. It's one that gets a lot of radio airplay; and 2. it sells a lot of records. The problem with this definition is that it consists of two elements that are beyond your control. Sounds to me like a perfect setup for frustration. Now, I'm not saying that hit songs *do not* have big sales and lots of radio play but let's assume that those things are the *result* of writing a hit song and not the definition of one. So, what *is* a hit song? For that matter, what is a song?

Most people would agree that the definition of a song is: *a melody with lyrics.* Many songwriters include chords in that definition (although the Copyright Office doesn't—melody and words are all that's required for a copyright). So, if words, melody, and chords are all that's needed, then is this a song?

What's the simplest and most useful definition of a song?

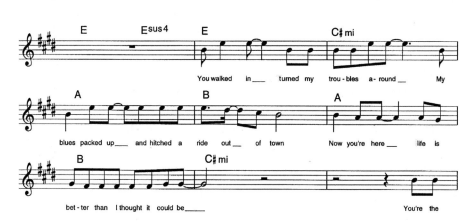

⇐ Not this!

It isn't! Why not? Because it's just a *representation* of a song. Looking at the dots and lines doesn't do anything for you emotionally—they just sit there on the page. A song does something to us, it changes our mood, affects our feelings. This picture doesn't.

A song evokes an emotional reaction

When you think about the songs you like best, you recall not only what they sound like, but how they make you feel. That's what a song is all about—*an emotional reaction* to the melody, lyrics, and chords. A song can evoke feelings of love, loss, joy, and grief, paint a picture and pull us into the scene, make us feel sexy or sad. It can be moving, compelling, satisfying, exciting, or seductive. So now, let's try another definition of a song:

A song is a highly effective means of communicating emotion.

⇐ This!

Hit songs with plenty of emotional punch:

"Who Knew"
(P!nk)

"Live Like You Were Dying"
(Tim McGraw)

"For A Moment Like This"
(Kelly Clarkson)

"Rise Above This"
(Seether)

"If I Ain't Got You"
(Alicia Keys)

If a song is emotionally effective—if it moves you, if it speaks to your feelings—you will want to hear it again. If a song moves *a lot* of people, then a lot of people will want to hear it again and *that* is a hit song.

A hit song is one that communicates emotion to a lot of people.

Unlike big sales and huge radio play, creating emotion in your listeners is something that *is* within your control. By bringing your own insights and inspiration to your song and communicating these clearly and effectively through the use of *song craft,* you can reach out to listeners and offer them a powerful emotional experience, the kind that will bring them back to your song again and again. The Shortcuts in this book give you a good idea of the various ways you can use song craft to help you communicate with listeners. The insights and inspiration are up to you! Put these all together and you're on the road to writing a hit!

Do It Now

Choose a hit song you like, the more recent the better, but oldies are all right, too. (Avoid songs you *don't* like; they will defeat the purpose of this exercise. And, anyway, it's just not as much fun.)

Observe your own emotional reactions as you listen to the song. What do you like about this song? How does it make you feel? Why do you enjoy listening to it? Try to identify a few specific things the melody and lyrics are doing that create a reaction in you.

See "Shortcut Resources" on page 261 for information on where to find current music charts, hit songs, lyrics, and legal downloads.

Shortcut #6

Be Sure You Really Want
to Write Hit Songs

Clear out any negative feelings you have about writing hits.

There are two kinds of songs: hit songs and album cuts.

Album cuts are anything you want to write. If you're the artist, you can write a 13-minute "Happy Birthday" song to your dog and put it on your album! Your loyal fans, the ones who hang on your every word, will probably buy it; after all, they love you and they are fascinated by everything about you, including your dog. However, radio is not likely to play it, especially mainstream radio. Film and TV projects are also not likely to use it unless they have a specific scene about a doggie birthday party. It's great that you wrote this song for your album but if album cuts are all you write, eventually you might notice that your music isn't creating any new fans for you, CD sales are not going well, the marketing campaign isn't creating any buzz, and your record label is giving you the "goodbye" look.

Why can't I just write album cuts?

Songs that use the kind of song craft described in this book—ones that sound like they *could* be hits—reach out to listeners, creating new fans who want to hear more of your music. That's a very good reason to have a couple of strong hit songs on every album. These are the ones that drive everything else: marketing, radio play, touring. Every artist needs them! Independent artists, I'm talking to *you*. You need them to get a deal with a major or even a mid-sized record label! Songwriters, I'm talking to *you!* This is what publishers need to hear from you! Planning on pitching your songs to film and TV shows? This is the type of song that will give you your best shot!

Trying to write the impossible song

Some artists feel that writing hit-style songs makes them "less authentic," that they're pandering to the whims of the masses, selling out to the almighty buck. Since this attitude makes it just about impossible to write a hit song, they don't really have anything to worry about. Writing a song you *don't* like or respect is hard to do. Why? Because every time you decide to keep or throw away a line, it's a personal decision based on your own taste and intuition. How can you make those decisions if you don't have an emotional connection with your song? *You can't.*

Read Shortcut 8 to find out why mediocre doesn't cut it.

As I mention in Shortcut 8 "No Hacks Need Apply," I don't want you to think of hit songs as "dumbed down" or mediocre. You're going to create a *great* song, your best song, *and* make it accessible to listeners. You're not going to hold back and write something only halfway decent; you're going to push yourself harder than you ever have before. That's the attitude it takes to write the hit songs *you* are going to write.

What do you want?

Ask yourself: Do I really want commercial success? Would I like to hear my songs on the latest hot TV series? Would I like to have one of my songs played on major college radio stations, then crossover to mainstream radio? If the answer is "yes," then clear your mind of any preconceptions or negative feelings you have about writing hit songs; these will only get in the way and make a difficult job that much harder. The "Do It Now" steps in this Shortcut will help you focus on the hit songs you want to write and create the attitude that will take you there. Good luck to you!!!

Do It Now

Make a list of hit songs you like, ones that have moved you. They can be from the past or present. There are plenty of Top 100 song lists and Desert Island lists online. Check out a few of those and see if they remind you of more songs to add to your list.

Pick a few of these songs and ask yourself what it is that makes them memorable for you? What moves you? What makes you want to hear them again? What do you remember most about them—a lyric line? Melody line? A whole chorus?

Listen to current hit songs and find at least one you wish you had written.

Now, tell yourself you are going to write songs *that good!* Because you are! Keep your favorite songs handy. Use them as ghost songs, especially the recent ones. Paint a bulls-eye around a title and put it on your wall. *This* is what you are aiming for.

See "Shortcut Resources" on page 261 for information on where to find current music charts, hit songs, lyrics, and legal downloads.

Shortcut #7

Make Song Craft Work for You

Use craft to make your song compelling, accessible, and memorable.

As songwriters, we sometimes think that if we feel an emotion or think a thought while writing a song, it will somehow, magically, be communicated to listeners. Occasionally, accidentally, that happens but, more often than not, listeners don't seem to get it. They're not as moved or as involved in the song as we think they ought to be. What's happening here? Perhaps, the emotion that launched the song is simply not being communicated to listeners in a way they can understand and feel. This is where song craft can be a lifesaver! Try using song craft to embed the emotional message of your song where listeners can't miss it!

Communication doesn't happen by accident!

The elements of song craft have been developed over centuries by songwriters who figured out what works by trial and error. The tools we use now are road-tested, proven techniques. You don't have to reinvent the wheel (or songwriting) every time you write. There are structural, melodic, and lyric writing techniques that we know work on listeners to get them involved. They're right here in the Shortcuts in this book! You can use these techniques to make your songs more exciting, moving, and memorable.

Song craft is at your service

Here's an example of song craft at work: Many times listeners fail to respond to a song simply because they missed an important piece of information; perhaps because you didn't have their attention when a crucial bit of emotional insight went by. Songwriters have noticed that creating contrast just before or during an important line, like the hook, can make listeners suddenly tune in and take notice. You might suddenly leap from a low to a high note (an interval jump) on the first word of the line or stretch out the pace of the words to create contrast in pace. Listeners will notice there's something different going on and they'll pay attention, it's just human nature. Now you've got them involved and whatever it is you want to say, they'll hear it! This is just *one* example of how craft can make your song more accessible and help get your message across.

Read Shortcut 22 for more on using contrast.

Keep in mind that craft is never a substitute for heart. It's *your* message, *your* story, *your* emotions that are driving the song. Song craft is there to deliver the message and make sure it gets heard. But the message, ultimately, is yours. If you've got an original, compelling, and authentic message, song craft can ensure your listeners hear and feel the emotion you want them to experience!

It's YOU!!!

There are two important things to remember about song craft:

*Important idea!
Think about
this one.*

**If you have something to say, but no song craft ...
listeners may not hear you.**

**If you have song craft, but nothing to say ...
listeners may not care.**

Craft is *always* at the service of the song, *never* the other way around. It's there to help you communicate effectively and memorably but it's no substitute for YOU!

What song craft can do for you

So let's get back to that song—the one that wasn't grabbing listeners and shaking them up—and see what you can do to change that.

- Are you giving listeners enough lyric information and developing it in a way they can follow?

- Is your melody memorable, fresh, and compelling?

- Are you using contrast to keep and hold attention?

- Is there enough repetition to provide a sense of structure but not so much that listeners get bored?

*What is a
hit song?
See Shortcut 5.*

All of these issues are addressed in the lyric, melody, and structure Shortcuts in this book. Read through a few of the Shortcuts then listen to one of your own songs to see if you can add impact and clarity for listeners by applying these ideas. Remember, a hit song is one that effectively communicates emotion to listeners. The tools of the song craft trade are there to help you do exactly that!

Do It Now

Listen to hit songs you like and notice how the songwriters use craft to keep and hold your attention. Some things to watch for are:

- Contrast between verse and chorus in note range or pace of the words

- Lyric lines that pull you into the emotion, characters, and situation

- A strong hook that sums up the emotional heart of the song

- A melody that's easy to remember yet fresh and supports the lyric well

If you don't know how to look for these things, read through some of the melody and lyric Shortcuts for more information.

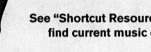

**See "Shortcut Resources" on page 261 for information on where to
find current music charts, hit songs, lyrics, and legal downloads.**

Shortcut #8

Don't Make the "Formula Song" Mistake

This is no place for hack writers!

In my songwriting workshops and classes, I'm often confronted with the belief that song craft is somehow *the enemy*, that if you write well-crafted songs they will somehow be mediocre, lifeless, lacking in inspiration, or mere exercises in writing to a "formula." And such a thing could *never* be an authentic expression of *you!* It's merely hack writing.

Excuse me while I take you on a short detour. Back in the good ol' 16th Century, the equivalent of today's big hit song was the sonnet. Every poet worth his Elizabethan salt did some serious sonnet writing. Talk about needing to have a command of your craft! This is a tough form that makes a lot of demands on the writer: a tight rhyme scheme, specific line lengths and meter. Sure, there were plenty of hack Elizabethan poets who wrote mediocre, lifeless but well-crafted sonnets. Then there was Shakespeare; he also wrote well-crafted sonnets but his soaring, evocative, deep, intriguing poems blew those hacks away. We don't think of Shakespeare as a guy who wrote "formula" sonnets. He was the master of his craft; it never mastered him. Hacks are writers who never rise above their craft. They don't use it; it uses them.

What is hack writing?

Song craft is not a formula

The majority of hit songs are well crafted—they have the kind of structure, lyric focus, and melodic dynamics that keep listeners involved. But does that make them "formula" songs? If that were all these songs had, if hit songs lacked the inspiration, energy, life, and heart we value so highly, they wouldn't attract listeners. You've got to have both.

One of my favorite Adult Contemporary (AC) hit songs is "Unwritten" sung and co-written by Natasha Bedingfield. This is a remarkably well-crafted song from its tight lyric palette of images (books and writing, indoors and outdoors, dark and light) to its rhythmically sophisticated melodic phrasing. The combination of message, originality, and proven song craft is irresistible. It was at the top of the music charts for many months so it obviously appealed to a lot of listeners. Emotionally it had a strong message and communicated it with intensity and honesty—a great blend of heart and craft.

Find a balance of heart and craft. Check out Shortcut 15 for ideas.

So why do songwriters equate song craft with hack writing? I think it's because when we hear a really good song, like "Unwritten," the craft is *invisible*, we don't even notice it. On the other hand, when we hear a mediocre song that doesn't move us, *all* we hear is the craft!

Be the master of your craft. Use it to give your songs clarity, structure, development, and dynamics. These are the things that pull listeners into your song. Once they get there, the message and the humanity are up to you!

Do It Now

Listen to some of your favorite hit songs, ones that truly move you. Ask yourself what elements of craft are being used in this song. For example:

- How does the lyric convey information about what the singer is feeling?
- How does the first verse pull you into the situation?
- How does the lyric develop?
- What is your favorite part of the melody?
- How does the melody work to support the lyric?
- What is the hook, how often is it repeated, and what makes it memorable?
- What is the structure of the song?
- How does the writer create that structure?

All these elements of craft work together to involve you in the song. The overall effect, though, is greater than the sum of the craft. Ultimately the song moves you because the writer had something to say and used craft to say it!

See "Shortcut Resources" on page 261 for information on where to find current music charts, hit songs, lyrics, and legal downloads.

Shortcut #9

Compete With the Front-Runners

To write at a level that gets you noticed, aim for the best.

Just imagine for a moment that you're a race car driver competing at the Indy 500. You and your hugely powerful car are tuned up to perfection. You're ready to prove you've got the right stuff. The starting gun fires and you peel out along with the rest of the competition. By the end of the first turn you are right where you want to be: lined up fender to fender with the *last* car in the pack. Your strategy is to remain inches ahead of him throughout the entire race and across the finish line. He's the guy you plan to beat!

Of course, this is a ridiculous scenario. No one competes with the last car in a race. A successful racing strategy would be to beat the car that's in front of the pack. Now, why would you settle for anything less in your songwriting?

Don't compete with the last car in a race!

If you're like most other songwriters, at one time or another you've said, "My songs are better than the junk that's on the radio!" It's likely that some of your songs *are* better than some of the songs on the radio. But imagine the Top 40 radio charts are a kind of racetrack. Are you competing with the song that's in slot number 40? That strategy would be about as effective as competing with the last car in a race. Perhaps, there's a song that's in slot number 10 that sounds fairly weak but that "car" is being driven by an artist with a huge fan base and a long string of hits behind her. Competing with that song is not a good strategy either.

Face it … you're not competing with the worst, you're competing with the best. For that matter, you're not competing with "the mediocre," either. If that's your goal, you will always be mediocre. You can be *better* than that. You have to be!

So don't toss off a half-written, unfocused song with the excuse that it's good enough because it's better than that TV show theme written by the producer's son-in-law. Your competition is the front-runner, the hit song that got to the top because it was well-crafted, emotionally evocative, and communicated its message effectively to a lot of listeners. That's what you're aiming for. So … study the best. Learn from the best. Push yourself to *be* the best!

Choose a winning strategy!

Shortcut #10

Learn to Reverse Engineer the Competition

Take apart the hits to see what makes them tick.

Any business that wants to compete successfully needs to know what the competition is doing. So what do they do? They buy the product made by the leader in their field and take it apart to see how it's made. It's called "reverse engineering." It doesn't matter whether the product is a car or a can of beans, reverse engineering will tell you what the components are and how they were put together to create a successful product. Guess what … *you* can do the same thing with hit songs! Of course, like the competition's product, you can't steal the components. There are copyrights involved. But you *can* learn from success and apply what you learn to your own songs.

How to reverse engineer a song

Take apart a successful song to see how it works.

Choose a recent hit song you admire, the kind of song you'd like to write. Listen to the song and note your reactions. (Read Shortcut 3 to learn more about how to do this.) Write down the lyrics. Get familiar enough with the song that you can hum or sing the melody. Now you're ready to take a look at the elements of this song that contributed to its success!

Structure

- Identify the different sections of the song. The majority of hit songs have both a verse and chorus section. Many have a bridge after the second chorus. On your lyric sheet, indicate where each section of the song begins.
- Notice how the sections are organized. Make a list of the song sections in the order they occur in the song.
- How does the song let you know which section you are listening to? Write down the differences between each section.

To find out more about basic song structure and organization, read the "Shortcuts to Hit Song Structure" section of this book.

Lyrics

- Read through the first verse and notice how the lyric introduces the theme or situation of the song. In your own words, sum up the information in the first verse.
- How does the first verse lead you to the chorus? In your own words, write your answer next to the first verse lyric.
- Read the chorus lyric. What information does it give you about the emotions or situation in the song? Write your answer next to the chorus.
- Is there a line that sums up the central idea of the song? What is it and where does it occur in the chorus?

Ask similar questions in each song section and write down your answers. You'll end up with a good idea of how this lyric developed and kept you, the listener, involved. You'll find more information in the "Shortcuts to Hit Lyrics" section.

Melody

- Hum or sing the verse melody, leaving out the lyrics (just sing "da-da" instead of the words).
- Within the verse, notice which melody lines repeat. On your lyric sheet, indicate which lines those are.
- Are there any lines in the verse that are not repeats of another line? Indicate those lines on your lyric sheet.
- Look at the melody lines just before the chorus. Do they build energy or anticipation?
- Hum or sing the chorus melody. Note the pattern of repetition and change in the chorus melody and indicate the pattern on the lyric sheet.
- What does the first line of the chorus melody do that sets it apart from the verse melody? Write that down.
- Does the last line of the chorus create a sense of completion?

There are Shortcuts that can tell you more about all of these melodic concepts.

Repetition and change in melody, building anticipation, and creating a sense of completion are important aspects of contemporary hit melodies. See the "Shortcuts to Hit Melodies" section to learn more about creating these effects.

Production

While production—the instrumental arrangement and mix—contributes to a record's success, in most cases the production is supporting *what the song is already doing*. For instance, the instrumental arrangement may increase in volume and complexity as the melody builds to the chorus or it may drop out instruments to enhance the more intimate lyric feel of a verse.

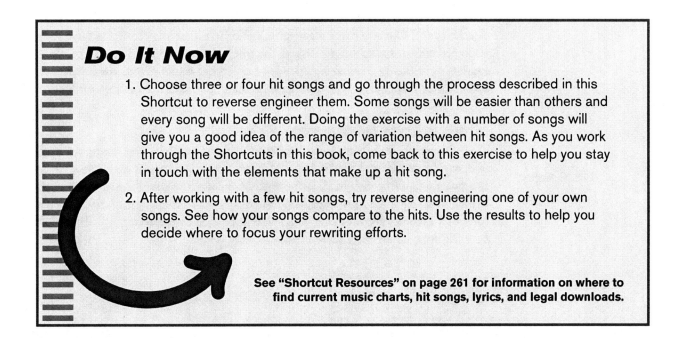

Do It Now

1. Choose three or four hit songs and go through the process described in this Shortcut to reverse engineer them. Some songs will be easier than others and every song will be different. Doing the exercise with a number of songs will give you a good idea of the range of variation between hit songs. As you work through the Shortcuts in this book, come back to this exercise to help you stay in touch with the elements that make up a hit song.

2. After working with a few hit songs, try reverse engineering one of your own songs. See how your songs compare to the hits. Use the results to help you decide where to focus your rewriting efforts.

See "Shortcut Resources" on page 261 for information on where to find current music charts, hit songs, lyrics, and legal downloads.

Shortcut #11

Choose a Genre

Learn and practice writing in one style at a time.

Music genres have been around for hundreds of years. A couple centuries ago, there were just a few genres: religious music, classical music, dance music, romantic ballads and folk songs. Today we have numerous genres with names like Country, Rock, Pop, Dance, Electronica, Alternative, R&B, Rap, Americana and sub-genres such as Neo-Traditional Country, Dance-Pop, Teen-Pop, EMO, and Neo-Soul. Wikipedia lists 26 sub-genres of Blues! How do you deal with all this?!!

Genres exist to help listeners find your music.

There's only one important thing to keep in mind: All of these genres have been separated, named, and identified because they appeal to different audiences. There's nothing inherently better or worse, more or less creative about any of them. But they differ markedly in melodic and lyric style, themes, chord progressions, rhythm, and production because each has an audience that likes a certain sound. Listeners who like Modern Rock generally aren't crazy about Neo-Traditional Country and vice versa. Think of your own likes and dislikes; there are probably certain styles of music you love and others you don't like at all. Each set of listeners wants to easily find the artists and music they like. Record labels, radio, and song publishers want to deliver it to them! So the music industry began classifying the music based on similarities of sound and audience.

So why is this important to you?

If you write a song that does *not* share the melodic, lyric, or thematic characteristics of a mainstream, commercial music genre, you're going to have a tough time when it comes to selling it. Publishers and record labels are looking for songs and artists who sound like they could be played on major radio stations. If your song doesn't sound like any particular genre, radio isn't likely to play it because their audience may not respond positively. You might have success selling it in a niche market or releasing it as an independent artist and seeking your own audience, but as far as it becoming a mainstream hit song, the odds are not in your favor.

Start with a genre you like

Choose a genre with songs you like!

There's nothing to prevent you from writing in more than one genre but each will require study and research so consider focusing on just one until you're thoroughly familiar with it. If you're unsure which genre you want to write in, go through the Song List on page 265. Listen to several songs in each style. Find a style that includes three or four songs you like. Then read Shortcuts 117 and 118 to learn more about the characteristics of that genre.

Shortcut #12

Acquire the Skills and Tools You Need

These six must-haves will put hit songwriting within your reach.

Just like a chef preparing to cook a masterpiece, you'll need to gather a few ingredients and acquire the tools of your trade to get started. Here's a list of the basic tools and skills you need in order to whip up a hit.

Acquire these six basic skills and tools

➤ **Knowledge of song craft**
The knowledge you need to write songs that have hit potential is right here in this book. It's the most important tool you have. Read "How to Get the Most From the Shortcuts!" for some good ideas on how to proceed.

➤ **Access to recent hit songs**
You're going to use hit songs to learn your craft, keep up to date with new techniques, and aim your songs straight at your target market. Check out "Shortcut Resources" on page 261 to find resources for locating and buying hit songs.

➤ **A small, easy-to-use recording device (cassette or digital)**
Even if you have an elaborate home recording studio, a small, handy recording device is a valuable tool. Use it to keep track of melody, lyric, and chord ideas, as well as works-in-progress and ghost song practice sessions. Look for a recorder (cassette or digital) that's easy to operate; you don't want to have to stop and set up equipment in order to get your ideas down. Make sure the recorder has number tracking or a file ID system so you can organize your ideas and keep track of them in a notebook or on computer.

Keep things easy & inexpensive to start with. You can upgrade later.

➤ **Internet access**
If you want to compete in the hit song market, Internet access has become a necessity. You can buy recent hit songs cheaply, find collaborators, and search for chord help at the click of a mouse. For music downloads and uploads a high-speed Internet connection (DSL or cable) may be required. If you don't own a computer, library computers will allow you to do research but not purchase and download music.

➤ **A keyboard or guitar**
If you're writing lyrics only, you can skip this step and the next one. For those who are writing lyrics *and* music, if you don't have a keyboard or guitar, check out the wide variety of instruments available in every price range. You don't need top-of-the-line sound quality for writing songs! Look for an electronic keyboard or acoustic guitar in your price range that's comfortable and easy to use. When buying a keyboard, get one that's capable of *transposing*, i.e., moving the chords and notes up or down. Guitarists, buy a *capo* so you can move chords up.

Optional: It's a good idea to get a keyboard with a MIDI input and output since you may want to work with a computer sequencer program at some point. Some keyboards come with built-in rhythms that can be useful when you're writing.

> **The ability to play six chords on keyboard or guitar**
> To write the chords that go with your melody, you'll need to be able to play six basic chords on guitar or keyboard. See Shortcuts 104 through 107 to learn chord basics.

No note-reading required

No note-reading needed!

Even if you plan on writing your own melodies and chords, *you don't need to read or write music notes.* Notes are just a convenient way to remember melodies. Use your handheld recorder and just sing your melody and lyrics into it. That will do just fine.

Music software is optional

There are some wonderful and inexpensive software programs on the market. These are a lot of fun and can spark plenty of creative ideas. Most include a library of drum loops that can provide a solid rhythmic feel for your song. For more information, See "Shortcut Resources" on page 261.

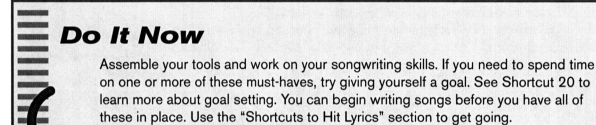

Do It Now

Assemble your tools and work on your songwriting skills. If you need to spend time on one or more of these must-haves, try giving yourself a goal. See Shortcut 20 to learn more about goal setting. You can begin writing songs before you have all of these in place. Use the "Shortcuts to Hit Lyrics" section to get going.

Shortcut #13

Make a Creative Space for Your Songwriting

Creative spaces come in all shapes and sizes.

If you have a home studio where you can close the door and work for hours, congratulations! If you've got a powerful computer with plenty of music software, a good microphone, and a guitar or MIDI keyboard, you're in great shape! But if all you have is a laptop and a desk, you can still claim a creative songwriting space for yourself.

You don't need to think of a creative space as an entire room with a door to keep out the rest of the world. There are many, smaller creative spaces in your life if you just look for them.

A creative space can be small, portable, and self-contained.

A notebook is a creative space

This is your chief creative space. Keep a notebook to write down titles, lines, and ideas as they occur to you. It's faster and it can be more easily integrated into your daily life than a computer. For instance, if you get an idea in the middle of a TV show or washing dishes or going for a walk, grab your notebook and write it down.

Don't depend on remembering a great line; it'll be gone before you know it. If a line strikes you with enough force to make you notice it, then it's trying to tell you something. Acknowledge that by putting it in your notebook. Later on, you can reassess whether it's useful or not.

Keep a second notebook in the car and periodically transfer your ideas from the car notebook to your master notebook. That way everything's in one place when you're ready to write. Choose a style of notebook you're comfortable with. A small spiral notebook or a three-ring binder—whatever feels comfortable for you.

A handheld recorder is a creative space

Whether you use a handheld cassette or digital recorder, just like a notebook it's a place where you keep your creative input. Keep it with you and whip it out for melody and rhythm ideas. Be sure to keep a logbook or computer file with a short description of your ideas and where they are located so you can go back and work on them.

Make sure your recorder is easy to use!

A table and chair can be a creative space!

A flat working space—whether it's a desk or the kitchen table—can be transformed into a mini-home studio. You'll need room to spread out your lyrics. Your studio equipment is your handheld recorder with the built-in microphone and, now, you're the engineer. If you do your songwriting on guitar, you're ready to go. If you write on keyboard, there are inexpensive instruments with built-in speakers that will keep your setup really simple and self-contained. You can set up for a writing session in a few minutes and take it down just as quickly.

A computer is a creative space

If you have a computer, you have a home studio. There are many music software programs that will record your voice, guitar or keyboard, create instrumental and rhythm tracks, suggest chord progressions and arrange tracks. Check the Internet and recent books on home recording for more information. See "Shortcut Resources" on page 261 for a few suggestions. If you haven't used one of these programs before, start with a low-priced version, or a free demo, and work your way up to the more expensive, complicated programs with all the bells and whistles.

Be sure to back up everything as you work and keep your back-up media in a safe place.

You've even got remote recording!

Sometimes a great idea for a song occurs to you when you're not anywhere near a creative space. If you're running errands, commuting, or at work and don't have your handheld recorder with you, call your voice mail or answering machine and leave a message for yourself. Sing your idea into the phone. Remember to include a count-off at the beginning so you know the starting beat and the tempo.

It's all inside!

Your creative space is in your head

You always have your creative space with you. It's your knowledge. It's your inspiration. It's the songs you love and listen to. It's your experience and practice. Everything else is just a means of getting it out of you and into a form other people can hear.

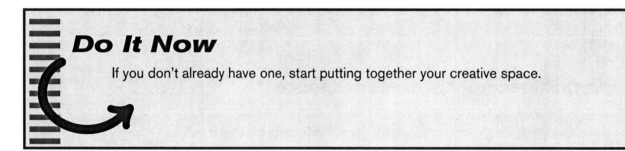

Do It Now

If you don't already have one, start putting together your creative space.

Shortcut #14

Learn Some New Habits

Make your songwriting habits work constructively for you.

After you've written a few songs, you may notice that you tend to write similar endings for sections, or you're using the same melodic patterns over and over, or there's a particular word or phrase you always fall back on to express a certain emotion. These are songwriting habits. All songwriters have them.

But that's my authentic voice!
No, it's not

Your habitual choices tend to be the first things that come up for you when you're writing. Because they come so easily, they feel natural and organic. But, while the melodies or lyrics that occur to you spontaneously may feel like an authentic part of you, these are actually a result of the music that imprinted itself when you were most impressionable, usually your late teens and early twenties. These are limited resources; there are only so many choices they can offer you. As you continue to write, it's essential that you *add to* this stockpile of influences and musical ideas by consciously embedding new ones. If you don't …

Don't mistake your habits for your authentic voice!

- Your songs will begin to sound dated.

- You'll stop growing as a songwriter.

- You'll lack the flexibility needed to work professionally.

Making habits work for you

Songwriting habits are not bad things to have, not by any means! They're an important part of your writing process. While your song is in the early stages and you're still forming the emotional content, you don't want to be thinking about things like, "Should I use an interval jump here or start my chorus two beats earlier than expected?" That kind of question is sure to distract you from the emotions at the heart of your song.

Instead, if you're continually embedding new habits and techniques based on current hit songs, you'll feel an *impulse* to do something new. Like all the old, outdated habits, it will just "be there," offering you an interesting, contemporary-sounding choice.

New habits can offer fresh choices when you're writing.

So get some new habits!!!

At first, using a new technique is something you have to consciously make yourself do. It's definitely *not* spontaneous. However, like riding a bicycle, the more you practice it, the more effortless it becomes. At a certain point the new technique will be something that occurs to you as a spontaneous choice while you're writing. It will be a new habit. That's the goal.

To create a new habit:

➢ **Step 1.** Choose a current hit song that sounds like something you'd like to write.

➢ **Step 2.** Identify what the song is doing that appeals to you. If the melody sounds fresh and exciting, spend some time studying how it's put together. (Shortcuts 74 and 75 can help you analyze a hit song melody.) Perhaps the lyric is vivid and compelling. Take a look at how the lyric creates that effect. Are there a lot of action words or images? Does the chorus payoff with strength? Check to see if you're using these melody and lyric techniques in your own songs. If not …

Use ghost songs to help you learn new habits.

➢ **Step 3.** Use the hit song as a ghost song. If your goal is to use more action in your lyrics, try using action words where the ghost song does. If your goal is to embed new melody writing techniques, start your melodic phrases where the ghost song does, emphasize the same beats. Read Shortcut 2 for a step-by-step guide.

➢ **Step 4.** Now, write a song of your own, without using a ghost song, and make an effort to use the new technique. You may find that it's already partially embedded and it's starting to come naturally. If not, repeat Step 3.

Thinking or feeling, which comes first?

When I'm analyzing a song in one of my workshops, showing people some of the amazing things that go on in today's hits, I'm frequently asked if I think the songwriter was focusing on those things while he was writing. My answer is no; the songwriter was most likely focused on the emotional message of the song. However, his habits were offering him intriguing, contemporary, workable choices. Naturally, plenty of things were tweaked during the rewriting phase but during the initial, roughing-out process, the songwriter was able to emphasize feeling over thinking because he had embedded useable, current-sounding habits. Keep your habits up to date by regularly going through hit songs, looking for new melody and lyric approaches and embedding new songwriting techniques.

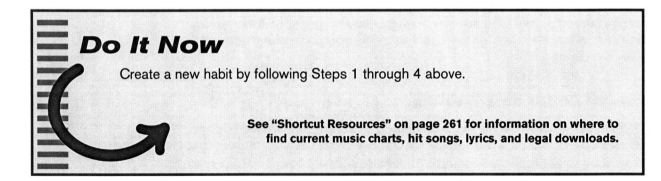

Do It Now

Create a new habit by following Steps 1 through 4 above.

See "Shortcut Resources" on page 261 for information on where to find current music charts, hit songs, lyrics, and legal downloads.

Shortcut #15

Left Brain and Right Brain: Good Songwriting Uses Both!

*Your analytical side and your creative side
need to work together.*

You've probably heard the phrases "left brain" and "right brain." These have become shorthand for two general ways of thinking: your left brain is logical, verbal, sequential, and judgmental while your right brain is intuitive, visual, inclusive, and generally non-judgmental. Although these are oversimplifications, they provide a useful and convenient way to refer to the two distinct approaches used by our brains to grasp ideas, communicate, and conceptualize. You need both of them to write a song!

*Left brain =
logical
verbal
judgmental*

Ideally, when you're writing, you let your right brain dominate in the early stages, allowing ideas to flow freely and creating the raw material for your song. Your analytical left brain can then sort through all of it and shape it into a song that clearly and effectively expresses the theme for listeners.

*Right brain =
intuitive
visual
non-judgmental*

That's the way it's supposed to work! Most of the time your left brain jumps in way too early, judging the material while it's still being created. Other times, the right brain falls so deeply in love with its own ideas and lines, it refuses to let go, ignoring sound advice from the left brain which is screaming that your song doesn't make any sense! They're like a couple of bickering children.

Too much of a good thing can be bad for your song

You need input from both the right and left brain—your creative and rational sides—to write an effective song. Too much logical, analytical left brain can make your song fall flat; the left brain never soars or reaches for the moon. Too much intuitive, visual right brain, though, can turn your song into unintelligible gibberish for listeners. So here are some ideas you can use for balancing left and right brain input on your song.

*Keep both sides
in balance!*

Games songwriters play

To get your judgmental left brain to relax while your right brain gets down to the business of creativity, try taking a lighter approach. Tell yourself you're just playing a game or doing an exercise rather than pursuing the more serious business of writing a song. Then invite your left brain in to do the rewriting.

➤ **Sing along with hit songs from any era and make up new lyrics.** Give yourself permission to come up with silly phrases. This willingness to be less than serious opens the door to right brain creativity.

> **Play the "Find-a-Title" game in Shortcut 42.** Develop your title by looking for the questions it asks (Shortcut 44) and creating raw material (Shortcut 45). Then let your left brain step in and decide whether to develop it further or not.

> **Record a TV show that has a relationship theme.** Choose a scene and quickly write a title and chorus that could be used to underscore it. You have 20 minutes to write lyrics and melody. Set a timer and GO! It doesn't have to be good; you just have to do it. Your left brain can polish it afterwards.

> **Find a headline in today's newspaper and write a chorus using all or part of the headline.** When you're done, throw it out. (Unless you like it! In which case, let your left brain go to work.)

> **Sing the chorus of a hit song and change the notes of the melody.** Change the pitches. Hold some notes longer or shorter. Add pauses or take them out. When you have a new melody, make up a lyric for it. Then put your left brain to work adding strength to both.

> **Use the "Do It Now" instructions in the Shortcuts and turn them into games by giving yourself a time limit.** Write down your initial ideas and impulses, knowing you can rework everything later during a rewriting phase.

Tell your inner critic to take a hike!

As you play the games or do the exercises, try not to judge what you come up with. Remind yourself that no one will see it but you. Feel free to throw everything away at the end of a writing session. If your "inner critic"—the judgmental left brain—wants to get involved, tell it to wait until you finish the game. Then, if you want to, sort through what you wrote and let your left brain decide what to keep, what to work on, and how to organize it.

Do It Now

Play any of the games and exercises included in this Shortcut. Try not to judge. If you write something you like, go ahead and develop it further using Shortcut 47 to create a sketch of your song and Shortcut 76 to get your melody started. Then use the rest of the Shortcuts for ideas on adding impact to your lyric and melody.

Shortcut #16

Follow Your Muse

Use "loud" and "soft" inspiration.

There are songwriters out there who think that writing a hit song is the exact opposite of following your muse. They feel that a muse-driven song must be obscure, difficult, make the listener work to get inside the song's heart; and that it must break all the rules to demonstrate its own brilliance.

This is a myth; it is simply not true and it will drive listeners away from your song. It's no coincidence that the songwriter who makes this mistake is often the one who hates the music business and the audience for failing to recognize his or her genius. A mistake like this can rob you of the success you deserve because it keeps listeners *outside* your song instead of bringing them into the emotion and theme you want to communicate. No one likes to be on the outside looking in.

Don't buy into this myth!

All great artists use inspiration as a guide. Often it's the initial impulse to create a work. Once the inspiration has jump-started the process, then discipline kicks in, molding and shaping the work into something that clearly conveys what the artist wants to say. Any work of art, whether it's a song, a painting, a sculpture, or a film, is a two-part process consisting of inspiration (which is one form of creativity), and craft (a different form of creativity). Craft is what helps you reach your audience but, for a song to be fulfilling for you as an artist, for you to love what you do, want to keep doing it, and grow while you do it, inspiration is *essential*.

Effective songs combine craft and inspiration!

Soft inspiration: what resonates for you

Of course there are the big, obvious inspired moments when an entire section of a song comes to you or the whole idea from start to finish is roughed out in a few minutes. I call this "loud inspiration"; it's the kind you can't miss. When it happens, thank your muse and then set to work crafting the rest so that it supports your initial impulse.

Then there are smaller moments, sometimes dozens of them in a single song, where inspiration is also at work. There are several places in this book where you'll be asked to look for a phrase or idea that *resonates* for you—one that sticks in your head, echoes for awhile, sounds intriguing, pulls you toward it, or suggests other thoughts. For whatever reason, this phrase *draws your emotional attention*. This is also your muse talking to you, saying, "Look over here. Pay special attention to this." It's just that the voice of the muse is somewhat quieter in these spots. I call this "soft inspiration." Learn to recognize it. Tune your antennae so you don't miss it. It can help lead you through your song while maintaining your initial inspired idea. (Read Shortcut 41 for more about finding phrases that resonate for you.)

How do you stay in touch with your muse?

Following your muse does *not* mean grabbing the first phrase that occurs to you and it does *not* mean that everything will suddenly be easy! It's a process that involves staying inside the emotional situation, seeking out phrases that effectively communicate your idea, and constantly adjusting your track—going backwards if need be—to maintain the connection with your original inspiration.

How do you know when you're losing touch with your muse? How do you recognize a false start or a wrong turn? Here are some danger signs:

- Clichés and generic phrases begin showing up.
- The song's focus starts to drift.
- Your own emotions become less involved.

Don't lose touch with your inspiration.

When you begin to see these signals, a caution flag should go up. Stop and go back through what you've written. Use "soft inspiration" to recognize those parts that feel true and vivid to you and let them lead you somewhere new. Once you're back on track again, you'll regain a sense of satisfaction and "rightness."

Remember that your muse may be working on more than one idea or song at a time. Muses are like that; they roam here and there at will. You'll need to be watchful. Stay open to ideas but if a line doesn't seem to fit and you're bending your idea out of shape to accommodate it, write it down on a separate page and save it for later.

Do It Now

1. Choose a hit song you like. See if you can identify the lyric line that originally inspired the songwriter to write this song.

2. Use Shortcuts 41 and 42 to find titles and lyric phrases that draw your emotional attention.

See "Shortcut Resources" on page 261 for information on where to find current music charts, hit songs, lyrics, and legal downloads.

Shortcut #17

Get in the Sandbox and Play!

Be creative. Try new things.
Don't be afraid to take chances!

Some writers work on their songs as if they're handling fragile, glass objects that might break if someone breathes on them the wrong way. Other writers dig right in, treating their songs like tough little works-in-progress. (The end product may still sound as fragile as glass.) The way you approach working on your songs can make a big difference, not only in how effective and commercially ready your finished songs are, but also in how practiced and confident you become as a songwriter.

Imagine you're in a sandbox with another kid and you're each building a sandcastle. The other kid has the fragile-as-glass mentality—he scoops up a mound of sand, it starts to drift back down, as sand will, so he backs off and doesn't touch it, afraid the whole thing will fall apart. You, on the other hand, with your tough work-in-progress attitude, gather a couple of Tonka trucks, a pail of water, and maybe some kitchen utensils, and go to work. You start with the same little mound of sand and try adding some water to make it stick together. That works except for one part that falls down. You reshape it with a spoon and then add more water and sand with your mighty dump truck. Who is going to end up with the better sandcastle? Who has learned more in the process? Who is more involved? And who is having more fun?!! That's a no-brainer but it's funny how many people will use the fragile-as-glass approach every time!

Take a hands-on playful approach to songwriting.

Creative playtime!

This book is full of ideas. Every one of them can provide you with hours of creative playtime in the sandbox—and give your creativity a real workout—but only if you're willing to explore them.

Choose a couple of songs you've already written or rough out new ones from scratch, then start applying the Shortcuts in this book to see what happens. Give the results the "fresh ears" test (see Shortcut 115). Ask yourself, as a listener, whether the changes you made added strength to your song or not. If not, then return to what you started with and try something else to see what happens.

Don't be afraid to play with your songs. Jump in the sandbox and have fun!

Shortcut #18

Don't Overthink!

Stay focused on the emotional flow of your song.

There's a scene in the movie *Bull Durham* where the rookie pitcher has lost his edge and is made to pitch an entire game wearing women's underwear. Keeping his conscious mind thinking about how odd, embarrassed, and generally uncomfortable he felt, left his unconscious mind free to do what it already knew how to do well.

In a similar way, overthinking your song can cause it to lose its emotional edge. Overthinking happens when ...

- Your inner critic steps in too early.

- You substitute craft in place of heart.

- You rework a song so much that you lose perspective.

Don't get stuck overthinking your song.

Here are some steps you can take to keep from overthinking your song.

➤ **Have song craft at your fingertips**
Remember, the rookie in *Bull Durham* already knew how to pitch well. He had all the skills he needed. Similarly, you will need to have the techniques and skills of your craft readily available to you. Shortcut 2 can show you how to use ghost songs to help you learn and embed current songwriting techniques.

➤ **Make work seem more like play**
Your inner critic is a product of your judgmental left brain. It bustles in and takes over whenever it considers there's serious work to be done. If it's kicking in too early in your creative process, try fooling it into thinking there's nothing important for it to work on, nothing that requires its formidable management skills; you're only playing a game. See Shortcut 15 for a list of songwriting games that will throw your left brain off the scent while your creative right brain gets down to work.

➤ **Give yourself plenty of choices**
When you run into a problem, try to avoid getting caught up in reworking the same section over and over. Identify the problem so you can look for a solution: Is it a predictable transition? Is it a lyric that's relying on clichés? Are you having trouble figuring out where your melody could go next? Spend some time listening to hit songs to see how they deal with that situation. Read through the Shortcuts that apply to that area and look for ideas you can use. Now go back to your song with fresh ears. Quickly run through a variety of solutions until you hear one that strikes you as workable then move on.

Shortcut #19

Do What You Love

Your best work is the work you love to do.

Here are three good reasons to do what you love:

> 1. **Things you love to do are things you spend more time doing.** The more you do something the better you are at it. Therefore, the things you love doing become the things that you are best at doing!

> 2. **The things you love doing are ones that have meaning for you.** They will lead you to discover inner resources and abilities, enriching your life and making you a happier person.

> 3. **You love doing it, so why *not* do it?**

That doesn't mean you love doing it all the time

Doing what you *love* doesn't mean just doing what's *easy*. A relationship isn't always easy even if you love the other person. Your relationship with your songwriting is like a love relationship: you want to be in it even though the ride can sometimes be a bumpy one. As long as you're getting something rewarding from it—enjoyment, a sense of accomplishment, the satisfaction of genuine self-expression—then you'll continue to have a satisfying relationship.

Do what you love

There's a funny thing about doing what we love: often, we can't seem to find the time to do it! There are just too many obligations and interruptions that demand our energy and attention. "I have a full-time job. I'm too tired to write after work." "I can't focus on songwriting when the kids are home." Keep in mind that you don't need a big chunk of quiet time in order to write a song. Many of the "Do It Now" exercises in this book can be done in 20 to 30 minutes. Of course, you can spend as long as you want, but try a mix of time spans. You may do an exercise in less than 20 minutes, come back later and rework it for another 20 minutes, then leave it alone for a day and revisit it for a final 20-minute polish.

Set some goals to keep your songwriting on track. See Shortcut 20.

Make songwriting an integral part of your life. Look for titles in the conversations around you, search for themes in your everyday life.

In the phrase "Do what you love," most people think the important word is LOVE but it's really DO. *DO it!*

Shortcut #20

Ready, Set, Goal!

*Nothing gets you moving faster
than knowing where you're going.*

Imagine yourself getting into your car. You turn on the engine—it's running smoothly. You check to see if there's gas in the tank; it's full. You back out of the driveway into the street. You sit there, engine idling as it suddenly dawns on you—you don't know where you're going! You have a vague notion of what your destination looks like but no real idea where it is or how to get there.

Obviously, this is no way to get where you want to go. Yet it's *exactly* the way many people treat their songwriting. They have a desire to write songs. They get ideas for songs—maybe a line or two or a concept—then they finish it the best they can, move on to the next one, and write it in the same way. Often, the songs rely on old habits, chords, and melodic styles picked up, perhaps, years earlier. These chords and styles feel "authentic" because they are the first ideas that come out. Working this way is the equivalent of idling a car in the middle of the street. Eventually it will just run out of gas.

Setting goals can help you get out of idling mode!

Wouldn't it be better to have a clear idea of where you're going, look at a map, then follow the directions and reach your destination? Of course it would and that's what *goals* are all about.

Techniques of effective goal setting

The metaphor of following a map to a destination is a useful one. Your Overall Goal is the destination you eventually want to reach. Along the way there are Step Goals, the equivalent of following a map. Drive down this street. Turn left at the corner. Drive one mile. Stop. Each of those is a Step Goal that you accomplish on your way to reaching your Overall Goal.

Make your goal something that's within your control.

There are just two rules for effective goal setting:

- Make sure it's something you want to do.

- Make it something that's within your control. If it's beyond your control, it's a wish, not a goal.

Set your Overall Goal

Your Overall Goal is your ultimate destination. You might, try something like this …

> **Overall Goal:** Write a song that expresses what I want to say and communicates it effectively to listeners.

That's a good goal and it's within your control but is that what you really want? Now that you see it in black and white, perhaps it feels like it's missing something. Let's try this …

> **Overall Goal:** Write a song that gets played on the radio and becomes a big hit.

Hmmm, that feels good. There's just one problem: it's mostly out of your control. It will depend on who's interested in recording the song and what other strong songs are being considered by that artist, whether the record company decides to pour lots of money into promoting it, and which competing artists are being released at the same time. So, try this one …

Your Overall Goal gives you the big picture.

> **Overall Goal:** Write a song that communicates effectively and sounds like it *could be* a hit.

That works. This is the kind of song that publishers and record labels eat for breakfast, lunch, and dinner; they need a constant supply. So if you write a song like that, you have a reasonable chance of attracting interest. In the meantime, the goal you've set is something over which you have control.

Set your Step Goals

One big overall goal can be overwhelming. By breaking it down into smaller steps you give yourself a clear map to follow and goals that are within your reach. Since I don't know where you're starting from, I can't tell you exactly what route to follow but here are some common Step Goals people set on their way to the Overall Goal we just looked at. You can adapt them to your own situation.

Break it into smaller Step Goals.

> **Skills, Tools, and Resources Step Goals:** Identify the songwriting skills and tools you need. Make acquiring each of these an individual Step Goal. See Shortcut 12 for a list of the six basic skills and tools you should acquire in order to improve your chances of songwriting success. Some will take more time and effort than others. Depending on where you're starting from, you may have three or four or more Step Goals in this area. Be sure to give yourself enough time to complete each one.
>
> See "Shortcut Resources" on page 261 for a list of useful Web sites, publications, and software. It's a good idea to gather the resources you need ahead of time so you don't have to stop once you get rolling. Make getting your resources together one of your early Step Goals.

> **Songwriting Step Goals:** For your first songwriting Step Goal, you could choose to write a new song or rework an old one. The Table of Contents in this book can help you define your goals. Depending on how much time you have, choose one or more Shortcuts from the Table of Contents to work on each week.

Write down your goals and organize them

Make a goal list and put it where you can see it!

Don't count on remembering what you decided to do. Write down your Overall Goal followed by a list of your Step Goals. Decide in what order you'd like to work on your goals. You can be working on more than one at the same time. Put the list where you can see it! Tape it to the bathroom mirror or stick it to the refrigerator door. It's too easy for the things we *have* to do to take over our lives and make us forget what we *want* to do. Make your goals a part of your life. And update your list as you complete your Step Goals!

Give yourself the time you need to achieve your goals

Just writing down your goals and looking at them won't get you where you want to go. Remember, you want to keep rolling forward toward your destination, not idling in neutral thinking about it! Decide how much time you can spend each week working on your goals and then *do it!* Step by step, you *will* get where you want to go.

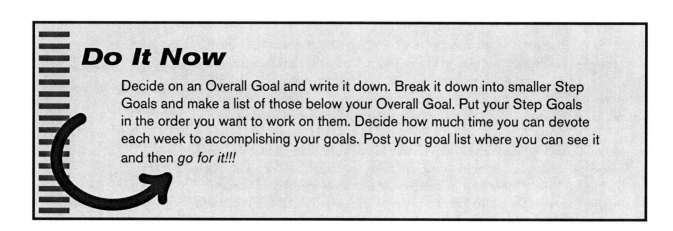

Do It Now

Decide on an Overall Goal and write it down. Break it down into smaller Step Goals and make a list of those below your Overall Goal. Put your Step Goals in the order you want to work on them. Decide how much time you can devote each week to accomplishing your goals. Post your goal list where you can see it and then *go for it!!!*

PART THREE

Shortcuts to Hit Song Structure

Learn the basic working parts of a song

and how to put them together

to give listeners a dynamic,

exciting experience they'll love …

Shortcut #21

Know the Basic Elements of a Song

*Learn to identify the parts of a song
and how they work together.*

Let's say you showed up for a physical exam and your doctor tried to listen to your heart by putting her stethoscope on your knee. Or you went to a mechanic to have your Ford sedan repaired and he opened up the trunk to check your engine. Pretty stupid examples, right? Why stupid? Because we expect most professionals to have a basic structural knowledge of whatever it is they're working on. Without that, their results would be pretty poor.

In much the same way, a professional songwriter needs to be familiar with song structure, the essential parts and pieces of a song and how they're put together.

Know all the working parts.

Verse: same melody, change the lyrics

The verse lyrics give the listener information. The lyrics change in each verse adding to the listener's understanding of the situation and emotional theme. The chord progression and melody remain the same in each verse with small variations in the melody to accommodate lyric changes. By keeping the melody essentially the same, you ensure that the listener recognizes this section each time it comes around, helping to define the song's structure. The verses in Brad Paisley's Country hit "Mud On the Tires" offer a good example of a verse melody with a changing lyric.

Verse

Chorus: same melody, same lyrics

The chorus is the high point of a contemporary song. In a Verse / Chorus song it occurs after each verse and again after the bridge. The chorus melody is catchy and memorable; the lyrics sum up and focus the overall theme laid out in the verses. The melody and lyric remain the same each time the chorus is repeated. Small changes may occur but be careful; once they've heard it, listeners look forward to a recognizable, repeated chorus section. This is important; the chorus acts as an anchor, giving the listener a "home base" between the other, more variable sections. Check out a hit like Matchbox Twenty's "How Far We've Come" to hear a strong, repeated chorus section.

Chorus

Hook: memorable, catchy lyric and melody

The hook is the most memorable line in your song. It often includes the title—so often, in fact, that I sometimes refer to it as the "hook/title line." It's called the hook because it does exactly that: it grabs attention and hauls the listener into the song. It's the line that listeners will remember long after the song is done. If it's a good one, they'll want to come back for another listen. To hear a solid hook/title line, listen to the opening of the chorus in Daughtry's "It's Not Over."

Hook

Refrain: an anchor for listeners

Refrain

The refrain is a phrase or line that occurs at the end or beginning of each verse in a Verse / Verse / Bridge / Verse song form. In this song form, the refrain is also the hook. Songs that have a refrain don't include a chorus. The refrain takes the place of the chorus as the anchor or "home base" for listeners. You can hear a hard-working refrain line in the Verse / Verse / Bridge / Verse song form in "Better as a Memory" by Kenny Chesney. The refrain is the last line of each verse and includes the title.

Bridge: a break from repeated sections

Bridge

The bridge occurs about two-thirds of the way into the song, after we've heard the verse or verse and chorus a couple of times. (This section is sometimes called the "middle eight." To keep things simple, I'm going to refer to this section as the "bridge" throughout this book.) The bridge provides variety and relief from the now familiar verse and chorus melodies. The bridge lyrics do not generally include the title of the song. Nickelback's "Photograph" includes a strong bridge after the second chorus that starts with the line "I miss that town …"

Pre-chorus: build intensity from verse to chorus

Pre-Chorus

The pre-chorus occurs at the end of a verse and provides a build up to the chorus. It adds to the intensity of the song, creating a sense of anticipation that gives us a greater sense of emotional release when we get to the chorus. To hear this concept, listen to Rascal Flatts' "What Hurts the Most." The first pre-chorus begins on the line "I'm not afraid to cry …"

They add up to an emotional experience.

These are the essential elements that make up a song. Used effectively, they create an emotional experience for the listener. That's why these song sections exist. If they didn't work to increase the impact and memorability of a song, we wouldn't use them. Period. Sure you'll find hit songs that don't use these sections in *exactly* the ways described. There's room to play around. Not every hit song has a pre-chorus; there are songs that don't have bridges. However, these are the basic building blocks of the structures you'll learn about in the following Shortcuts, so keep them in mind.

Do It Now

Choose a few hit songs you like. Listen and identify the various sections: verse, chorus, and bridge. Some songs have instrumental bridges or an instrumental verse instead of a bridge. Pre-choruses can be hard to spot. Just look for a line or two at the end of the verse that feels like it builds anticipation leading into the chorus.

See "Shortcut Resources" on page 261 for information on where to find current music charts, hit songs, lyrics, and legal downloads.

Shortcut #22

CONTRAST works EVERY time

*Grab attention and create that all-important structure
with contrast.*

Imagine you and I are standing in a room full of people. If I start yelling suddenly, I will get everyone's attention. But if I keep on yelling at the same volume level, what will happen? Pretty soon everyone will get bored and stop listening (and probably leave). It's natural to think that being loud is an attention-getter, but if loudness becomes the norm then it ceases to be something in which we are interested.

We are "hardwired" to notice change. When something changes, we check it out. What's happening? What's different? It's buried deep in our brains, like the "fight or flight" response. After all, for a few hundred thousand years, noticing a sudden brown patch of lion against the smooth green of the plains could save your life. Things are not so different now: a siren or a shift in the traffic pattern are all we need to put us on alert. Once we're satisfied that everything is safe, we no longer need to devote energy to it and we disengage our attention. When I started yelling, everyone noticed the change; when they determined that I wasn't a threat, even though the yelling continued, they disengaged their attention.

Humans are hardwired to notice change.

So, let's try this. What happens if I yell for 30 seconds, then speak softly for 30 seconds, then yell again? Each of those changes in volume level will attract attention. It's the change itself that creates the effect, the *contrast* between loud and soft. The greater the amount of contrast—the more difference there is—the more it will grab attention. By using contrast strategically within your song, say, between verse and chorus, you can keep listeners involved and interested.

And there's something else that contrast can do …

THIS ain't THAT!

Contrast refers to things that are not similar; when associated with one another, they are easily distinguishable: loud/soft, high/low, fast/slow, smooth/choppy. (There are degrees of contrast: blue and green exhibit contrast though not as much as black and white.) Because contrast is based on differences (*This* is not *that*), it can be used to create organization and structure. One of the areas where we need plenty of both—organization and structure—is communication.

Contrast can be used to create structure.

Pick up any magazine and take a look at an ad. If it's an effective ad that communicates well, it has plenty of contrast. The most important words are in large type. The secondary information is in smaller type. There will be open space between lines to give your eye a rest and bold graphics to direct your attention to the next important thing the advertiser wants you to notice. This is how contrast is used to create organization and structure.

Use contrast to create structure in your song

You can do the same thing in your songs: grab the listener's attention with your hook line, direct it to the next important point, and create a coherent structure—all by using contrast.

Take my example of yelling for 30 seconds, then being quiet for 30 seconds, then yelling again. If I sing in a loud, urgent tone of voice I'll certainly grab attention, especially if the words are emotionally compelling—let's call that a "chorus." Then, if I employ a softer tone and the words reveal intimate details, I pull listeners closer, still keeping them involved because I'm doing something different. I've used contrast to create a new section. Let's call this the "verse." Then, when I return to the loud, urgent tone, I've got their attention again and it's clear that we're not in the verse any more, now we're in the chorus. Thus, I've created a structured experience, directed the listener's attention, and successfully kept them involved in what I want to communicate. And I used contrast to do it!

Shortcuts 80 and 81 can help you add contrast to your songs.

This example of yelling and whispering is fairly basic and primitive. In a song, there are transitions that help us move between the loud and soft sections. Plus, you can create contrast in other ways besides the obvious one of volume—note range, word pace, and phrase length are a few.

What about relying on production to provide contrast? You can, and there are hit songs that have done this. However, if you write contrast into the song itself and let the production *support* it, you'll be reinforcing a strength rather than adding it as an afterthought.

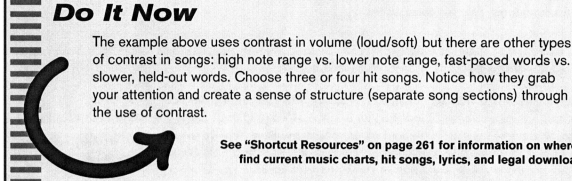

Do It Now

The example above uses contrast in volume (loud/soft) but there are other types of contrast in songs: high note range vs. lower note range, fast-paced words vs. slower, held-out words. Choose three or four hit songs. Notice how they grab your attention and create a sense of structure (separate song sections) through the use of contrast.

See "Shortcut Resources" on page 261 for information on where to find current music charts, hit songs, lyrics, and legal downloads.

Shortcut #23

The Original Hit Song:
The Folk Song Form

It's a time-tested song structure. Try an update!

Ever since the troubadours, songwriters have been figuring out what works and what doesn't, mostly by trial and error. For example, if you were a strumming, strolling bard-guy in medieval times and you showed up at the local royal court, you wanted to be sure to make a good impression. You quickly figured out that the ladies liked love stories and the men liked battle sagas, so you put together a song in which a battle-hardened hero falls in love. It worked! You sang a few dozen verses and then discovered that if you repeated the same lyric line or group of lines every few verses, your audience remembered the line and the song. Next time you strolled through town, they demanded to hear it. You had a hit on your hands!

Here's the beginning of today's Pop song structure.

The Folk song form

That line—the one that's repeated every few verses—is called the refrain line and it was an important step toward today's popular song forms. It took listeners into account, giving them a familiar reference point and underlining the focus of the lyric.

The basic song structure developed by the troubadours, a string of verses with a refrain line, remained unchanged for hundreds of years. That's how effective it was. Everything we do now grew from it so, even though we don't use it very often in its original form, it's definitely worth looking at. It's very simple:

Verse / Verse / Verse / Verse / Verse / Verse, etc.

Some or all of the verses include a refrain line; a line that, once established, remains unchanged throughout the song. A good example can be found in the traditional Folk ballad, "Scarborough Fair," a version of which was popularized by Simon and Garfunkel in the 1960s. The refrain—"parsley, sage, rosemary and thyme"—occurs on the second line of each verse:

Are you going to Scarborough Fair?
Parsley, sage, rosemary and thyme
Remember me to one who lives there
For once she was a true love of mine

The refrain line is the hook in this form.

There are only a few examples of the pure Folk song form in modern songs: Donovan's "Catch the Wind" released in 1965 and Bobbie Gentry's huge hit, "Ode to Billie Joe," in 1967. Both of these songs are now over forty years old, which begs the question: Is there any room on the current music charts for this song structure?

Meet the updated, hit song version

Try this idea!
⟹

Many of today's mega-hit songs rely on soaring chorus melodies and plenty of contrast between song sections to capture listeners. The Folk song form, with its repeated verses, just can't deliver that kind of attention-grabbing contrast. Or can it? "Iris," a record-breaking Pop hit for the Goo Goo Dolls in 1998, used the Folk song form but adapted it for today's contrast-hungry Pop audience by raising the melody up an octave on the third verse to create a powerful chorus. The higher melody grabbed attention with contrast in note range and volume, adding emotional urgency and making that section function as a legitimate Pop chorus. "Iris" is not, strictly speaking, in the Folk song form but it's close and might provide some inspiration for a song of your own in this style.

Do It Now

Try exploring the Folk form by using a folk song melody and adapting the lyric or creating an original lyric for it. Write a complete chorus melody and lyric of your own. Or add weight to the refrain line by repeating it or extending it in some way. You might also raise the verse melody up an octave and use that as your chorus. Be sure to write a chorus lyric that sums up the emotional heart of your song and pays off for the listener. Read Shortcut 50 for more tips on writing a successful chorus lyric.

Shortcut #24

Build It on Solid Ground:
The Basic Song Form

Use a proven song structure: Verse / Verse / Bridge / Verse.

For hundreds of years, most popular songs were in the Folk song form, the one we looked at in the previous Shortcut. The structure was a simple series of verses with a recurring refrain. However, in the late 1800s, songwriters began focusing more on emotion and less on storytelling. When that happened, the weakness of the Folk song form became apparent; with no story to propel it forward and keep the listener involved, the simple repetition of a verse/refrain melody quickly became boring. So some bright songwriter came up with the idea of varying the melody after a couple of verses, in fact, after exactly two verses.

Shortcut 23 has more on the folk song form.

This turned out to be just what listeners wanted to hear. The ever-popular refrain line remained embedded in the verse section and the form became: verse, then another verse, do something else, then come back to the verse again. The "something else" is called a "bridge." So the first contemporary song form looks like this:

Verse / Verse / Bridge / Verse

This form is sometimes referred to as "AABA" where the verse is indicated by the letter A and the bridge by the letter B. (I avoid using As and Bs to refer to song sections because the more complex song forms end up looking like alphabet soup.)

Do it, do it again, go away, then come back

The Verse / Verse / Bridge / Verse structure has been used in countless hit songs. *All* of the great hits from 1900 to 1960 by writers like Irving Berlin, George and Ira Gershwin, Cole Porter, and Rodgers and Hammerstein were written in this song form. The Beach Boys had hit after hit in this form, as did Elvis and The Beatles.

Something in our brains likes this particular mix of repetition and variation: Do it (verse). Do it again (verse). Go away (bridge). Come back (verse). It strikes just the right balance. Hearing a verse melody, then hearing it again, establishes familiarity *but* if we heard it a third time—three times in a row—we'd be bored. The bridge section provides something fresh and new just when it's needed. Returning to the original verse melody after the bridge feels good, like going home, back to a familiar place.

Use the right mix of repetition and variation.

The refrain line is an anchor

The refrain line occurs either at the beginning or end of every verse in almost all songs in this form. It acts as an anchor for listeners, providing them with a secure sense of place within the song and something familiar to look forward to. Because of its position of importance, the refrain line usually includes the title of the song.

Here are a few hit songs in the Verse / Verse / Bridge / Verse form.

The refrain provides a home base for listeners.

"Somebody Like You" (Keith Urban)
Refrain: The title is included in the refrain.
Location: last line of every verse

"Better as a Memory" (Kenny Chesney)
Refrain: The title is the refrain.
Location: last line of every verse

"Streets of Philadelphia" (Bruce Springsteen)
Refrain: The title is included in the refrain.
Location: last line of every verse

"Don't Know Why" (Norah Jones)
The title is included in the refrain line, which appears at the end of the first and last verses, like bookends. An interesting variation on the basic form.

Variations on the form

Paul McCartney and John Lennon used this song structure in many of their early songs like "I Saw Her Standing There," "And I Love Her," and "Things We Said Today." Later on, McCartney played with it in interesting ways in songs like "The Long and Winding Road" and "Yesterday" in which he didn't write a consistent refrain lyric. Stick with a simple, repeated refrain unless you're feeling extremely confident.

Make sure to master the form before trying these variations.

Eric Clapton used this form in "Wonderful Tonight." He varied the front end of the refrain line as the song progressed but he kept enough of the line (including the title) to provide an anchor for the listener.

Hit song tip

This form doesn't have the big, undeniable, scene-chewing choruses that mainstream radio likes to hear these days but it can still be used as the basis for a hit song. It works best for ballads and mid-tempo songs. Be sure your refrain line packs plenty of punch. Aim for a lyric that sums up the heart of the song's theme and try adding a twist to the melody in that spot to catch the listener's attention. Keith Urban's Country smash, "Somebody Like You," contains a good example of a strong refrain line with an internal repeat that helps to make it more memorable.

The best way to give this form contemporary commercial appeal is to write a blockbuster bridge. Sometimes the bridge in one of these songs is so compelling, it feels like a chorus. Again, the Keith Urban hit provides a good example.

While this song form gave birth to the song structures used in today's biggest hits, you rarely find a current hit song in this form in the Pop or Rock genre. It's still possible to have a hit with it in the Country genre and it occasionally turns up on the Adult Contemporary charts for an artist like Norah Jones.

Do It Now

1. Listen to hit songs in the Verse / Verse / Bridge / Verse form. See the list above for some suggestions. Try stopping the song just before you get to the refrain line in the second verse. (Remember, it's the one that usually has the title in it and will be the first or last line of each verse.) Ask yourself how you would feel if the song did *not* go to the refrain line. What if it went to a different melody or lyric? What are your expectations? What would feel good to you as a listener?

   Try playing both verses then stop just before the bridge. How would you feel if the next section were another verse? Now play the bridge and stop before the next section. What do you want to hear next? A brand new section you haven't heard before? Another bridge section? Another verse with a refrain?

2. Using the melody of the song you've just been listening to, make up a new lyric to the hook/title line. Sing along with the original song, singing your lyric in place of theirs. When the song goes to the bridge, write a new lyric for the first line of the bridge. These are the key points in this song form. Singing your own lyrics at these points will help reinforce the feel of this form.

   See "Shortcut Resources" on page 261 for information on where to find current music charts, hit songs, lyrics, and legal downloads.

Shortcut #25

Monster Hits: The Chorus Form

The song form that drives today's biggest hits:
Verse / Chorus.

"It's Alive! ALIVE!" Dr. Frankenstein shouts as his bulky creation slowly rises and takes its first steps on its own. In the search for a monster hit song, you, too, want your creation to have a powerful, well-built, muscular frame that can stand up on its own. If you've done your work well you, too, may find yourself dancing around the house shouting, "It's alive!"

Well-defined structure gives your song muscle! The kind of muscle that will help it elbow its way into a publisher's office. This strength and clarity of form is also attractive to listeners; they like the solid sense of location and anchoring that good song form provides.

Remember!
Use contrast
to define your
structure. Read
Shortcut 22
for more.

The monster's bio

How were the current mega-hit song forms developed? In the previous Shortcut, you got a look at the Verse / Verse / Bridge / Verse song form. While this form produced hundreds of hits in earlier decades, it accounts for only a small number of today's hit songs. It has been overtaken by the "Monster Hit," a song form with a huge, hook-driven chorus. Yet, these modern mega-hits evolved from that earlier form.

What happened went something like this: The Verse / Verse / Bridge / Verse song form has a refrain—an unchanging melody and lyric line that occurs in the same place in each verse, often the last line of the verse. Songwriters noticed that people liked and remembered the refrain line so they made sure it included the title of the song. (Think Billy Joel's "Just the Way You Are," or Eric Clapton's "Wonderful Tonight.")

It was only natural to wonder what would happen if they did more with this refrain line that everyone liked so much. The Beatles built on this idea in "I Want to Hold Your Hand" when they repeated the refrain three times in a row in every verse! Songwriters soon realized they could create an entire song section around the title/refrain line. Thus was born that unforgettable line of poetry: "Don't bore us, get to the chorus!"

The chorus-driven hit song form

The mega-hit chorus form looks like this:

Verse / Chorus / Verse / Chorus / Bridge / Chorus

(I'll just call it the "Verse / Chorus" form.)

The lyric and melody of the chorus remain the same each time the chorus section is repeated, giving listeners a strong "home base" to return to after every verse. The most prominent and memorable line in the chorus is the hook; it appears at least once during the chorus and is often the title of the song. The chorus lyric sums up the song's emotional theme while the verses develop the situation and characters. Some songs in this form, such as "Dani California," begin with two verses. This can be tricky—if the double verse delays the arrival of the chorus for too long, your listeners may get restless.

Often, the bridge provides an emotional high point, a reveal, or twist to the lyric, in a sense doing the work of a strong third verse, so you may want to take your listeners straight into the final choruses of your song after the bridge. A few hit songs go to a third verse or half verse. The choice is up to you; it depends on what feels right emotionally. (See Shortcut 33 for some suggestions.) Instrumental bridges are not a good idea if you're aiming for a radio hit; once you've got the listener involved in your lyric, keep them there by writing a vocal bridge.

Here are a few examples of the Verse / Chorus song structure in different genres:

Genre	Title	Performer
Country	"Live Like You Were Dying"	Tim McGraw
Pop	"Say"	John Mayer
R&B/Soul	"I Remember"	Keyshia Cole
Rock	"Dani California"	Red Hot Chili Peppers

Do It Now

1. Take a listen to the hit songs listed above or find other hits in the Verse / Chorus song form. Just before the end of Verse 2, stop listening and ask yourself how you would feel if the song did not go to the chorus next. What if it went to another verse? Would you feel satisfied?

2. Use a song in this form as a ghost song and write a new lyric to embed the feel of the structure. See Shortcut 2 for more on using ghost songs.

See "Shortcut Resources" on page 261 for information on where to find current music charts, hit songs, lyrics, and legal downloads.

Shortcut #26

Build 'Em Bigger and Better: The Pre-Chorus Form

Supercharge your structure: Verse / Pre-Chorus / Chorus.

When you were a child, you learned an important lesson from the Three Little Pigs. Build a robust, carefully constructed house from the strongest materials and it will still be standing no matter what life (or the music industry) throws at it.

In the previous two Shortcuts, you were introduced to the song forms that have given us the vast majority of hit songs from 1900 to the present day. The Verse / Chorus form of Shortcut 25 is still the primary song form for the mega-hit.

One of the proven draws of the Verse / Chorus form is the powerful emotional release that happens at the beginning of the chorus, that sense of "ahhhh" you get when a hit song launches into the first line of the chorus. So some bright songwriter came up with the idea of building tension and anticipation just before the chorus to give the emotional release—the "ahhhh"—even more impact. It's hard to resist getting caught up in the emotional roller coaster this song form evokes; it's a real powerhouse, the unbeatable House Built of Bricks.

Check out tension & release in Shortcut 79.

The blueprint for the house of bricks

From the Verse / Chorus song form it's but a short hop to this new form; just add a section between the verse and chorus, called a pre-chorus. The pre-chorus is just what its name says: a section that precedes the chorus and transitions the listener from the verse to the chorus. This transition often takes the form of a building up of tension and energy that can then be released in the first line of the chorus. For example, a rising melody line in your pre-chorus can raise expectations, leading the listener to anticipate the chorus. The more anticipation you build, the bigger the payoff when the chorus finally arrives!

The complete pre-chorus form looks like this:

Verse / Pre-chorus / Chorus / Verse / Pre-chorus / Chorus / Bridge / Chorus

(I'll refer to it as the "Verse / Pre-chorus / Chorus" song form.)

See Shortcut 33 for ideas on where to go after the bridge.

As in the Verse / Chorus song form of the previous Shortcut, you can come out of the bridge into either a pre-chorus or final chorus. You can even go to a verse or half verse, just be sure to maintain the energy and momentum of the song. Again, instrumental bridges are not recommended if you're looking for a radio hit; keep your listeners involved in the situation you're laying out in your lyric.

Constructing the pre-chorus

As with other song sections like the verse and chorus, there is no preferred or predictable number of lines for a pre-chorus. A pre-chorus can be as short as a single line or as long as four lines. It all depends on what you feel will build up the listener's expectations for the chorus.

Sometimes the pre-chorus is not a clearly separate section from the verse. Don't drive yourself crazy wondering whether a particular song has a pre-chorus or just a verse that builds tension at the end; it's more important to look at *how the lines function* just before the chorus. Is there a strong build-up of anticipation, emotional energy, or forward momentum? If so, then you could probably refer to those lines as a pre-chorus.

With so many sections, this song form can be a challenge to handle. If you've got a long verse or chorus, be careful about using a four-line pre-chorus; your song could easily turn into a six-minute marathon! In this case, consider limiting your pre-chorus to one line or two short phrases.

Feel the build!

A pre-chorus is all about building energy, anticipation, and momentum leading up to the chorus. It's the ultimate emotional roller coaster! Check out some of these songs to hear pre-choruses that work!

"What Hurts the Most" (Rascal Flatts)
The first pre-chorus begins with the line "I'm not afraid to cry …"

"Unwritten" (Natasha Bedingfield)
The first pre-chorus begins with "Staring at the blank page before you …"

"Someday" (Nickelback)
The first pre-chorus begins with "Nothing's wrong, just as long …"

"Truth Is" (Fantasia)
The first pre-chorus begins with "And all the feelings that I thought were gone …"

"Paralyzer" (Finger Eleven)
The first pre-chorus begins with "I am imagining …"

Listen to these songs. Feel how the anticipation builds going into the chorus!

Pre-choruses come in many sizes

In the examples above, there are hit songs from all four of the major genres— Country, Pop, Rock, and R&B/Soul. The pre-chorus elicits such a strong response from listeners in all genres that it has become an important tool for hit songwriters. As you listen to the examples, notice that each of these pre-choruses varies in length and style, from Nickelback's powerful single line build to Rascal

Flatts' slow but unstoppable freight train. There are a lot of interesting and creative ways to set up your listener for a big chorus. You can find suggestions in Shortcut 86. Just remember that the pre-chorus has only one reason for existence—to build excitement and anticipation leading up to the chorus. Be sure you give your listeners a big payoff when your chorus finally arrives!

Do It Now

1. Choose a few hit songs to listen to; any of the songs referred to in this Shortcut will do. Listen to the first verse and pre-chorus then, just before the chorus starts, pause the song. Ask yourself how you would feel if the song went to another verse at that point. What are you hoping for or expecting? What has the song led you to want at this point? Now play the chorus and notice how there's a sense of "resolution," how your desire to feel a release of tension was satisfied.

2. Try adding a pre-chorus to one of your own songs, just a line or two to increase the build-up to your chorus.

See "Shortcut Resources" on page 261 for information on where to find current music charts, hit songs, lyrics, and legal downloads.

Shortcut #27

Use the Pattern Listeners Can't Resist!

Why we "Do it, do it again, go away, and then come back."

As a group, humans are not very enthusiastic about chaos. If there's too much of it in your life—when things are out of control and unpredictable, when you don't know what's going to happen next—you feel anxious and frustrated. That's no fun! It's the same with songs: Listeners don't like chaos. They like to have an idea of where they are and what to expect or they start to feel anxious.

A regularly repeated phrase or section can provide a sense of organization and intention for listeners. It gives them something solid to hold onto, an anchor. If a song has little or no repetition, if it meanders here and there, listeners will soon become uncomfortable. They sense the song lacks coherence and purpose; chaos might be lurking just around the corner. *Repetition averts chaos and creates a recognizable pattern for listeners.*

Too much repetition, of course, invites boredom. Like wallpaper patterns, repeated images quickly become predictable and fade into the background. You don't want that to happen to your song! You want to keep your listeners involved and interested while at the same time giving them a sense of organization and intention.

The pattern that listeners love

So what's a songwriter to do? It seems like you're caught between the need for familiarity versus the desire for something fresh and new. You need to find the "sweet spot," the point at which there's enough repetition to keep listeners feeling anchored in familiar territory with enough variety to keep them interested. Songwriters have experimented with various combinations of repetition and variation and the one that has proven to work best in terms of overall song structure is: Do it, do it again, go away, then come back.

Do it, do it again, go away, then come back!

Using the pattern in song structures

The Verse / Verse / Bridge / Verse form is the most obvious example of this pattern. In terms of melodic structure, it looks like this:

Verse 1	Melody 1	Do it.
Verse 2	Melody 1	Do it again.
Bridge	Melody 2	Go away.
Verse 3	Melody 1	Come back.

You can think of the other two contemporary song forms in much the same way. For instance, if you imagine Verse and Chorus (or Verse, Pre-chorus, and Chorus) as a single section, then you end up with the same "Do it, do it again, go away, then come back" form, with the bridge, again, being the "go away" section. Here it is:

Verse 1 / Chorus 1	Melody 1	Do it.
Verse 2 / Chorus 2	Melody 1	Do it again.
Bridge	Melody 2	Go away.
(Verse 3) / Chorus 3	Melody 1	Come back.

This pattern is used in hit songs in all mainstream melodic genres.

Notice that the third verse is in parentheses. When you've established the first part of this pattern—Do it, do it again, go away—you can come back to any repeated section: verse, pre-chorus, or chorus. Once you've established the pattern, your listener trusts that the song has cohesiveness and direction and you can play with the section order a bit.

The best way to get familiar with this important pattern in songwriting is to listen to hit songs. You'll hear it over and over again, across the board, in hits in all mainstream genres. Here are a few:

Genre	**Title**	**Performer**
R&B/Soul	"Irreplaceable"	Beyoncé
Pop	"Breakaway"	Kelly Clarkson
Country	"You're Gonna Miss This"	Trace Adkins
Rock	"Vertigo"	U2

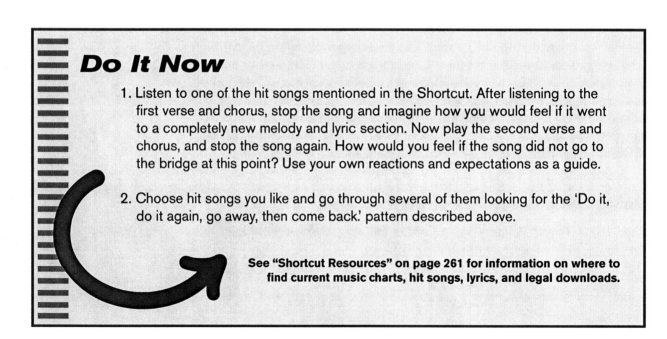

Do It Now

1. Listen to one of the hit songs mentioned in the Shortcut. After listening to the first verse and chorus, stop the song and imagine how you would feel if it went to a completely new melody and lyric section. Now play the second verse and chorus, and stop the song again. How would you feel if the song did not go to the bridge at this point? Use your own reactions and expectations as a guide.

2. Choose hit songs you like and go through several of them looking for the 'Do it, do it again, go away, then come back.' pattern described above.

See "Shortcut Resources" on page 261 for information on where to find current music charts, hit songs, lyrics, and legal downloads.

Shortcut #28

Which Song Structure Is the Right One?

Choose the structure that will work best for <u>your</u> song.

Rather than reinventing the wheel (or songwriting), you've made the wise decision to use one of the song forms described in Shortcuts 24, 25, or 26: the Verse / Verse / Bridge / Verse form, the Verse / Chorus form, or one with a pre-chorus. So which one will it be? Is one better than another? Is one more likely to deliver a hit song? While all three have proven appeal and share an underlying pattern, there are differences you can use to your advantage. And, as always, the real question is: Which form will add the most emotional impact and memorability to the song you are writing? Here are some suggestions that might help you decide.

Song Form #1

Verse / Verse / Bridge / Verse

1. **This is a tightly focused song form with a single, repeated refrain line that forms the core of the lyric.** The refrain is going to be the first or last line of every verse so all other lyric lines must relate to it and lead the listener toward it. Check out Kenny Chesney's "Better as a Memory" to hear this type of lyric.

2. **This form works well if your verses are around six to ten lines with your refrain at the beginning or end.** If you're writing a twelve-line verse or your verse has very long phrases, the listener may not get a chance to hear your refrain often enough for it to have maximum impact. In this case, you might try singing your refrain line twice at the end of each verse, using melodic variation to keep it interesting.

   Keep your lyric tightly focused on your refrain line.

3. **To aim this song for the contemporary hit market, try creating a powerful bridge with a lot of melodic contrast between bridge and verse.** Listen to Keith Urban's "Somebody Like You" to hear a mega-bridge in this song form. Although the bridge doesn't include the song's title or hook line, the soaring melody gives it the kind of ear-catching appeal that's needed to propel a song in this form to the top of the charts.

Song form #2

Verse / Chorus

1. **This form features two sections—verse and chorus—and, often, a vocal bridge.** It works well when you have a situation or theme that develops over the course of the song. For instance:

Verse 1:   We were together and so happy.
Verse 2:   But now you're gone and I miss you.
Bridge: I'll cherish what we had.

In between each of these "scenes" the chorus evokes the central emotion of the song. To hear an example, check out P!nk's "Who Knew," or Christina Aguilera's "Beautiful."

Use the chorus to evoke the central emotion and the verses to develop the situation.

2. **Because the chorus provides plenty of emphasis on the central theme and emotion of the song, your verses can be more complex than in the Verse / Verse / Bridge / Verse form.** Greater phrase lengths or number of lines in your verse give you the chance to spend time evoking the characters and painting the scene. Try this form when you have character and/or situations that need development. Shortcut 53 can give you some ideas on how to create a development path that will carry you through this song form.

3. **Verse and chorus are tightly tied together in this form.** A chorus may be repeated as many as four or five times in a song. To tweak this form for the hit market, be sure to maintain interest in your chorus by giving additional information in each verse. In this way, each time your listeners hear the chorus it means something more.

Song Form #3

Verse / Pre-Chorus / Chorus

1. **This form works well when you want to build a lot of dynamic changes into your song.** It's a form that builds excitement and tension in the pre-chorus and releases it in the chorus. Like a roller coaster, the pre-chorus lifts the listener from the level of the verses, slowly climbing up the hill as we anticipate what's to come, and then flying down the other side in the chorus. Two good examples are "First Time" by Lifehouse and "Should've Said No" by Taylor Swift. Both have a powerful pre-chorus that creates a sense of expectation leading up to a big chorus.

2. **This form works best when your chorus wants to have a lot of emotional energy and your verses need to be more conversational and intimate.** An abrupt shift between these two levels of intensity can be difficult for listeners to make on their own. The pre-chorus helps to create a smoother transition as well as build anticipation. Note that many of these songs are in the first person: the singer is telling us something intimate and personal in the verses then allowing his or her emotions full rein in the choruses.

There's plenty of emotional build and release in this form!

3. **There's more lyric and melodic "real estate" here than in the previous forms.** This can be both a plus and a minus. Your listener has to get through a verse and pre-chorus before finally arriving at the heart of your song—your chorus. Then get through another verse and pre-chorus before getting to a repeat of the chorus! To make this form work for you, maintain the energy

and keep the situation rolling forward throughout the verse and pre-chorus sections. Fill these with plenty of vivid character, information, and situational development in your lyric along with contrast, variety, and dynamic build in your melody.

Do It Now

Listen to the examples given above or hit songs you like and notice how the song form works to support the theme and lyric content. Write down the situation in each verse and notice how it changes. Look at how each verse leads to the chorus or refrain.

See "Shortcut Resources" on page 261 for information on where to find current music charts, hit songs, lyrics, and legal downloads.

Shortcut #29

Your Blueprint for Success:
The Layout

Visualize your song structure to help you stay on track.

Sometimes a picture really *is* worth a thousand words. On the following pages are "blueprints"—just simple diagrams—of two very successful song forms. Having an image of the whole structure, "a layout," in your mind as you write your lyric can help you organize your ideas and create a strong framework for your song right from the start.

The layouts can help with melody, too; even if you haven't got a lyric, you can picture the emotional rise and fall of the song's structure and create a melody to support it. See Shortcut 77 "Raw Material: Write Your Melody First" to find out more.

To use the Verse / Verse / Bridge / Verse or Verse / Chorus layout follow the steps below. You're just looking at song *structure* for now, trying to get an idea of how your song will flow, so don't worry about rhymes or line lengths as you work. (If a rhyme happens, that's fine. Keep it.)

Picture the song structure as you write. Think of your song as a whole.

> **Step 1.** What is the heart and soul of what you want to say? Write one or two lines that sum up the essence in the box marked "Chorus" or write a single line after "Refrain." Don't worry about how poetic or fresh your lines are. This is just a blueprint.

> **Step 2.** If you were telling a complete stranger about this situation, what would you say first? How would you introduce your situation? Write a couple lines in the box marked Verse 1.

> **Step 3.** How can you take the listener deeper into this situation or emotion? What happens next? Write that in the box for Verse 2.

> **Step 4.** Copy the lines from the first chorus or refrain to the second.

> **Step 5.** If there is one hope, lesson, or desire that has evolved from this situation, what is it? Write that in the box marked "Bridge."

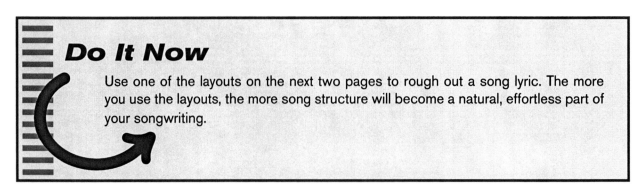

Do It Now

Use one of the layouts on the next two pages to rough out a song lyric. The more you use the layouts, the more song structure will become a natural, effortless part of your songwriting.

Song Layout: Verse / Verse / Bridge / Verse

Verse 1: Bring the listener into the situation.

Refrain:

Verse 2: Take us deeper into the emotions and situation.

Refrain:

Bridge: Provide an emotional peak, new insight, or summary.

Verse 3: You can take us deeper, show us another angle, or build on your bridge info.

Refrain:

VARIATION: After Verse 3 you can go to an instrumental verse or half-verse, then repeat the bridge and close with a final verse. If your verses are long, you may want to go straight to a repeat of the bridge and wrap up with a final verse or just a repeated refrain line.

Song Layout: Verse / Chorus / Verse / Chorus / Bridge / Chorus

Verse 1: Bring the listener into the situation.

Chorus: Give us the emotional heart of the theme.

Verse 2: Take us deeper into the emotions and situation.

Chorus: Repeat the first chorus.

Bridge: Provide an emotional peak, new insight, or summary.

Repeat chorus to fade out.

VARIATION: You can use this layout for a song with a pre-chorus. Just write your pre-chorus ideas at the bottom of each verse box or draw your own layout with a separate box for the pre-chorus between each verse and chorus.

Shortcut #30

Make Your Song Sections the Right Length

Keep your song rolling forward at a pace listeners can follow.

In my songwriting workshops, I'm often asked how long a verse or chorus should be. There are two answers: the complicated one and the simple one.

The complicated answer goes like this: Each of the three contemporary song structures offers plenty of flexibility. If you're counting measures—see Shortcut 74—a verse can be from eight bars to sixteen bars (in a mid- to up-tempo song). Pre-choruses range from four to eight bars. Today's choruses can be anywhere from eight bars up to fourteen or sixteen bars long. A refrain is usually a single line, often four bars long.

That's the complicated answer. The simple answer is: *Each section should be as long or short as it needs to be!*

Of course I prefer the simple answer. But what does it mean? How do you know what length it *needs* to be?

What length does it need to be?

If you have something compelling to say and you're moving the situation forward at a good pace, then you'll keep the listener involved no matter how long your verse or chorus! But if you're stalling, if you're repeating information you've already revealed, if you're leaving yourself nowhere to go in your next section, then, no matter how short your sections are, listeners are going to be bored at some point. When listeners are bored, the shortest of sections can seem interminable (and tune-out-able).

How long will it take you to tell listeners what they need to know?

Instead of trying to fit what you have to say into a pre-determined number of lines, think in terms of the most effective way to present it. How much time will it take for you to give your listeners the information needed to understand and emotionally connect with your song? And at what point will you be saying too much? Between those two points lies the perfect length for the sections of your song.

Find the perfect length for your song sections

Let me give you some suggestions for finding that perfect length.

- Use Shortcut 47 "Create a Rough Sketch of Your Song" to get an idea of what you want to say in each section: verse, chorus, and bridge. Try using one of the development paths suggested in Shortcut 53.

- Choose the layout sheet for the structure you want to use. (See Shortcut 29.) Make a copy of the layout and fill it in so you can visualize the flow of your song.

The results are in!

Once you've sketched out your lyric idea a funny thing happens. You notice that your first verse probably isn't going to be twenty-four or thirty-two bars long—if it were, you'd end up giving away the whole song, leaving nothing for Verse 2 or the bridge. It probably won't be just three or four bars long, either. Your listener is likely to need more information before getting to the all-important chorus or refrain. So, to give your listener the best experience, the verses will probably end up being between eight and sixteen bars long. (Once you've decided on a verse length, keep it consistent. All the verses in your song should be the same length.)

Section length supports good lyric flow & development.

A similar thing happens to the chorus when you lay out your song. If you say too much in the chorus, you leave the verses with nothing new to offer. You're also likely to lock in the meaning of the chorus too early, instead of allowing it to be reinterpreted and more deeply understood over the course of the song. So your chorus will probably end up being anywhere from eight to fourteen bars long.

If you approach the length of your song sections from this angle, they won't feel arbitrary and you won't need to ask the question, "How long should they be?" They'll be as long as you need. They'll support good lyric development and flow throughout the entire length of the song, keeping your listeners involved and interested in what you have to say.

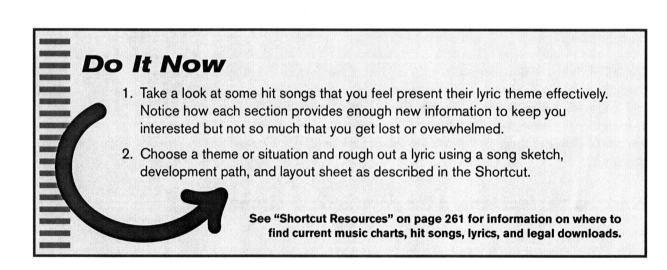

Do It Now

1. Take a look at some hit songs that you feel present their lyric theme effectively. Notice how each section provides enough new information to keep you interested but not so much that you get lost or overwhelmed.

2. Choose a theme or situation and rough out a lyric using a song sketch, development path, and layout sheet as described in the Shortcut.

See "Shortcut Resources" on page 261 for information on where to find current music charts, hit songs, lyrics, and legal downloads.

Shortcut #31

Add Dynamics:
Build a Structural Roller Coaster

Create the "whooooooosh" effect
with tension and release.

Just for a moment, think back to the unforgettable musical underscore in the movie, *Jaws*, especially that bit you heard each time the shark was about to attack. Before you ever saw the shark, you heard the music and *that* was enough to start your pulse racing, building tension to an explosive climax.

Now, I'm not suggesting that you go to this extreme in any song! I just want to make the point that music can create tension and a sense of increasing anxiety and stress in your listeners. So, what success-seeking songwriter would want to do *that????* Tension, stress, and anxiety aren't anyone's favorite feelings. Ah, but it feels so good when they're released! And it's that experience of rising tension followed by the release of that tension—emotional dynamics—that makes people want to hear a song over and over again. It's like riding the Cyclone roller coaster. Once you've experienced the thrill, you want to get that feeling again.

It feels great to release tension!

The Emotional Roller Coaster

If you think of your song structure as the peaks and valleys of the coaster's track, you'll have a pretty good picture of the dynamic build and release of tension in a song. Imagine the first verse of your song as the start of the ride. Slowly it rises up the first hill—*click, click, click*—building anticipation and tension. By the end of the verse, you're at the top of the hill and then—*whooooooosh!*—down you fly to the bottom as you launch into the chorus, releasing all of the built-up energy.

As you begin the slow accumulation of tension in the second verse, you expect the release that's coming. You're waiting for it, which makes the anticipation that much greater. And sure enough, it happens when the chorus takes off for the second time. Oh, that feels so good!

What next? You could do that climbing/falling thing again but any self-respecting roller coaster provides a new experience at this point: a steep, G-force curve ought to do the trick. Think of this as the bridge. Then, create that wonderful feeling of release one more time on the final downhill plunge before the ride is over. If your song gives the listener an experience like this, you can bet they'll buy another ticket and ride again.

D R
  L   E
I   L
               E
U   A
                 S
B   E
	D R
	  L E
	I L
	               E
	U A
	                 S
	B E
		R
		U V
		C E
			R
			   E
			      L
			         E
			            A
			               S
			                  E

Verse 1 Chorus 1	Verse 2 Chorus 2	Bridge	Final Choruses

Think of your song as a roller coaster ride.

What's amazing is how easily and effectively a melody can create emotional dynamic changes like this. A faster pace in the notes, or steadily rising pitch can build anticipation; an interval jump or slower, smoother pace can release tension. To hear the roller coaster effect in action, check out hit songs like "Remedy (I Won't Worry)" (Jason Mraz), "Live Like You Were Dying" (Tim McGraw), and "Because of You" (Kelly Clarkson).

Different genres treat tension and release differently

The Pop and Rock genres are the ones that rely heavily on huge releases of tension in the chorus. These are the mega-coaster rides! The Country genre is a little more restrained but uses similar techniques. Urban genres like R&B/Soul and Urban-Dance lean more on changes in melodic rhythm and pace to build and release tension rather than climbing, soaring melodies.

Find out more about using melody to create dynamics in Shortcut 79.

Why you can't rely solely on production to create the effect

When you listen to the examples given above, you'll notice that the production—instrumentation, mix, and arrangement—builds up to the chorus, hits a peak at the top of the chorus and releases energy slowly. Obviously the elements of production can heighten the experience of tension and release. However, relying solely on production means you'll be missing out on the opportunity to create an even bigger impact. If you build your roller coaster right into the song's melody, the production will give it support, increasing the effect.

Do It Now

Listen to the examples listed above and other recent hit songs. Notice the difference in the emotional energy levels between verse and chorus. The verses build energy and the choruses release it. Radio hits use this dynamic "ride" to give listeners an experience they like, one that keeps them listening and wanting to hear more. As you listen to these songs, see if you can feel the changes in dynamics yourself.

See "Shortcut Resources" on page 261 for information on where to find current music charts, hit songs, lyrics, and legal downloads.

Shortcut #32

Make Your Transitions Sizzle

Keep the momentum and interest going between sections!

Ever heard the phrase "Nature abhors a vacuum"? It means if there's a space with *nothing* in it, the cosmos will fill it with *something!* This law of nature currently applies to hit songs. When one song section ends and another begins, it creates a transition point. Transitions occur between a verse and chorus or at the end of a chorus going into the next verse or bridge. If there's an empty space between one section and the next, today's hit songs want to rush in and fill it!

In previous decades if the lead singer dropped out for a few beats between the end of the verse and start of the chorus that was okay. Hey, the guitar player could fill it! That's all changed now. Today's hit songs create forward momentum in the lead melody and keep it going ... nonstop!

TRANSITION #1:
End of the verse, going into the chorus

> **Fill the space with a phrase**
> Many of today's hits add a short phrase to fill space between the end of the verse and start of the chorus. Sometimes the phrase kicks off the chorus with added energy. To hear this type of phrase check out the transition from verse to chorus in "Irreplaceable" (Beyoncé). The fill phrase is "You got me twisted." In "Complicated" Avril Lavigne simply adds a "Tell me ..." to keep the momentum going.

> **Shorten the space between sections**
> Often the last line of a verse or pre-chorus is an ascending line that ends with the singer holding out a high note. In previous decades that note might have been held for a full four beats or more, followed by a pause, before the chorus kicked in. No more! In today's hits you'll rarely hear a note like that held for more than two beats and, if it's followed by a pause at all, it's not more than one or two beats. Listen to Daniel Powter's hit single "Bad Day" to hear this type of transition. You can also hear it in Nickelback's "Far Away" and numerous other hits. The message is: Pare your transition time down to the minimum.

> **Start early**
> Sometimes the transition between verse and chorus is blurred or eliminated altogether by starting the chorus early. You can hear this in the Rock hit "It's Not My Time" by 3 Doors Down. Notice how the last line of the pre-chorus ("Can you save me from this?") runs right into the first line of the chorus. This is a very effective way to build forward momentum going into your chorus.

Keep the momentum going through your transitions.

TRANSITION #2:
End of a chorus, going to
the second verse or bridge

The transition out of the chorus and into the second verse usually offers listeners a chance to catch a breath. There may be up to four bars of instrumental while listeners regroup before heading off into the second verse. A complex, relentless song like The Fray's "Over My Head (Cable Car)" *needs* a four-bar break after the first chorus. However, in this song, as in many other recent Pop-genre hits, the break is eliminated going into the bridge.

> **Keep the break short**
> Be careful about allowing the after-chorus break to go on longer than four bars. No matter how good your guitar player is, these days, listeners come to the party for the vocal. Many hits have shortened this break to two bars, like Nickelback's "Someday" or Foo Fighters' "The Pretender."

> **Eliminate the break**
> There are some songs that eliminate the after-chorus break altogether, like Seether's "Rise Above This" which dives straight into the second verse. Matchbox Twenty's "How Far We've Come" jumps abruptly from the choppy, short phrases and high note-range of the chorus into the steady pace and lower range of the second verse, a contrast that's guaranteed to catch the listener's attention. Both songs add a short instrumental break between the second chorus and the bridge. Rihanna's "Take a Bow" moves swiftly and without a break from the first chorus into the second verse and from the second chorus into the bridge.

Eliminating a break can create contrast that grabs attention.

In today's big hits, eliminating or minimizing transitions and instrumental sections keeps the forward momentum going, encouraging listeners to stick around for the entire ride!

Do It Now

1. Listen to hit songs and look for the transitions between sections. Notice how the forward momentum and energy is preserved.

2. Check the transitions in your own songs and see if you can increase the momentum by using some of the techniques described in this Shortcut.

See "Shortcut Resources" on page 261 for information on where to find current music charts, hit songs, lyrics, and legal downloads.

Shortcut #33

Keep Listeners Involved
All the Way to the End

Use structure to keep momentum going after the bridge.

You've got a powerhouse chorus, a couple of strong verses, a solid bridge, and you've kept your listener with you through it all. You are somethin'!!! You've got just one more decision to make before you're home free: Where do you go *after* the bridge?

Suggestions for transitioning out of the bridge

In the post-bridge part of your song, you've got an opportunity to catch your listeners and pull them into the song for the big finale. So think *contrast!*

➢ **If your bridge has an energy level similar to your verses, try going straight to your chorus afterwards.** This will give your listeners one more chance to hear a strong chorus release. Check out Kelly Clarkson's "Breakaway" or Rob Thomas' "Ever the Same" to hear examples.

➢ **If you wrote a big emotional bridge with a peak moment, one that tops your verses and maybe even your chorus, try going directly to your chorus afterwards but changing the feel of the first couple of lines, using a quiet, intimate delivery.** Then come out swinging on the third line and keep it at that level to the end of the song. Daughtry's "Over You" takes this approach. "Whatever It Takes" by Lifehouse does the same and even changes the second chord of the chorus (on "to turn this around") to strengthen the effect. Tricky to do but it works here.

➢ **If your song has a short pre-chorus, you can head there after the bridge and give listeners one final build-up and release into the chorus.** You can even use a half verse before the final chorus as Ashlee Simpson does in "Pieces of Me."

Get attention with one final blast of contrast!

Do It Now

1. Check out the bridges and closing sections in hit songs you like. Notice how they handle the transition out of the bridge and what follows it: chorus, pre-chorus, or verse. Try imagining a different choice. Do you think it would have a different emotional effect?

2. Look at what comes after the bridge in one of your own songs. Could you keep the momentum going more effectively with a different choice?

See "Shortcut Resources" on page 261 for information on where to find current music charts, hit songs, lyrics, and legal downloads.

Shortcut #34

Use a Ghost Song as a Guide to Good Structure

Try this technique for practice in writing song structure.

Ferrari builds great cars. They look cool. They go fast. The engine is a work of art. Nevertheless, it's what we don't see, and don't think about, that is the key to the strength and streamlined beauty of these cars: the chassis, the framework on which the car is built.

Structure is the framework on which you build your song.

To the average person, that framework is invisible. However, if you design and build racecars, then you're likely to use that framework as a model on which to construct your own car. The same holds true for songs. The average listener is unaware of song structure—it's invisible. If you've been listening to songs like the average listener, then you probably haven't noticed song structure either. But without a solid, muscular structure, your song will fall apart as soon as it hits the racetrack. Conclusion: You've got to start driving a Ferrari!

Use a hit song to provide a time-tested framework

Hit songs are built on solid song structures. Try hitching a ride on one of these racecars to get the feel of it. By following the steps in this Shortcut, you can use a hit song as a ghost song to provide a structure for songwriting practice. (REMEMBER: The lyric and melody of the ghost song are copyrighted. Do not use them in any song of your own.)

> **Step 1.** Pick a hit song that has a clearly defined structure. Listen through the complete song a few times to make sure you know which structure is being used. (Read through Shortcuts 24, 25, and 26 to help you identify the three primary hit song forms.) If you're not certain what the structure is, choose a different song. Although hit songs rely heavily on recognizable structures to capture those big audiences, you might come across one that's more complex or less focused than you want to deal with. Take your time deciding on the song you want to use. Listen to several before you pick one. For this exercise, a recognizable, solid structure is a must.

> **Step 2.** Write out the lyrics of the ghost song in a way that clearly reveals the structure of the hit song. Leave a few blank lines between each verse and chorus and before and after the bridge. You're going to use this structure as a framework on which to practice writing a well-built song.

> **Step 3.** Write a new lyric to the chorus melody of the ghost song. Try coming up with a title you can sing comfortably where the ghost song title is, then fill in the rest of the lyric around it. Read Shortcut 73 to learn more about writing a lyric to a ghost song melody. (If you're writing melody first, see Shortcut 102.)

➢ **Step 4.** Once you have a title and chorus lyric, move on to your verse and bridge lyrics. Use Shortcut 47 "Create a Sketch of Your Song" to map out the development of your song's theme and situation. Continue to use the ghost song melody and structure to guide you through your lyric.

Try letting the ghost song structure suggest the emotional dynamic of your lyric. If the ghost song builds anticipation just before the chorus, try to incorporate that increase in energy into your lyric.

➢ **Step 5.** If you're writing just a lyric, no melody, you can go ahead and complete your practice song. Notice how the structure of the ghost song affected the development of your lyric, how the length of your verse and chorus may be different from what you might have written without the ghost song.

If you're writing both lyric *and* melody, read Shortcut 103 which will walk your through the process of creating a new melody to your ghost song lyric.

(!) The lyric and melody of the hit song are protected by copyright. This exercise is for practice only.

Do It Now

Follow the steps above to practice writing songs with solid structure.

See "Shortcut Resources" on page 261 for information on where to find current music charts, hit songs, lyrics, and legal downloads.

Shortcut #35

Avoid the *Blah Zone*

*Start thinking about structure
in the early stages of your song.*

*Does this ever
happen to you?*

Here's a songwriting scenario that is probably familiar. (It is to me!) You've got an idea for the first verse and things are flowing easily; you're being carried along on a wave of sheer inspiration! The verse finds its own length as the initial rush of energy carries you through the beginning of the songwriting process. You write eight gorgeous lines and that's your first verse. One of those lines suggests a title, and you decide to use it in your chorus as the hook—not a bad idea—so you repeat that line four times and call it your chorus.

Plenty of songs have been written this way and sometimes they actually, accidentally work out. But more often than not—Uh oh!— you reach the second verse and find you don't have enough inspiration to fill another eight lines. No problem. You'll just repeat some ideas from the first verse in a slightly different way, then repeat your repetitive four-line chorus. For the bridge, your screaming Marshall-stack guitar player can take yet another solo.

This song is headed toward the *Blah Zone*. The second verse threatens to become static in terms of development. The chorus sounds like it will quickly become predictable. And the bridge … I'll leave that to your imagination. Possibly the production will save this mess. But wouldn't it be better to have a solid, well-built song to begin with?

How to stay out of the *Blah Zone*

A tight, well-focused song structure with plenty of definition between sections (contrast) and good dynamic flow (the roller coaster in Shortcut 31), plus solid lyric development will make your song compelling and keep listeners interested from beginning to end. Start thinking about your song's structure early on. Use one of the layouts in Shortcut 29 to sketch out your song's lyric and melodic structure. By using this "whole song" approach rather than the linear, "I wonder what comes next" songwriting process you can avoid falling into the *Blah Zone!*

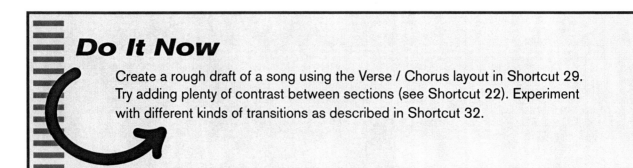

Do It Now

Create a rough draft of a song using the Verse / Chorus layout in Shortcut 29.
Try adding plenty of contrast between sections (see Shortcut 22). Experiment
with different kinds of transitions as described in Shortcut 32.

PART FOUR

Shortcuts to Hit Lyrics

A theme and a title—that's all you need to get started.

The theme will give your song a clear focus.

The title will provide a source of raw material

and give you the questions that your lyric

is going to answer. Once you've got a theme

and a title, you're in business!

Shortcut #36

Themes That Hit Home Runs

Check out this list of themes that listeners love.

> *Whatever she may offer you,*
> *Whatever she may say*
> *Remember the time when our love began.*
> *God knows, I will always be true.*

("I Must Sing" Beatrice, the Countess of Die)

These lines were written 800 years ago but they could be on the Pop charts today. Why? Because this is a theme listeners never get tired of. In a few simple words, this lyric conveys jealousy, yearning and fear of losing a lover—a time-tested, proven winner of a theme!

The vast majority of hit songs are about love relationships: *I love you. I lost you. You lost me. We fell in love. You fell out of love. I'm so lonely. You cheated. I didn't. It's over. It isn't over. I'll never give you up.* I sometimes think that all hit songs are about the first five seconds of a relationship or the last five seconds. That's an exaggeration but not by much! Why? Because that's where all the drama is. The moment of falling in love or the moment of breaking up, these are the emotional peak points in relationships. The warm, comfortable times in between—or the endless wrangling—are harder to write about because there's no single focus, no one moment that tells the whole tale.

Most hit songs are about relationships.

Why do we respond to certain themes?

So why are we so fascinated by these dramas of the heart? The easy answer is that humans are social beings; we're curious about other people, we want to know what they are feeling. In a way, we're all voyeurs. However, there's more to it than that. As songwriters, we tend to choose those moments that offer drama, insight, and change. In life, these moments are often the most difficult to get through and the scariest. Listeners can live these moments vicariously, safely, within the context of the song and know they are not alone in feeling the same things.

Listeners can experience emotions safely within the framework of a song.

Even though the majority of hit songs focus on themes that circle around love relationships, this is not as limiting as it may seem. There are an infinite number of ways to treat these themes—as many as there are songwriters. By using *your* insights and experiences, you can make these themes your own. Always write what is true for you. Be present in your songs, otherwise you'll end up writing the same old song with the same old theme. Exactly what you want to avoid.

Here's a list of themes that are common to many songs in many eras. Check out some of the lyrics to these songs to learn how different songwriters handle the same theme in very different ways.

- **First Encounter / Falling in Love**
  "When I See U" (Fantasia)
  "First Time" (Lifehouse)
  "Somebody Like You" (Keith Urban)

- **Let's Get Together**
  "Want To" (Sugarland)
  "Realize" (Colbie Caillat)
  "Touch My Body" (Mariah Carey)

- **Deep in Love / Our Love Is Special**
  "Bless the Broken Road" (Rascal Flatts)
  "For a Moment Like This" (Kelly Clarkson)
  "Like You'll Never See Me Again" (Alicia Keys)
  "Everything" (Michael Bublé)

- **Lost-In-Love Songs (hurt, jealousy, guilt, suspicion, anger)**
  "You're Beautiful" (James Blunt)
  "You'll Think of Me" (Keith Urban)
  "Truth Is" (Fantasia)
  "What Hurts the Most" (Rascal Flatts)
  "Moving Mountains" (Usher)

- **Love Is Over**
  "So Happy" (Theory of a Deadman)
  "Take a Bow" (Rihanna)
  "Rise Above This" (Seether)

- **Love Endures All**
  "In a Real Love" (Phil Vassar)
  "Ever the Same" (Rob Thomas)
  "White Flag" (Dido)

Many songs share the same theme. How you handle it makes your song unique!

Other relationship themes

Of course the idea of relationships is not limited to love relationships. You are also in a relationship with your own self-image and the world around you: *I'm changing. I'm growing up. I want to be more like this. I want get away from that.* So a relationship song can also be about your relationship with life, relationship with society, or relationship with family. Just be aware that love relationships tend to dominate the hit song charts in all genres.

- **Christian**
  These songs sometimes sound like mainstream love songs. The loved one is God or Jesus but this may not be stated specifically in the lyrics, allowing the listener to interpret the song.

  "I Will Be Here For You" (Michael W. Smith)
  "Overjoyed" (Jars Of Clay)
  "Will You" (P.O.D.)
  "The Last Night" (Skillet)

- **Society**
  "Waiting On the World to Change" (John Mayer)
  "Remedy (I Won't Worry)" (Jason Mraz)
  "How Far We've Come" (Matchbox Twenty)

- **Life & Self**
  "Unwritten" (Natasha Bedigfield)
  "Live Like You Were Dying" (Tim McGraw)
  "New Shoes" (Paolo Nutini)

- **Family & Friendship**
  "Breakaway" (Kelly Clarkson)
  "How to Save a Life" (The Fray)
  "Photograph" (Nickelback)

Songs can be about many kinds of relationships.

Do It Now

Listen to hit songs in the genre in which you're interested. Make a list of the themes of 15 of the Top 20 songs. If you're unclear about a theme, skip it and go on to the next song. See how many of the themes fit within the list given in this Shortcut. Among those songs that share a theme, notice how it is treated in different ways.

See "Shortcut Resources" on page 261 for information on where to find current music charts, hit songs, lyrics, and legal downloads.

Shortcut #37

Tracking Down a Blockbuster Theme

Where to find themes that will work hard for you.

Some songwriters spend a lot of time waiting. Waiting for inspiration. Waiting for an idea. I don't want you to wait. I want you to start doing, writing, and creating right now!

One of the things songwriters frequently wait for is an idea that will launch them into the deep emotional waters of a song. Although these ideas do turn up from time to time, it's hard to build a substantial body of work on such an unpredictable resource. And it's funny how, once an idea has worked, it tends to show up over and over again, leading to repetition and stagnation of your creative muscle. It's not necessary to hang around hoping an idea will magically appear—there's a whole world of inspiring, intriguing ideas out there waiting to be discovered if you just go looking.

Tip: Don't wait around for inspiration. Go out and find it!

Hunting the blockbuster theme

You might have noticed that successful songs use many of the same themes that drive all types of dramatic entertainment. Just check out any list of popular films or today's favorite TV dramas. While hit songs tend to focus on relationships and emotions rather than car chases and special effects, they share many of the same dramatic elements with contemporary films and TV shows: Who is involved? What will happen next? Who is doing what to whom? You can use popular movies and TV shows, especially ones that focus on romance or relationships, to lead you to themes that pack a big emotional punch both for you and your listeners.

Look for themes that resonate for you

So, yes, I'm telling you to watch TV and go to the movies to find ideas. But remember, it's important for *you* to be present emotionally in your song. Start by looking for a scene that draws your emotional attention. When did you find yourself getting involved with a character? When did you identify with the character? What was the peak emotional moment for you in this character's story? Any of these points in a storyline can provide a theme for a song.

Look for themes and characters that intrigue you.

For example, here's a scene: The lead character sits alone in a dark room after running into an ex-lover who is now involved with someone else. If you were watching this scene and you felt moved by it, consider creating a song based on it. Use your imagination to create dialogue, background, and specific examples, whatever you need for your song. Think of your song as underscore for the scene.

There are a number of advantages to finding themes this way. Using movies and TV shows for inspiration works well because you gravitate to ideas that resonate for you, ones that are free of personal biographical "baggage" and have proven, universal appeal. And, by giving yourself new material to react to, you'll discover emotional angles and insights that might never have occurred to you otherwise.

You don't have to limit yourself to the characters and incidents in the film or TV program; feel free to make them your own. Imagine a different outcome or additional details to fill out your song. What emotional message do *you* want to communicate based on this situation? Try turning that idea into your hook. Make your song as unique or unusual as you wish. But, stay with the emotional essence that drew you to the scene and character in the first place; keep that central to your song.

Give yourself something new to react to.

Do It Now

Pick a movie or TV show with a dramatic story. Make it one you like to watch. Look for a scene with emotional content, maybe it's a scene where one character finds out something about another that changes the way they feel, or realizes something for the first time. Write down this idea in a single sentence. Look for a short phrase that expresses this theme. Make it your title. Use Shortcuts 44 through 47 to sketch out the development of your song.

See "Shortcut Resources" on page 261 for information on where to find current music charts, hit songs, lyrics, and legal downloads.

Shortcut #38

Themes: Make Them Your Own

Use a fresh approach or insight to pull your listener in.

As you can see from the themes list in Shortcut 36, the same idea can provide the starting point for very different songs. You'll probably write several songs on a single theme and they will all be different. The trick is to find new ways to approach it and to make emotional discoveries that keep the theme compelling for you and your listeners.

So how do you take an idea that has been used by dozens of songwriters and give it something uniquely your own? Here are three approaches that will help you explore your theme and find fresh perspectives. By using one or, better yet, a combination of all three, you'll end up with a song that expresses the concept in a distinctive way.

1. Seek out new insights.

Take some time to really get inside your theme. Imagine yourself in the situation. If it's a personal experience, recall what it felt like when you went through it. Write down your feelings. What is the most important thing you can say about it? What caused it to happen? What happened that you didn't expect? What did you learn from it?

Explore your theme by putting yourself inside it.

Think of yourself as an explorer; by putting yourself into the situation and living or re-living it, you are mapping out the terrain. Although others have been over this territory before, *you* will discover things they missed. It's this process of discovery that makes songs interesting and compelling for listeners. If you simply repeat familiar phrases, although they may have truth in them, you're going over old ground. Listeners have been there already and they'll put their emotions on autopilot. Show them a new way to experience this place.

2. Use fresh language and images.

You know the phrase, "A picture is worth 1000 words"? In songwriting, this concept is at the heart of what we do. Just take a look at the first line of "You've Lost That Lovin' Feeling," one of the greatest lost-in-love songs ever written. The writers, Cynthia Weil and Barry Mann, could have said something like "I can tell you don't love me anymore." That would certainly explain the situation but it wouldn't make us feel it, see it, and experience it like the image of a woman who doesn't close her eyes when her lover kisses her. This theme has been the subject of countless songs but, by using small, vivid details, the writers brought it to life for us.

For tips on using images, read Shortcuts 57, 58 & 61.

In songwriting, *how* you say something is as important as *what* you say.

That's because *how* you say it can convey more information than you would ever be able to cram into a straightforward explanation. An image, example, or telling detail can communicate everything the listener needs to know in order to grasp the heart of a situation, rediscover it, and feel it as if for the first time.

3. Try a new approach or angle.

Take a new approach to a familiar theme. In Carrie Underwood's huge Country hit "Before He Cheats," the songwriters took a predictable, familiar theme and gave it a vivid, fresh coat of paint! We hardly notice the old "he's cheatin' on me" chestnut underneath.

We've almost come to expect these types of thematic ploys in the Country genre but you can find them in Pop, R&B/Soul, and Rock, too. "So Happy" by Theory of a Deadman is a brutally honest look at the end of a bad relationship. It's a rough lyric, but it works for the Rock genre of this band and takes this theme to the limit, pushing the song up the charts. Alicia Keys creates a unique approach to the theme of enduring love relationships in "Like You'll Never See Me Again" by reminding us of the impermanence of life.

Choose a theme and try looking at it from different points of view. Make a list of ideas based on your theme. Be inventive. Ask yourself "what if?" Imagine different scenarios and reactions. Write down everything that occurs to you no matter how unusual. When you have ten or so ideas on your list, pick one and try developing it using the sketch method in Shortcut 47.

Make a list of possible angles and character reactions!

Do It Now

1. Look up the lyrics to several hit songs in your genre and check the themes. Are they ones you've heard before? How did the songwriter make the theme fresh? Was it the language, the insights, a new approach, or all three?

2. Choose a theme from the list of themes in Shortcut 36. Decide how you would approach this theme in a unique way. What's the situation? What kind of language would you use? What new insights could you bring to it? Try making a list as suggested at the end of this shortcut.

See "Shortcut Resources" on page 261 for information on where to find current music charts, hit songs, lyrics, and legal downloads.

Shortcut #39

Make Your Title
the Peak of the Pyramid

For real staying power, build 'em like the pharaohs.

Of the Seven Wonders of the World, only the Great Pyramid of Giza is still standing. Tourists today can still see something close to what the pharaohs actually built. So what is it that gives the pyramids their immense stability and longevity? Let me share a little secret: There are more than two million blocks of stone in the Great Pyramid and every single one of those blocks supports the pinnacle, the single peak at the top of the structure.

This works!

There are plenty of ways to write a song. However, if you want to end up with something that will last like the pyramids and attract listeners like a tourist magnet, the most efficient and dependable method is the one that begins with the title. Once you have your title, you know what you are building and every word and every note can be fitted in so that it leads toward and supports a single focus point. Now that's a rock solid song!

Instructions for Building Your Pyramid

➢ **Step 1.** Choose a title that intrigues you, one that makes you say, "I wonder what that's about!" Shortcuts 40 through 42 can help you find a strong title.

➢ **Step 2.** Write down the questions the title asks. Every good title suggests questions that need to be answered. Read Shortcut 44 to learn more.

➢ **Step 3.** Make a list of related and contrasting phrases, images, and words. See Shortcuts 45 and 46 for more on how to make your list.

➢ **Step 4.** Sketch out your song using Shortcut 47. When you finish, you'll have the raw material you need to create a memorable song that's focused on and supports your title.

Do It Now

1. Look at hit song lyrics and notice how the chorus and verse reinforce the title as the song progresses. What questions are asked and answered?

2. Pick a short phrase to use as a title, then use the steps in this Shortcut to start developing the pyramid that will support it.

See "Shortcut Resources" on page 261 for information on where to find current music charts, hit songs, lyrics, and legal downloads.

Shortcut #40

Use Images, Action Words, and Phrases in Your Title

Give your title the edge! Be vivid and memorable.

In a well-constructed song, the title is the one lyric phrase that I guarantee your listeners will notice and remember! More than that: It will be the guide and the goal toward which all other lines lead. It will be the hook that grabs people and pulls them deep into your song. It will sum up the heart and soul of your theme. So, right from the start, think about choosing *a memorable title with potential for development.*

Length: Most titles are one to five words in length. Titles longer than that are hard to remember and are usually shortened by listeners anyway, so you might as well do it for them and ensure your title maintains its punch. There's no hard and fast rule about title length. Do what feels right but go short if you can.

What makes a title memorable?

Let's try out a title. How's this: "Love Relationships Can Be Difficult." As a song title, this one is a real loser. Of course you knew that but *why* is it so bad? The statement is certainly true and it's what the song is about, so why is it so weak and forgettable? Because it's an *abstract statement.* Abstract statements are ones that are not connected to a specific action, concrete example, or image. This type of statement goes right in one ear and out the other. Listeners may agree with it but it doesn't make them feel anything; it has no relevance and doesn't raise curiosity, so it's forgettable.

Avoid abstract statements in your title.

What if we gave that same song a title like "Our Love Is a Battleground"? Now the title is specific ("our love") and it has a concrete image ("a battleground"). The listener is automatically involved, curious about what these individuals are feeling while mentally picturing a battleground. This has become an intriguing story or situation rather than an abstract statement. Which title would you, as a listener, find more compelling and memorable—"Love Relationships Can Be Difficult" or "Our Love is a Battleground"?

Getting the title edge!

➤ **Let images do the work**
   Here some examples of hit song titles that use concrete images to create a mental picture for the listener.

   "Smoke Gets In Your Eyes"
   "Gangsta's Paradise"

Read Shortcut 57 to learn about the power of images!

"Shadow of the Day"
"Mud On the Tires"
"When Stars Go Blue"

And here's a title I'll be using later on in the lyric Shortcuts ...

"Give Me the Moonlight"

Use action words

Action words
are covered in
Shortcut 62.

Action words are both visual and energetic. They not only help us picture what's happening, they make us physically feel it. Here are a few examples of hit song titles that use action words.

"Stealing Cinderella"
"Jesus Walks"
"Rise Above This"
"Jump"
"Don't Blink"

➤ **Say it to someone**
Add intimacy to a title by speaking directly to "you." Here are some hit song titles that use this type of direct address to get our attention.

"You're Gonna Miss This"
"Love Me If You Can"
"You're Beautiful"
"I Just Called to Say I Love You"
"Hey There Delilah"

➤ **Use a conversational or idiomatic phrase**
The one exception to short titles (up to 5 words) is the case of familiar, well-known phrases. A long title like Stevie Wonder's "I Just Called To Say I Love You" is memorable because people are familiar with it. Conversational or idiomatic phrases can make good titles.

"I Don't Want To Miss a Thing"
"I Heard It Through the Grapevine"
"Who Knew"
"What Was I Thinkin'"
"Truth Is"

Feature your
title prominently
in your song.

Title exceptions: Are you feeling lucky?

Not all hit songs have memorable titles but these are the exception. The Goo Goo Dolls hit song "Iris" does not fit the title guidelines suggested here. You may not even recognize the song by this title; most people refer to it as "I Just Want You To Know Who I Am." But you won't find it under that name at iTunes! Perhaps the Goo Goo Dolls can afford to be hard to find. However, if you haven't already sold a few million records—like they have—give your title every advantage. It's going to need to compete in a tough world; give it the edge!

86   SHORTCUTS TO HIT SONGWRITING

Do It Now

1. Look for effective titles in hit songs. Does the title use one or more of the following: images, action words, direct address, a conversational phrase?

2. Try rewriting the following phrases using the techniques in this Shortcut to convey the same information in an emotionally appealing and memorable way. Have some fun with them! Try to make your titles as appealing as these are *un*appealing!

   "Love Is a Basic Human Emotion"
   "A Supportive Friend Is Useful"
   "Dealing with Rejection Can Be Challenging"
   "Loneliness Is Difficult on Weekends"
   "I'm Feeling Optimistic About the Future"

3. Look through some of your own song titles to see if you can add memorability and impact using the ideas in this Shortcut.

See "Shortcut Resources" on page 261 for information on where to find current music charts, hit songs, lyrics, and legal downloads.

Shortcut #41

Find Great Titles:
Follow Your Emotional Attention

Use a title to launch a process of discovery.

John Wayne once explained his acting technique by saying that he didn't act, he only reacted to what others in a scene were doing. Where did John Wayne come up with this idea of reacting instead of acting? Most likely, one day on the set, he noticed that if he chose his actions himself (if he *acted*), his choices eventually became repetitious and uninteresting to both the audience and himself. Whereas, if he *reacted* to others, his performance was always fresh and real. By staying involved with his surroundings, he was part of an evolving situation, doing what we all do in real life—react to things around us.

*Don't act ...
react!*

How does this relate to songwriting? You may have started writing songs because you experienced an emotion or situation that evoked a strong reaction in you. It could take five, ten, twenty or more songs to exhaust the possibilities of that event; it could even be something you write about for a lifetime. But it can't be *all* you write about. Eventually, you risk getting stale and repetitive. Instead of *reacting* with genuine emotion, you start *acting*—doing what you already know how to do, falling back on old habits, and writing the same song over and over.

Look outside for inspiration

To keep your songs fresh and real—both for yourself and your listeners—make certain your songwriting process provides you with new ideas and insights. There has to be an opportunity for you to discover other things your muse wants to say, things you may not even be aware of. This is how you keep growing as a songwriter. It's exciting. It keeps your art alive. The interesting thing is, rather than turning toward the inside for new ideas, you need to turn outward to do this exploring. To begin the songwriting discovery process, you have to give yourself something new to react to.

A great title can launch
the discovery process

Because a strong title can provide the basis for a cohesive, effective lyric, it's an excellent place to begin exploring new song ideas. Rather than turning inside for the inspiration for your title, try looking to the world around you for ideas.

- Read headlines in newspapers, online news sites, and magazines.
- Listen to talk shows, commercials and cable news channels.
- Watch classic movies, TV dramas, and reality shows.
- Listen to your own conversations.
- Play the Find-a-Title Game in Shortcut 42.

These will all give you new ideas, words, and phrases to react to. Of course, much of what you hear and read won't be of use to you. You're looking for those few short phrases (one to five words) that stand on their own, phrases that have a meaning beyond the context in which they appear.

The trick to finding titles as you read the newspaper or watch a film is to stay focused on your songwriting objective—finding a title that suggests a fresh song idea. Avoid getting caught up in the content of what you're reading or watching. If it's a film or TV show, keep reminding yourself that you're listening for bits of dialogue, not a theme or plot line. The same holds true when you're sifting through a newspaper, online blogs, or magazine articles. You're not interested in the subject matter, just single words and phrases. Let your eyes skim over the page. Look at the headlines first.

Phrases that interest you or raise questions are worth working on. Look for phrases that resonate for you.

Important:
Follow your emotional attention

A title is not going to be just any bunch of words. It's important that you tune into your own reactions in order to find a phrase that will inspire and support an entire song. Be on the alert for a phrase or word that jumps out at you or sticks in your memory. Look for lines that intrigue you, or a phrase that makes you think, "I wonder what that's about." When you hear one of those, *write it down*. Let it knock around in your head *and* heart. Use Shortcuts 44 and 45 to develop the phrase further and find out if it continues to hold interest for you.

If a phrase doesn't captivate you, don't use it—no matter how much you may think it sounds like a hit song title. Such a song is likely to end up lacking the passion and excitement of emotional discovery. When you find a phrase that does hold interest for you, that's an indication that there's something worth exploring. You may not know what it is, but you can find out by writing that song.

Look for phrases that resonate

The world is continually tossing song material your way. Some sources are more productive than others. For instance, the entertainment section of the newspaper has more usable phrases than the business section … but you never can tell what you'll find, so keep your eyes and ears open! Here's a list of phrases I gathered from online news sites and TV shows.

> Can't Hide It from Myself
> Shining Alone
> Stay Till I'm Gone
> You Gave Your Word
> Stars Don't Lie
> Cloudy Now, Sunny Later
> Smart and Sexy
> Tell Me What You're Looking For
> Stumbling On
> If You Say It Softly
> Don't Take Me Too Seriously

Each of these "found phrases" suggests song possibilities. Any one of them could be a strong title. They raise questions that can be developed and answered in a lyric. However, what's important is whether any of these phrases *attract you.* Read through them one at a time and take a moment to notice your reaction. Is there one that strikes you as more interesting than the others? Is there one that suggests questions you'd like to answer or evokes an emotional reaction? If so, this is a phrase that "resonates" for you. It has an effect that goes beyond being a mere collection of words. Consider using this phrase as a title and developing it into a lyric using Shortcuts 44 through 47. Stay close to the feeling that initially drew you to the phrase. As you work on your lyric, you'll begin to uncover the answers to your questions. Stay in touch with your responses. This is the process of self-discovery that will lead you to new insights, ideas, and themes.

What if the same title that intrigues you also appeals to someone else? That's not really a problem. Many songs share the same title and the two of you will end up writing very different songs. The same title resonates in each of you for different reasons based on personal experiences and emotions. As you write, you'll follow your own journey of discovery which will be different from anyone else's.

Do It Now

Look through a newspaper or magazine, watch a TV show or movie, go online, or listen to conversations. Be on the lookout for short, usable phrases. Ignore the context; it's only the phrase you want. This is a different way of listening and reading than you're used to, so try doing it for short periods of time at first. Write down all the potential titles you find, then choose one or two that interest you. Use Shortcuts 44 through 46 to develop one of these into a rough lyric.

Shortcut #42

Play the Find-a-Title Game

Use this word list to stimulate fresh ideas.

In the previous Shortcut I described a songwriting process that begins with an external source such as a phrase from a headline or a conversation. Using these external cues can give you something new to react to and stimulate fresh ways of looking at things. It's like having a collaborator throw ideas at you except, in this case, your collaborator is the whole world!

To give this process a tighter focus, I created a game using a word list. The following two pages contain a list of words that can help you find fresh titles. Here are two ways to play the Find-a-Title game:

1. **Let a single word suggest a title**
   There are plenty of hit songs with one-word titles ("Help!" "Angel" "Jump" "Amazed" "Still" "Hero"). Let your eye scan the word lists on the next two pages. See if there's a single word that draws your attention, one that makes you pause. Write it down if you feel it's a possible title. Don't limit yourself, though, feel free to add any other words it suggests to you. If a word in the list suggests a whole phrase, write *that* down! The word list is here to inspire ideas, not take the place of or limit your creativity.

2. **Choose any two words from the list and create a phrase**
   Again, let your eye run easily over the list until you see a word that draws your attention. Write it down. Go back to the list and repeat this process until you have three or four words. Now, try putting a couple of them together. Some combinations will be pure nonsense, but others will suggest an emotion or idea to you. Play with combinations of the words on your list by adding short words to link or modify them. See what kinds of interesting phrases you can come up with.

   You can add words to the Find-a-Title list to customize it. Many songwriters have words that have a special resonance for them. As you tune your ears and eyes to look for song titles in the world around you, go ahead and add other words that appeal to you.

Go PLAY!!!

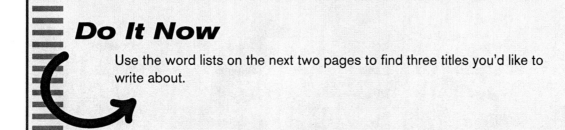

Do It Now

Use the word lists on the next two pages to find three titles you'd like to write about.

Act	Breathe	Do	Follow	Hold
Affair	Breathless	Doesn't	Fool	Home
After	Bridge	Don't	Foolish	Honest
Again	Call	Down	For	Hopeless
Against	Can	Dream	Forever	Hot
Ain't	Can't	Dreaming	Forget	House
Air	Careless	Drive	From	How
Alive	Carry	Edge	Get	Hungry
All	Caught	Emotion	Ghost	Hurt
Almost	Chance	Empty	Girl	Idea
Alone	Cherish	End	Give	If
Always	Child	Endless	Glad	Impossible
Amazing	Close	Enjoy	Glory	In
And	Closer	Escape	God	Inside
Angel	Color	Eternal	Gone	Inspiration
Any	Come	Even	Good	Into
Anymore	Completely	Every	Goodbye	Invisible
Anytime	Cool	Everybody	Goodnight	Is
Anywhere	Could	Everyday	Got	Isn't
Arms	Cover	Everything	Groovy	It
Ask	Crash	Eyes	Grow	Join
Away	Crazy	Fade	Half	Joke
Baby	Cross	Faithful	Halfway	Journey
Back	Crush	Fall	Hand	Just
Beautiful	Cry	Falling	Hanging	Keep
Because	Daddy	Far	Happy	Kiss
Bed	Dance	Farther	Hard	Kind
Believe	Dangerous	Fast	Has	Know
Belong	Dark	Feel	Have	Last
Best	Dear	Fever	Head	Late
Between	Decide	Find	Hear	Lay
Big	Deep	Fire	Heart	Leaving
Black	Desire	First	Heaven	Lesson
Bless	Destiny	Flame	Help	Let
Blind	Different	Fly	Helpless	Letter
Break	Distance	Flying	Here	Life

Light	Not	Sad	Stay	Try
Like	Nothing	Safe	Steal	Twilight
Living	Now	Said	Still	Two
Longer	Nowhere	Save	Stop	Understand
Look	Ocean	Say	Storm	Until
Looking	Once	Search	Strange	Up
Losing	One	Secret	Substitute	Use
Lost	Only	Sexy	Suddenly	Vanish
Love	Open	Shadow	Sun	Vision
Lover	Our	Shame	Sunshine	Voice
Loving	Out	Share	Survive	Wait
Lucky	Own	She	Swear	Walk
Mad	Perfect	Shine	Sweet	Water
Made	Picture	Should	Swim	Way
Make	Places	Show	Take	We
Mama	Play	Simple	Talk	What
Man	Please	Single	Taste	When
Maybe	Power	Sky	Teach	Whenever
Meet	Pretend	Sleep	Tears	Where
Midnight	Promise	Slow	Tell	While
Million	Quit	Smile	Tender	Why
Miss	Rain	So	Thank	Wild
Missing	Reach	Some	That's	Will
Moon	Ready	Somebody	Then	Wings
Moonlight	Real	Someday	There	Wish
More	Reason	Someone	These	Without
Music	Release	Something	Think	Woman
My	Remember	Sometimes	This	Words
Name	Remind	Somewhere	Thousand	World
Near	Rest	Song	Time	Years
Need	Rhythm	Soul	Today	Yes
Never	Right	South	Together	Yesterday
Next	Risk	Speak	Tonight	Yet
Night	Room	Spend	Too	You
No	Rose	Stand	True	Young
Nobody	Run	Stars	Truly	Your

Find-a-Title Notes

Use this page to keep a record of titles you want to work on or use it to customize the Find-a-Title word game by adding more words.

Shortcut #43

Make Your Title an Original

Give your song a recognizable, unique title.

You might have noticed that there are many songs, even hit songs, with the same title. For instance, Huey Lewis had a hit with "The Power of Love," Celine Dion did well with another "Power of Love" as did a band called Frankie Goes To Hollywood. Another popular title that has done well: "Angel" for Sarah McLachlan, Aerosmith, Dave Matthews, Dru Hill, and Jimi Hendrix—all different songs. In fact, the ASCAP online database lists 436 songs with the single-word title "Angel"! So, what's happening here? Should you call your song "The Power of Love" or "Angel" and hope to increase your chances of a hit?

It's what you say about your title that makes it powerful

Although the title is an essential and featured element of a hit song, *it's what you say about it and how you say it* that gives your song the compelling quality that makes listeners want to hear your song again and again. There have been plenty of songs called "The Power of Love" or "Angel" that *weren't* hits! In other words, it's your fresh insights, emotion, and ability to use song craft that will make your song a hit. That's why you should *always* look for a title that engages your emotional attention, one you want to explore.

Your title can help listeners remember your song

So why are there so many songs with the title "Angel"? Perhaps because the image of a luminous, protective, healing figure is so universally appealing and evocative. Perhaps, at some point, *you* may want to write a song about an angel. You might even want to use "Angel" as your title. Go right ahead. However, here's a suggestion: Add a couple of additional words to make your title distinctive and memorable, like these songwriters did: "Angel in My Eyes," "Angel of the Morning," "Heaven Must Be Missing an Angel." The longer title not only distinguishes these songs from others, it recalls more of the melodic hook, refreshing the listener's memory and acting as a reminder of the theme of the song. Help listeners remember *your* song by giving them a title that is distinctively yours!

Unique titles help listeners recall your melodic hook and lyric theme.

Do It Now

From the word lists in Shortcut 42, choose some single words that might work as titles. Try adding one or more words to make them more descriptive and uniquely your own. Notice how the longer title suggests a possible lyric situation, even a melody line.

Shortcut #44

Answer the Questions
the Title Asks

When it's NOT a good idea to leave them wanting more.

That old cliché "Always leave them wanting more!" does *not* apply to songs. If you leave your listeners hanging, if you leave them in the dark, if you leave them with unanswered questions, they will not be happy. Why? Because.

I could end this chapter with that line and *you'd* be a frustrated reader. The title of this Shortcut drew your attention. Hopefully it intrigued you a little bit. Now, if I abandon that title—and you—without answering your questions, you'll have every right to feel that I let you down.

A good song title works the same way; it suggests questions that you, as a songwriter, need to answer. If you don't, your listeners will be disappointed.

Find the questions the title asks

Choose a title that suggests questions to be answered in the song.

What kinds of questions am I talking about? Take a title like "Heartbreak Hotel." It immediately suggests questions: What is a "heartbreak hotel"? What happens there? Who stays there? How do you get there? How do you get out?

When you've got an intriguing phrase that listeners want to know more about, *that's* a good title! Here's another: "Amazed." Take a moment before reading on to think about what questions this song will need to answer.

Done? I'll bet you came up with questions that are similar to mine: "Who or what is the singer amazed by?" "Why is it so amazing?" A song with this title, for example the hit by Lonestar, has *got* to answer those questions in some way! (And, of course, it does.)

Here's a short list of questions that might be raised by a title. There are plenty of others! Don't limit yourself to these. (See the worksheet in Shortcut 46 for more.)

- Why do you say that?
- What happened to make you feel that way?
- What will you do about it?
- What does that mean?
- Why is it important?

Make the title questions work for you

The title of any song is likely to be at the heart of the chorus and probably repeated, so the questions it raises are bound to haunt the song—lurking in and around the entire lyric. You can't ignore them (and neither can your listener) so why not make them work *for* you.

The questions raised by the title can lead you through your song, helping you develop the situation clearly. For example, if your title is "Please Don't Leave Me" it raises questions that could be handled in the following way:

Verse 1:	Why does the singer think the other person is leaving?
Chorus 1:	Why is the singer saying this? ("Please, don't leave me.")
Verse 2:	What can the singer do about this?
Chorus 2:	Same as Chorus 1.
Bridge:	What will happen next?
Chorus 3:	Same as Chorus 1.

Title questions can help you develop your lyric.

Finding the questions will help you stay focused

Knowing what the questions are that the lyric needs to answer will help you stay focused on the central theme of your song. You need to know what your song is about. If you don't have the answer to that, chances are your lyric will get into trouble. Make a list of three or four questions you want to answer and stick with them. Make sure your lyric keeps leading back to them, giving us more information that helps to answer those questions. If more questions come up while you're writing, check to be sure they lead back to these primary questions. If you introduce something into your lyric that raises a different set of questions, consider saving it for another song.

Do It Now

1. Look up hit song titles and lyrics. Find questions raised by the titles that were answered in the lyrics. Make a list of these questions. It's also interesting to note where they were answered: Verse 1 or 2, a chorus, or a bridge?

2. Try making up a few titles of your own. (See Shortcuts 40 through 42 for a little inspiration.) Write three questions for each title.

See "Shortcut Resources" on page 261 for information on where to find current music charts, hit songs, lyrics, and legal downloads.

Shortcut #45

Raw Material: Create Lists of Related and Contrasting Words

Mine a ton of ore with lyric gold inside.

Sometimes I wish I were a painter, a sculptor, or a potter instead of a songwriter. These lucky artists have raw materials to draw on for their work: paint, stone, metal, and clay. Songwriters have nothing but a blank page and a silent keyboard or guitar. Creating something out of nothing is a real challenge!

What if there were some kind of clay or paint for lyric writers, some raw material you could shape into a chorus and verse, or chisel away to form a bridge. There is! In this Shortcut, I'll show you how to develop the raw material for a song lyric. You'll create plenty of words, phrases, images, and ideas to draw on and inspire you. You won't end up using all of them, of course; like a potter, you'll work over what you want and throw away what doesn't belong. What you're aiming for is a very rough shape, an initial something that you can form an opinion about. It's always easier to react to something—clay, colored paint, stone, words—than to create something out of thin, sometimes *very* thin, air.

Create your raw material: Start with your title

In the previous Shortcuts, I've been suggesting that you start your lyric with a title. The title will help you keep your song focused and provide questions the song needs to answer. You can also use it as the starting point for developing the raw material from which to build your song.

As an example, let's use the title, "Give Me the Moonlight." We're going to make a list of words, images, and phrases that are *related* to the title. Then a list of opposite or *contrasting* words and phrases.

> ➢ **The list of Related Words**
> Words that are "related" to your title are ones that you associate with any word in the title or the whole title itself. Write a list of words, as many as you can think of. If a word in your list suggests another one, go ahead and write it down. Follow the trail of associations; don't worry if the connection isn't perfectly clear. You won't use all these words and phrases; some of them may suggest others that you *will* use. For this title, my list would look something like this.
>
> • "Give Me the Moonlight": *night, twilight, moon, deep blue sky, stars, evening, quiet, romance, romantic, couple, lovers, alone together, touch, kiss, lips, eyes, look, sharing secrets.*

Use the title to create a list of related words, phrases & images.

Your Related Word list may look somewhat different but it probably included some of the same words as mine. Many of us share the same associations; the differences will help to make your song unique. Put yourself in the song, imagine your emotions, and feel them. Then see what comes up for you.

> **The list of Contrasting Words**
> After you've made your Related Word list, make another list of opposite or contrasting words. Include words that contrast with your title as well as with the images, phrases, and words in your Related Words list. My list of contrasting words for this title would look like this:

- "Give Me the Moonlight": *day, morning, sun, bright, hot, noisy, crowded, strangers, busy, job, money, boss, frustration, alone in a crowd.*

Make a list of contrasting words, phrases & images.

How to use your raw material

When you combine these word lists with the questions your title asks (See Shortcut 44.), you're ready to start writing, adding more words and images to your lists as you create the song.

Here's how I might do it: Writing a song with the title "Give Me the Moonlight," suggests these questions to me: "Why do I want the moonlight?" and "What will I do when I get it?" The word lists give me a place to start my song. Here's a useful tip: By starting with the contrasting words, you tell your listeners what the problem is! So I might start with the image of a crowded, rush-hour street scene for my first verse: *When the sun is beating down / everybody's rushing 'round / Trying to make a buck / there's no time for love.* All of those images and ideas were derived from my list of Contrasting Words.

Tip: Start with the Contrasting Word list to set up the conflict or problem.

Now, when I get to the chorus, I know I'm going to use my title, so I'll lean on the Related Words list, because those words will support it. My chorus might go something like this: *Give me the moonlight, give me the night / When the world is still then I can tell you all the things I feel inside / Give me the moonlight give me the night. / Give me the stars but make them the ones that I see shining in your eyes / Give me the moonlight.*

Now I have contrast between the verse and chorus. I've developed a lyric that's cohesive, while giving listeners the information they need to stay inside the song. Instead of staring at a blank page and wondering what to do next, I started a song with just a title and the word lists derived from it.

Do It Now

Using Shortcut 41 or 42, find a title you want to work with. Now, use the "Develop Your Title Into a Lyric Worksheet" in Shortcut 46 to help you create the raw material for a lyric.

Shortcut #46

Develop Your Title Into a Lyric Worksheet

Assemble the raw material for a lyric based on your title.

1. Find the title questions

A good title suggests questions that need to be answered in the lyric. (See Shortcut 44 to read more about title questions.) A lot depends on your title, of course, but here are a few suggestions:

Why did you do that?	Why do you want that?
What does that mean?	What happened to make you say that?
What does that look like?	Why do you feel that way?
Why is that important?	Why are you doing that?

Title Questions. (Write your title and questions here.)

2. Related words, phrases, and images

Make a list of words, phrases, and images related to your title and any other words that these suggest. Write freely. Don't worry if the associations aren't exactly clear. You won't be using all of them in your song. See Shortcut 45 for more information.

Related Words. (Write your related words, phrases, and images here.)

3. Opposite or contrasting words, phrases, and images

After you've made a list of related words, make a list of contrasting words, phrases and images. The words can contrast with your title or with the words in your Related Words list. See Shortcut 45 to find out more.

Contrasting Words. (Write your contrasting words, phrases, and images here.)

4. Developing your lyric

- Rough out a chorus lyric first. Try using your title in the first line or last line or both. Answer at least one question you wrote in the Title Questions box. Use one or two (or more) of the words you wrote in the Related Words box. Don't worry if your lines are just rough ideas. This is only a start!

- For your first verse, check out some of your contrasting words to set up a problem or conflict and see what happens. Again, try answering a question from the Title Questions box.

- Use Shortcut 47 "Create a Sketch of Your Song" to help you continue to develop your lyric. As you work, add to your lists of related and contrasting words. If you think of more title questions that need to be answered, add to those, as well.

- Once you've roughed out your lyric, use the other Shortcuts in the "Shortcuts to Hit Lyrics" section to add strength, impact, and focus. You can also use this lyric development process with a ghost song melody. See Shortcut 73 for a step-by-step guide.

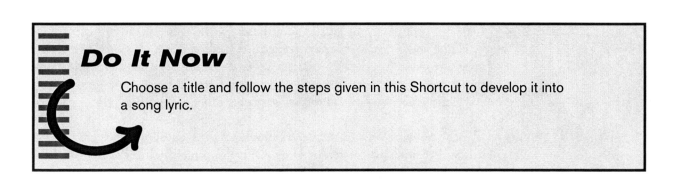

Do It Now

Choose a title and follow the steps given in this Shortcut to develop it into a song lyric.

Shortcut #47

Create a Sketch of Your Song

Before you invest your time and energy,
try Leonardo's bright idea.

I figure any idea that was good enough for Leonardo da Vinci is good enough for me. So here it is: Before Leonardo applied all that expensive, hand-mixed paint, he took a few pieces of chalk and drew a rough sketch. He laid down the forms, identified the focal points, and mapped out the composition of the scene. He even made changes, shifting images to create a clean, well-balanced painting with the strongest impact on the viewer. Of course, he didn't invent this idea—it's called "underdrawing" and a lot of artists did it—but if it's got LdV's stamp of approval, I'm on board!

You can probably see where I'm going with this. The idea of underdrawing or sketching is not only a great way to make a painting, it's also a great way to make songs! Like Leonardo, try working out a rough sketch of your lyric; know where you're headed before you make the expensive investment of hard work and hours of your time.

Why sketch out a song?

Create a sketch of your song to maintain focus, development & organization.

A song sketch will give you the opportunity to check out the following:

- Does your song develop at a good pace and flow well?
- Have you left out something that listeners need to know?
- Is there a solid relationship between verse and chorus?

A sketch can also help you find a place for that inspired line—the one you can't bear to not use. Maybe it doesn't belong in the verse you're currently working on but you can see that it will work in the bridge. Put it there and continue working on your verse.

When to create your song sketch

Leonardo worked up his sketch after he knew what the theme of his painting would be and who or what was going to be featured in it. As songwriters, this means we work up a sketch only after we have a clear idea of the theme and a title that expresses the heart of that idea. (If a completely different concept occurs to you while you're working on this song, start another one!)

If you're not sure of your theme, try developing the questions suggested by the title and creating raw material before you begin your sketch. Read Shortcuts 44 and 45 to find out more about these ideas.

How to create a song sketch

Let's try working up a song sketch based on a title and theme. The title we've been using in the lyric Shortcuts is "Give Me the Moonlight" so let's stick with that one. Based on the questions this title asks and the raw material I created, the theme is going to be: "Love is nourished in the quiet, intimate time I spend with you." Here we go …

Verse 1: An effective way to introduce a theme is to show what happens when there's a problem involved.

> *When I'm caught up in the craziness of my job and day-to-day stress*
> *I lose touch with what makes me happy.*

Chorus: I have to use the title in the chorus, so I'll put it in the sketch then flesh it out.

> *Give me the moonlight and I'll be fine because when I'm with you*
> *in the quiet of the night all my cares melt away.*

Verse 2: In the next verse, it's obvious I should explain why being "with you" in "the moonlight" solves the problem, right?

> *I can drop the mask I wear in the daytime, be myself, and share my*
> *doubts and fears. You listen and put your arms around me.*

Chorus: Repeat the lines from the first chorus.

> *So give me the moonlight and I'll be fine because when I'm with*
> *you in the quiet of the night all my cares melt away.*

Bridge: The bridge often provides a peak emotional moment so what would be the strongest emotion here? How about …

> *You and I together in the warmth and beauty of the moonlight is*
> *what I live for.*

Chorus: And the bridge has set us up for the final choruses.

> *So give me the moonlight and I'll be fine because when I'm with*
> *you in the quiet of the night all my cares melt away.*

Tip: Use one of the layouts in Shortcut 29 as a template for your sketch.

Using the sketch technique with other song forms

I chose to demonstrate the sketch technique on a song with a Verse / Chorus structure but it can be used with the other two contemporary song forms as well.

Verse / Verse / Bridge / Verse song form: Treat your verses as in the previous example. Try making your refrain line the final line of each verse and put the title of your song in it. Make sure the information in each verse leads the listener toward the title in your refrain line.

Verse / Pre-chorus / Chorus song form: Use the sketch as in the Verse / Chorus form, but add a pre-chorus section. This section builds anticipation leading up to the chorus. Look for an idea that gets the listener ready for the chorus. In the example above, it might be something like, "But as soon as I can get to you I know things will be fine because …" The word "because" is a good way to find the line that leads into your chorus. You don't have to say it or sing it, just *think it* right before launching into your chorus and then look for the line that leads up to it.

Suggestion: Take a straightforward approach to the language in your song sketch. In the actual lyric you can be as poetic and unique as you want, just be sure you get all the points in your sketch across to your listener!

Do It Now

1. Look up recent hit song lyrics and create song sketches based on them. Notice how the verses add to your knowledge of the situation and how the chorus gives you the emotional heart of the song's theme.

2. Create a title, determine the theme, and sketch out a song.

See "Shortcut Resources" on page 261 for information on where to find current music charts, hit songs, lyrics, and legal downloads.

Shortcut #48

Write a Hook That Sticks

Three ways to write a hook
that gets inside your listener's head.

A "hook" is exactly what its name implies—a phrase that catches your attention and hauls you into a song like a fish on a line. And once you're hooked, it's hard to get free. A good hook hangs around long after the song is over.

Some songwriters feel there are several hooks in a song: a primary hook, secondary hooks, and instrumental hooks. In my opinion, for a song to be a hit in today's competitive market, *every* line in your chorus needs to be as catchy as you can make it. You can call them all "hooks" if you want to. However, I'm going to focus on the single, most memorable line—the one you don't have to make an effort to remember because it just sticks in your head. That's the one I'm going to call the "hook."

Much of the easy instant replay quality of a hook has to do with the lyric phrase you choose. The trick is to get inside the listener's head and compete with everything else that's going on in there.

Your hook has to compete with everything that's going on in the listener's head!

1. Make your hook a conversational phrase

Aim for a phrase that sounds natural and conversational, one that's constructed in a way we would actually say it. By doing this, you make your phrase believable and mimic something that's already going on inside the listener's head. Our minds are filled with internal dialogue. When another conversational phrase comes along—your hook—it fits right in with what's already there. Coupled with a melody that emphasizes the key words in the phrase, it becomes stronger and more vivid than the average internal dialogue, making it easy to recall. Here are a few conversational hook phrases:

Truth is I never got over you. ("Truth Is"—Fantasia)

You had a bad day. ("Bad Day"—Daniel Powter)

You're gonna miss this. ("You're Gonna Miss This"—Trace Adkins)

2. Use images and action phrases

Besides holding conversations with ourselves, we also run scenarios in our heads. We've got plenty of images and action going on. Adding these to your hook can help it compete with the rest of the activity in our minds. If you're going to use a well-worn image like 'angel' in your hook, surround it with some qualifiers that make it more specific or describe the scene: "You're my angel in a red dress." "Talk to me, street angel."

Image: I will go down with this ship. ("White Flag"—Dido)

Image: Get a little mud on the tires. ("Mud On the Tires"— Brad Paisley)

Action: Hey, I put some new shoes on. ("New Shoes"—Paolo Nutini)

Be conversational.
Be pictorial.
Be intriguing.

3. Use a phrase that intrigues your listener

Be tantalizing. Raise questions. People are naturally curious. If your hook suggests an impossible or unusual situation, it will tend to stick around and urge listeners to go back to the song.

What if I say I'm not like the others? ("The Pretender"—Foo Fighters)

Hate me if you want to, love me if you can. ("Love Me If You Can"— Toby Keith)

This is Radio Nowhere. Is there anybody alive out there? ("Radio Nowhere"—Bruce Springsteen)

Do It Now

1. Play a hit song. Go do something else. Later on, try to remember a line of the song. What line was it? Where did it occur in the song? Why do you think you were able to remember the lyric? Did it use one or more of the three techniques described in this Shortcut?

2. Try playing one of your own songs for friends. After a couple of minutes, ask them what line or lines they remember. If it's not your hook, consider reworking your hook phrase to add more impact using the concepts in this Shortcut.

See "Shortcut Resources" on page 261 for information on where to find current music charts, hit songs, lyrics, and legal downloads.

Shortcut #49

Make Your Hook
a Mini-Version of Your Song

Lure your listeners back
with an unforgettable hook.

Ever had a commercial jingle running through your head, keeping you awake at night, or just generally driving you crazy? Getting rid of it is like getting rid of the hiccups—no one is exactly sure how to do it but there are plenty of crazy remedies. We all want to avoid those annoying repeating loops!

So what's the difference between a song hook that keeps running through your head and a jingle that's driving you nuts? Not much if it's a banal hook line from a song you don't like. However, there's a *big* difference if the hook evokes the emotional world of a song, especially a song you *do* like. This is what you want your hook to do so I'm going to suggest that you turn your hook into a mini-version of your song, offering listeners a taste, a reminder of what they enjoyed, and making them want to listen again.

Create a mini-version of your song in the hook

Here are a few examples of hit song hooks that offer listeners a quick and effective reminder of the whole song experience.

> *Use your hook to give listeners a reminder of the whole song experience.*

> ➤ **Focus on the song's central emotion**—In Rascal Flatts' "What Hurts the Most," the hook line is the title of the song. The song lyric focuses on hurt and how the singer copes with it day to day, as well as the moments when it's most painful. So, when you recall the hook—"what hurts the most"—it pulls you right back into the song's emotional theme.

> ➤ **Give us a summary of the situation**—In Avril Lavigne's hit "Complicated," the song lyric revolves around the changes the other character is going through and the singer's reaction to them. The hook, which is the first line of the chorus, gives us a taste of the whole story in miniature.

> ➤ **Emphasize the message of the song**—In Beyoncé's "Irreplaceable," the title of the song is not really what the song is about; in fact, the male character in the song is *very* replaceable. The hook is actually the first line of the chorus: "You must not know 'bout me" which is repeated for emphasis. The lyric centers on how the male character underestimated the singer and what she's going to do about it. By the end of the song we know plenty about her! This is an example of underlining the most important aspect of your theme in a hook line.

Know what your song is really about

To write a knockout hook, *you need to know what your song is really about at its core.* This may sound obvious. Of course you know what your song is about ... don't you?

Know what your song is about, then make sure your hook expresses that idea!

Sometimes songwriters figure things out as they go along, so the theme tends to drift a little. Or they bend their theme to include lines that don't really belong. However, if you're going to feature a compact hook line that sums up the entire song, then the song needs to be tightly focused around a clearly defined theme. It takes discipline and rewriting to keep your message on target. Go through your song and make sure that every line leads back to your hook, even those inspired lines you're in love with! Any line that isn't tightly woven into the song's central message needs to be replaced. You can always use those great but off-topic lines in other songs.

Make sure your hook expresses your theme

If you have a lyric with a clear, focused theme but you're not sure whether your hook is expressing it effectively, ask yourself: What is the singer going through emotionally during the song? Summarize that idea in a single sentence then see if your hook conveys the same idea. If not, try looking for another line in the song that would make a better hook, or write a list of phrases, words, and images that express the central concept, then use the techniques in Shortcut 48 to help you choose one of those phrases and increase its impact.

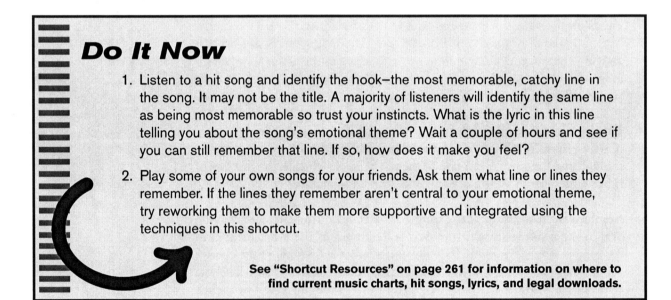

Do It Now

1. Listen to a hit song and identify the hook—the most memorable, catchy line in the song. It may not be the title. A majority of listeners will identify the same line as being most memorable so trust your instincts. What is the lyric in this line telling you about the song's emotional theme? Wait a couple of hours and see if you can still remember that line. If so, how does it make you feel?

2. Play some of your own songs for your friends. Ask them what line or lines they remember. If the lines they remember aren't central to your emotional theme, try reworking them to make them more supportive and integrated using the techniques in this shortcut.

See "Shortcut Resources" on page 261 for information on where to find current music charts, hit songs, lyrics, and legal downloads.

Shortcut #50

A Hit Chorus: From Big Opening to Payoff Line

Cook up a winning chorus with this recipe.

Listeners love the high energy of the chorus and today's big hits give them plenty of it! Many top ten hit songs have choruses of six, seven, eight lines or more. As a lyric writer, the challenge is to fill all those lines with relevant, supportive information that sustains interest through repeated listens. So, what goes into the mix?

Lyric Ingredients for Cooking Up a Hot Chorus

Just as your whole song has a structure made up of sections, a chorus has its own internal structure. It often starts with an ear-catching opening line, followed by a series of lines that build on it, and then ends with a payoff line. Mix these in the right amounts and you're good to go!

> 1. **The big opening line.** This is the perfect opportunity to write a line that announces your theme and draws listeners into the heart of your song. It could be the song title itself, a line that includes the title, or it may be an intriguing line that sets us up for the title later in the chorus. Take a listen to Daughtry's "It's Not Over" for an example of a strong, opening hook/ title line. Check out Matchbox Twenty's "How Far We've Come" for a powerful line that sums up the singer's attitude and makes us wonder what he'll say next.

> 2. **The follow-up line.** On the second line of your chorus, stay focused on the theme you laid out in your opening. Try a different way of stating the opening line or answer the question, "What did you mean by that?" In Trace Adkins' song, "You're Gonna Miss This," the first line of the chorus is the title, the follow-up line is "You're gonna want this back." By stating the theme in the first line and restating it in the second, the song gives listeners enough time to grasp this important piece of information.

> 3. **The mid-section.** Stay close to your theme. Imagine yourself talking to strangers; what would you tell them next to help them understand the *emotions* the singer is feeling? Write down your ideas. Don't try to rhyme or fit them to a rhythm, just get your thoughts down. Then work with them, play with the words; try other ways of saying things until you've got something that goes deeper into your theme. To see this technique at work, and the others in this Shortcut, check out the chorus of Kelly Clarkson's "Because of You."

Put every line of your chorus to work! Each line has a job to do.

➤ **4. The payoff line.** Although you certainly don't want to think of your chorus as a joke, it does share an important structural element with comedy: Both jokes and choruses build to a payoff line that gives the audience a sense of satisfaction and completion. In today's hits, this is sometimes where the title appears or where it is repeated if already used in the opening line. Take a look at the Tim McGraw hit "Live Like You Were Dying" for an example of a great title/payoff line in the chorus. Notice how the rest of the chorus leads you right to it while giving you plenty of information about the emotional theme of the song.

You need to give listeners enough information in the chorus so they can grasp the essential meaning of your hook. They don't need a detailed explanation or examples—save that for your verses. Stick with the heart of your theme; make the chorus the emotional center of your song.

Do It Now

1. Read over the lyrics and listen to hit songs in the Verse / Chorus form. Stick to recent hits because chorus styles have evolved over the last ten years. Look at the lyric structure in the chorus of each song. Notice where the hook occurs, how the theme is stated and reinforced, and how the last line creates a sense of completion or payoff.

2. Write or rewrite a chorus lyric of your own using the structural elements in this Shortcut. If you found a hit song you liked in Step 1, try using it as a ghost song and write new lyrics to the chorus. (See Shortcut 2 for more on ghost songs.)

See "Shortcut Resources" on page 261 for information on where to find current music charts, hit songs, lyrics, and legal downloads.

Shortcut #51

Define Your Title and Theme in the Chorus

Don't keep listeners guessing.
Tell them what it's all about in your chorus.

Let's say I've decided the title for my new song will be "Shining Alone." I came up with some lines for my chorus. They go like this:

> I was shining alone
> Then you came along
> Now two lights shine as one.
> Strong in the sun
> I can stand on my own
> I'm not afraid of shining alone.

But now I'm having trouble writing my verses and I don't know why. Hmmmm. Maybe it's because I haven't decided what my song is about! Now there's a setup for disaster.

What's happening is this: A song title can suggest several themes, as "Shining Alone" does. In fact, I have two different themes going. In the first three lines, the theme is "Finding Love." In the next three, it's "Learning to be Independent." Both are legitimate themes and both could be developed from this title. I've got to decide which one I'm writing about and be certain that the chorus lyric conveys that choice. If I don't, my song will be confusing and lack emotional impact for listeners.

A song title can suggest several themes. Pick one!

Get to know your title; make an "in other words" list

The title is the engine that drives your chorus. It's likely to be the all-important first line or payoff line or both. Be sure you're clear about what your title means to you. Here's a great way to find out: Write your title at the top of a piece of paper. Next to it, write "in other words …" Below that make a list of things you could say that would explain your title. Now read through your list and make sure all of your lines mean *the same thing!* Delete any that don't.

Take the title "Love Me If You Can," from the hit by Toby Keith, and make an "in other words" list. It might read, "I'm not easy to love," "I've got some issues you'll have to deal with if you want to get close to me," "I dare you to love me," "I'm not about to change for you; you'll have to put up with me." If you keep your "in other words" list handy while writing your chorus, it will help you stay focused on your title and define your theme clearly.

Four ways to ensure
that your chorus defines your theme

➤ **1. Answer a question raised by the title**

Use Shortcut 44 to identify the questions your title raises. Choose at least one question to answer in your chorus. You can take care of the rest in your verses and bridge.

Check to see if your chorus communicates your theme.

➤ **2. Use related words and images**

In Shortcut 45, you learned how to create a list of words, phrases, and images that are related to your title. Try using some of these in your chorus.

➤ **3. Use your "in other words" list**

Replace a line in your chorus with one from your "in other words" list. Does your chorus still make sense? Try replacing other lines in your chorus with lines from the list. If the meaning of your chorus remains intact, you can feel confident that it defines your title.

➤ **4. Test it out**

A good test of a chorus lyric is whether it can stand alone without any verse or bridge information and still get an emotional idea across. Try showing your chorus lyric to a friend and ask what feeling is being described. If it isn't the one you meant to convey or he can't tell you what the emotion is, then rework it to add more clarity.

Do It Now

1. Listen to hit songs and notice how the chorus defines the title and emotional theme (the "how I feel") of the song.

2. Choose a title in which you're interested or find one using Shortcut 42. Create an "in other words" list and write a chorus using some of the suggestions in this Shortcut.

See "Shortcut Resources" on page 261 for information on where to find current music charts, hit songs, lyrics, and legal downloads.

Shortcut #52

Verses: Take Us Deep Inside the Situation

Give listeners plenty of information and insight.

Once upon a time, song verses told stories. Folk songs recalled great deeds and memorable events in verse after verse. Of course, today's songwriters know that verses no longer consist of epic tales told in rhyme, but if you ask them to explain what contemporary verses do instead of that, the answer isn't very clear. So, here it is …

Today's hit song verses *develop a situation and personalize a theme.*

There's a difference between developing a situation and telling a story. Stories feature an account of an event or series of events that take place over time. Development of a situation, on the other hand, takes us deeper into a single event or emotion, offering insights by showing us how the main character is affected. In song verses, this is all tied together by a theme embodied in the singer's experience.

Verses bring your theme to life

There's nothing more persuasive than making an audience *feel* what you want them to understand. For instance I could say to you, "Young women have big dreams." You'd probably just shrug and say, "So?" Why should you care? I made a generic, abstract statement that has little impact on you. But if it's personalized, that's a different matter. To bring this theme to life, the writers of "Breakaway," Kelly Clarkson's huge hit, made us see it through the eyes of a young girl dreaming of escape from small town life. Here's how the verses and bridge portray this theme:

Use a situation and characters to bring your theme to life.

> *Verse 1:* I was lonely growing up and yearned to escape the confines of a small town.
>
> *Verse 2:* I want to experience faraway places, as far away from that small town as possible.
>
> *Bridge:* I know it won't be easy. The world can be a confusing place.

Every word of this lyric works to personalize the theme, to bring the character to life for us, and reveal her feelings.

- The first verse sets up the singer's motivation and tells us something about who she is. Without that, we wouldn't care about her.

- The second verse takes us into the singer's dreams, giving us a picture of what she wants so we don't have to guess.

Take us deeper into your theme in each song section.

• The bridge acknowledges the seriousness of what she is about to do, anchoring it in real experience, giving the singer credibility.

Because the song is in the first person, we actually hear the singer's tone of voice, how she talks, and what she thinks about. We enter her world and begin to feel what she is feeling. The theme becomes real for us because we've been invited inside the emotional life of someone who is living it.

Never run out of things to say!

When I hear a song that repeats the first verse later in the song, uses the same lyric in every pre-chorus, and has an instrumental bridge, I know the songwriter missed a great opportunity to reveal a situation and character. There's already plenty of repetition built into contemporary song structures, leaving very little lyric "real estate" to work with. Every bit of it is needed to give listeners enough information to understand the theme and empathize with what the main character is going through.

Be sure your lyric does all this!

• Show us the problem or situation.
• Let us know how it affects the singer.
• Give us some background, so we have a context.
• Convey the personality and voice of the singer.
• Let us know who is involved, what happened, and why it happened.

We're all voyeurs. We love to know other people's intimate feelings. Plus we like to see our own experiences reflected in our favorite songs. Use the verses to open up the situation and make your theme come to life. Details, insights, revelations! Take us all the way inside and let us live it!

Do It Now

1. Look at the lyrics to hit songs in the genre you are interested in and notice how the lyric takes you into the world of the singer. What details, events, hopes, and background information are you given? If the song is about a relationship, what do you learn about the people involved and what's happening in their relationship?

2. Choose a theme you want to write about. Give it a personal dimension by creating a character in a situation that demonstrates your theme. Answer the questions: Why did the singer do that? What does the singer hope will happen? What steps does the singer plan to take?

See "Shortcut Resources" on page 261 for information on where to find current music charts, hit songs, lyrics, and legal downloads.

Shortcut #53

Verses & Bridge:
Try a Development Path

Keep things moving forward for your listener.

Imagine a deep, dark forest. At the edge of the forest, a listener stands gazing into the trees considering whether to go forward. She sees a path that looks inviting and takes a few steps into the woods. It's a different and mysterious world; she would be lost without the straight, well-marked path to guide her. She starts along it, enjoying the sights around her. Suddenly the path veers sharply to the left. She nearly stumbles but continues on. The path doubles back on itself. She's not happy about this. The path does more strange things: it makes a complete circle around a tree and a couple of zigzags. Our listener is now worried that the path is not going anywhere, but still she keeps on. The path finally narrows, it's overgrown and hard to find. She begins to feel abandoned and alone. What started out as a nice walk in the woods is turning into a nightmare!!!

Don't let *this* happen to your listener!

As you write your verses and bridge, keep the path through your song clear. Make sure things are moving forward, taking the listener along with them.

Lead listeners through your song by giving them a clear path to follow.

It can be tough to find the balance between giving listeners too much information too quickly and not giving them enough or repeating information they've already heard, taking them in circles.

Use Shortcut 47 "Create a Sketch of Your Song" to get an idea of what you want to say in each verse. It's a good idea to make notes on a song layout sheet (Shortcut 29) so you can visualize the flow of your song.

Create a "development path"

Here are some development paths your song might take. Notice that each path leads the listener *into* and *through* a situation, keeping the momentum rolling forward and giving information as it's needed. The chorus is integrated into the song as a natural extension of the verses and bridge. (The vast majority of hit songs are written from the point of view of the singer—the first person "I"—so I'll use that approach in these examples.)

Path #1 – Deal with a problem

Verse 1:	This is the problem.
Chorus:	Here's how I feel about it.
Verse 2:	This is what I tried to do about it.
Chorus:	Repeat chorus.

| *Bridge:* | Here's how I hope to find a way through this. |
| *Chorus:* | Repeat chorus. |

Path #2 · Give us a history

Verse 1:	I remember the beginning.
Chorus:	This is what it felt like.
Verse 2:	Things changed. Everything is different now.
Chorus:	Repeat chorus.
Bridge:	Can we get back to the way things were?
Chorus:	Repeat chorus.

Path #3 · Build it up

Verse 1:	I took a chance.
Chorus:	Now my life has changed.
Verse 2:	I risked everything for happiness.
Chorus:	Repeat chorus.
Bridge:	It was worth it.
Chorus:	Repeat chorus.

You can find more development paths by listening to well-written hit songs. You'll notice that some songs share similar paths. It's how the path is personalized by the songwriter that makes it unique and gives it strength. A path is just the outline of a song. How you flesh it out is up to you. Make each path your own with the details and emotions of your specific situation and characters.

Do It Now

1. Look for development paths in recent hit songs. Write out a few of the ones you find.

2. In 20 minutes, write a lyric based on any of the development paths in this Shortcut. Don't bother about rhyming. Don't worry about how good it is. Just do it!

See "Shortcut Resources" on page 261 for information on where to find current music charts, hit songs, lyrics, and legal downloads.

Shortcut #54

The Bridge: Give Your Song a Peak Moment

This is the place to bring it all together.

In your verses, you've described the setting, the characters, and the details of the situation—everything needed to understand what's happening. In the bridge, you've got a chance to build on your verses and go beyond them to deliver a peak moment or a different perspective for your listeners. Remember, these are the lines that launch the final choruses of your song. If you don't say it here, it won't get said! Try these techniques to make your bridge a springboard for your final wrap-up and leave your listeners with some memorable thoughts.

> **Offer a different perspective**
> Give listeners another angle on your theme. Is there a different way of stating what the song is about? If your verses offer a lot of detail, try a more philosophical bridge lyric. Check out "Live Like You Were Dying" recorded by Tim McGraw, or Keyshia Cole's "I Remember" for good examples of this type of bridge.

> **Turn your bridge into the "reveal"**
> Today's listeners like to feel they've gotten a real look inside the heart of the singer. The bridge is a great place to reveal the singer's true feelings. To hear this type of bridge, check out Nickelback's "Photograph," Fantasia's "Truth Is," or P!nk's "Who Knew."

> **Take it to the limit**
> If your chorus and verses circle around your theme without coming right out and saying it, now's your chance. Listen to Rihanna's "Take a Bow" for a wonderful example.

Try these ideas! Make your bridge a memorable experience.

Do It Now

1. Check out the bridge lyrics in the hit songs mentioned above. What is it about these lines that sets them apart from the rest of the lyric? How do they work to increase the impact of the final choruses? The majority of hit songs have vocal bridges, especially in the Country and Pop genres. Look for vocal bridges in your genre and notice how they are handled.

2. Rewrite or add a bridge to one of your own songs using the techniques in this Shortcut.

See "Shortcut Resources" on page 261 for information on where to find current music charts, hit songs, lyrics, and legal downloads.

Shortcut #55

Lead-In Lines Make Your Lyric Transitions Work

Make sure your listeners follow you from the verse to the chorus.

Lyrically your verse and chorus are doing two different things. While the verses are busy giving us the details of the situation, the chorus takes us deep into the emotional heart of your theme. Changing gears between these two sections can be challenging for listeners. If the difference in tone and content is too great, they may not stay with you. While it's a good idea to create a big attention-grabbing shift in your *melody* at the top of the chorus, consider a smooth, easy-to-follow *lyric* transition to help your listener make the leap. Think of the last line of your verse (or pre-chorus) as a lead-in line, one that deposits the listener right on the doorstep of the chorus!

Make your lyric transitions easy to follow.

Test your lead-in lines

Check your transition lines as you write. This applies to all transitions into a chorus whether it's from a verse, pre-chorus or bridge section. To see if your lead-in lines are working, try speaking the last line of your verse or bridge and the first line of your chorus; in between, insert one of the following phrases.

Try these lines to test your lead-in!

> What I really mean to say is …
> You see it's like this …
> What I want you to understand is …

If a line like this makes sense in the transition, then your lead-in line is working.

Lead-in lines and the effectiveness of your chorus

Although *all* of the lines in your verse should lead to and support your chorus, if the lead-in line is wandering or unfocused, the overall impact of your chorus could be undermined. A weak lead-in line forces your chorus to work harder to create an effect. On the other hand, a strong lead-in line can give a weaker chorus a much-needed boost!

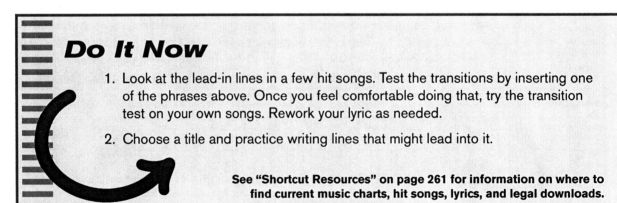

Do It Now

1. Look at the lead-in lines in a few hit songs. Test the transitions by inserting one of the phrases above. Once you feel comfortable doing that, try the transition test on your own songs. Rework your lyric as needed.

2. Choose a title and practice writing lines that might lead into it.

See "Shortcut Resources" on page 261 for information on where to find current music charts, hit songs, lyrics, and legal downloads.

Shortcut #56

"Key Lines": The Lyric Lines They Always Hear

Who says audiences don't listen to lyrics!

People *do* listen to lyrics. Want proof? How many million-selling hit instrumentals have you heard lately? Just about … none. Lyrics have an advantage over instrumental performances; they allow the listener to identify with a character and be drawn inside an emotional situation. Of course an instrumental can be emotionally moving but it can't tell you the *details* of what happened that made the composer or performer feel that way.

So, listeners do hear lyrics; but they don't always hear them in the order we wrote them, and they don't give *all* the lyric lines in a song equal weight or equal attention!

Here's a common scenario: It's rush hour and you're driving home from work. You've got the radio on. There's a song playing but you're still thinking about what happened earlier that day, not really paying any attention to it. Suddenly, there's an ear-catching jump in the melody, the pace of the words changes. You turn your attention to the song to check out what's going on. What you hear is the first line of the chorus; it's also the title of the song and sums up the heart of the song's theme. If you like what you hear, there's a good chance you'll keep listening.

Contemporary song structures are geared to catch attention at certain key points, most obviously the opening line of the chorus. *This is the lyric listeners always hear. If you do your job well, they'll stay for more.*

The "key lines" in your lyric

Here's a list of the key lines in the Verse / Chorus song structure used in the majority of today's hit songs:

Listeners hear the key lines in your lyric!

➤ **The opening line of the chorus**
This is the line that listeners *always* hear so make it an ear-grabber! Use a vivid image or action word; make a strong emotional statement that tells the listener something about the singer and the theme. "Unbreak my heart …" "Feeling alive all over again …" "You were everything, everything that I wanted …" In hit song after hit song, the opening line of the chorus makes its point with strength.

➤ **The second line of the chorus**
In today's hits, we often hear a repeat of the first line melody *but with a new lyric.* This is your chance to draw your listeners deeper into your song while they're hearing a repeat of the melody that grabbed them in the first place.

Be sure to follow up your opening line with one that progresses naturally and easily. Don't force your listeners to have to figure out something at this stage; they may not have enough information.

> **The payoff line: the last line of the chorus**
> Even if you captured your listeners in the opening lines of the chorus, they may drift away over the next few lines. You can pull them back in with a satisfying payoff line. Frequently, in contemporary hits, the title is repeated at this point.

> **The first lines of Verse 1 and Verse 2**
> The first line of Verse 1 should be intriguing. Give the listener an interesting setup, location, or situation. Poetic language can get attention, but make sure it isn't so opaque that listeners get lost right away.
>
> After all your hard work in the chorus, be sure to give the opening line of Verse 2 plenty to keep listeners interested. Use it to pull them forward and deeper into the situation. Remember, the first time they hear your song they may not have been paying attention to Verse 1, so try to make this line one that can stand on its own.

> **The refrain line**
> If you're working in the Verse / Verse / Bridge / Verse song form, your refrain line will be the first or last line of every verse. This is the hook of your song, so treat it like one. Use the suggestions for the first or last line of the chorus as described above. The refrain line should *always* include the song's title—make sure your title is distinctive and memorable. Sometimes the refrain line is all the listener remembers, so make it the kind of lyric that draws them back to your song.
>
> Little by little, listeners will hear your whole lyric—give them something worth listening to! If you've got a strong melody and nothing to say, your audience will drift away. Don't underestimate the power of words. A hit song needs both—a powerhouse melody *and* a knockout lyric!

See Shortcut 49 for ideas you can use to write your refrain.

Do It Now

1. Test the key lines for yourself. Play hit songs in the background while you're working, driving, or talking on the phone. Notice the lines that jump out and catch your attention.

2. Look at the key lines in songs of your own. See if you can make them more noticeable or memorable by using images, action, or a strong emotional statement.

See "Shortcut Resources" on page 261 for information on where to find current music charts, hit songs, lyrics, and legal downloads.

Shortcut #57

Images: Make Your Lyric Come to Life

Pictures are vivid, expressive, and memorable.

You know those magazine quizzes that ask a few questions and then reveal all kinds of deep things about you from the answers? Here's a quiz that may not reveal any deep stuff but it *will* offer up a few insights into both you and your listeners.

Which line do you find more interesting?
    a) Let's have fun.
    b) Let's get a little mud on the tires.

Which line makes you want to find out more?
    a) I've changed my attitude and I feel better.
    b) I put some new shoes on and suddenly everything is right.

Which line do you believe?
    a) I can take the rain on the roof of this empty house.
    b) I can handle loneliness.

Which line makes you want to take action?
    a) Live your life with arms wide open.
    b) Embrace life.

If you're like most listeners, you answered b, b, a, a. These lines came from mega-hit songs. The other lines ... didn't.

Images are more effective than abstractions

What's the difference between the winning and losing lines in this quiz? The winners use images to communicate an *abstract* idea. In each pair of lines, the same idea is expressed but it has more impact when an image is used to convey it.

Images get your brain actively involved; abstract ideas don't! For example: seeing someone smile—or even just imagining it—gets your brain zinging and crackling all over the place. But the abstract idea of 'happiness' doesn't have the same effect. Check it out for yourself: Take a moment to imagine someone you like giving you a big, warm smile. Notice how your body and emotions react. Now, stop imagining that and read this word: HAPPINESS. Doesn't feel quite the same, does it?

Use images to express abstract ideas.

So, how does this apply to your songwriting? Well, if you write a line like "I feel happy," and it manages to get inside your listener's brain, it pretty much sits there like a lump, being forgettable. If you want to engage your listener and hit them with a memorable, evocative line, try using images. Like this ...

I'm grinning as I dance down the street. The sun sparkles on the pavement, throwing diamonds at my feet.

Back up your images with more images to add support.

Whoa, happy!!! I get it! *Here's why:* The images of grinning and dancing are physical expressions of happiness, the kind of thing your brain can get involved with; it then sends messages to your body that feel good. The picture of diamonds, especially diamonds being thrown at your feet, tells your brain these are times of wealth and plenty, another physical expression of *wellbeing*—it feels good! Now you're brain and body actually *feel happiness.* If you want your listener to get involved in your song, *make them feel the emotions in the song by using images!*

Suggestions for using images

➤ **1. Use images to replace abstract ideas and general statements about emotions.** Instead of "I love you" or "I'm so sad," substitute the physical and visual cues we use to recognize these emotions.

➤ **2. Try adding other images that evoke similar emotions, the more the better!** For instance, if you want to tell your listeners that the singer is falling in love, try two different types of pictures: images of things that evoke happiness, excitement, and desire—the emotional components of falling in love—and images of falling or flying to evoke the dizzy, unbalanced physical sensation of emerging love.

➤ **3. Use images to describe the situation and events in your song.** Rather than simply telling listeners that something happened, paint a picture. In this way, you create an experience similar to watching a movie— bringing listeners into the "scene" and letting them experience it for themselves. Check out Nickelback's "Someday" and notice how images like "unclench your fists" and "unpack your suitcase" paint a picture of the situation.

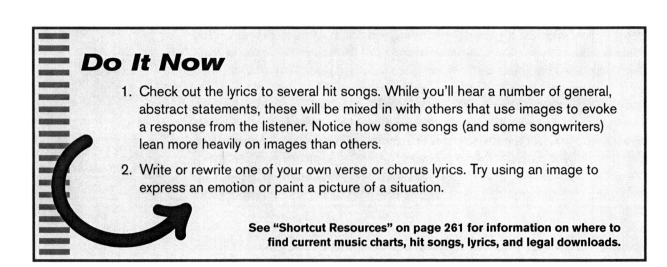

Do It Now

1. Check out the lyrics to several hit songs. While you'll hear a number of general, abstract statements, these will be mixed in with others that use images to evoke a response from the listener. Notice how some songs (and some songwriters) lean more heavily on images than others.

2. Write or rewrite one of your own verse or chorus lyrics. Try using an image to express an emotion or paint a picture of a situation.

See "Shortcut Resources" on page 261 for information on where to find current music charts, hit songs, lyrics, and legal downloads.

Shortcut #58

Images: Let a Family of Associations Work for You!

Images never arrive alone;
they bring their friends and relations.

One of the most potent elements of speech is the *image*. It's impossible *not* to see a mental picture when we hear an image word. If I say "car," you imagine a car. If I say "rain," you picture rain. But that's not all that happens. Along with that picture of rain, comes all the associations you have with it: a grey sky, the physical sensation of humidity, cold and wet outdoors, and cozy indoors. Images don't arrive alone. They are always accompanied by a gaggle of related images, ideas, sensations, and experiences. Think of it as a family that stays together.

As a songwriter, you can use this family to your advantage. While you can't control *all* of the responses your listener will have to an image, there are plenty of shared associations you *can* count on. These associations add depth and richness to your lyric with no extra effort on your part. Play with them, use them to underscore your theme; you can get a lot of use out of an image that's got a big family.

Use image families: related images, ideas, associations & sensations.

Use images to draw your listener into the song

"I miss you. I really miss you. I really, *really* miss you." Obviously the person speaking this phrase is sincere, so why don't I feel anything? Maybe it's because the phrase isn't activating my emotions. It's simply a statement of fact and, worse than that, it's one that doesn't have anything to do with *me*.

What could a songwriter do to get me more involved in this lyric? In "Missing" by Everything But the Girl, the hook line compares missing you to the way the "deserts miss the rain." I have a whole group of associations with deserts and with rain, as do most people. I can see and feel the dry, arid, thirsty desert. I can imagine yearning for that thirst to be slaked by the rain. Ah! That's how "missing you" feels! Yes, *now* I know what you're talking about. It reminds me of a time when I felt that way myself. Now, not only am I picturing the images and feeling the sensations, the song has turned out to be about something that happened to ... *me!*

Make it about ME, the listener!

Support your characters and theme with images

An excellent example of an image family that supports the theme and lead character in a song can be found in Brad Paisley's "Mud On the Tires." The image of muddying up the tires on a new car suggests a whole group of associated ideas—freedom, joy, youthful high spirits, and light-hearted rebellion—giving us a lot of information about the central character and his world and providing the song with a sense of solidity and believability.

On the flip side, be alert to images with associations that *conflict* with your theme or with each other. These can create a distraction that drags your song down. If the singer drives a "flashy pink Cadillac" with its suggestion of ego and impulsiveness, it will be difficult for us to believe he's also "the salt of the earth" or "dependable as the rising sun." Your listeners will spend a lot of time trying to reconcile these two sets of images instead of listening to your song. This is an extreme example; look for more subtle occurrences where one image is undermining another. Of course, it's fine to have contrasting images when you want to demonstrate the difference between two people or things.

Use an image family that supports your character and theme!

Freshen up your images

An image like "I'm a prisoner of your love" can work for and against you. The image of a "prisoner" has a lot of associations with it that might add depth to your theme but it's become such a cliché that listeners don't "see" it anymore. To make an image like this work for you, freshen it up by varying the image itself: "Your love is holding me hostage." Or, give us a new insight or twist on the image in the surrounding lines: "I'd give up my freedom to become a prisoner of your love." Keep the family of associations but use it in a way we don't expect.

A variation on this idea involves using a family of images that isn't usually associated with your theme. Again, this creates a twist or insight that catches the listener's attention. Check out Usher's "Moving Mountains" to hear this approach. He describes a troubled love relationship using images like "my stock is down" and "I used to be worth my weight in gold." It's clever, fresh, and gets his point across.

Do It Now

1. A strong hit song lyric often makes use of an image and its family of associations. Check out "Radio Nowhere" (Bruce Sprinsteen), "Before He Cheats" (Carrie Underwood), or "New Shoes" (Paolo Nutini). Notice the way an image and its family of associations communicates and supports the theme of the song and the central character.

2. Choose an image to use as your song title. Make a list of any associated images, words, feelings, and experiences you have with that image. Write a chorus and verse making use of that family of associations.

See "Shortcut Resources" on page 261 for information on where to find current music charts, hit songs, lyrics, and legal downloads.

Shortcut #59

Use Right Brain Language:
Make Your Listener Feel, Not Think

Connect with the emotions and start communicating.

There's a kind of language that isn't our regular, everyday speech. It isn't factual. It isn't used to give directions or explain how a car engine works. Sometimes it says things that sound ridiculous, even impossible. When it's used in songs, we listen to it and love it! It's the kind of language we use to communicate things that are hard to put into words, things like emotions. I'm going to call it "right brain language."

Right brain vs. left brain language

The phrases "right brain" and "left brain" are creative jargon for two different ways of thinking. Your left brain is rational and judgmental; your right brain is intuitive and inclusive. When it comes to language, the differences become very clear indeed. Your rational, analytical left brain is very good at rattling off facts and figures and making statements that are either true or false. Right brain language, on the other hand, is a riot of images, a cascade of connections, a swirling tornado of action, sensations, and associations.

When the literal, rational left side of your brain hears a phrase like "My love is as deep as the wine dark sea …" it wants to know exactly how deep in feet and inches! The right side of your brain, however, is capable of making an intuitive leap. It can visualize the image while connecting the emotions attached to one thing (the wine dark sea) with another thing (love). It understands that the phrase "My love is as deep as the wine dark sea" means something like "I have profound feelings for you that are unlike anything I have experienced before."

Why you want to reach
your listener's right brain

If I say to you, "Relationships are very painful." You might reply, "Sometimes they are, but sometimes they can be wonderful." In other words, you can argue with me. That's your rational left brain talking, remembering times when a relationship worked well for you and assessing whether or not you might have that experience again. I've made a rational, general statement, the type that engages the left side of your brain. We could debate this all day and neither of us would ever feel the emotion at the heart of my statement.

Don't give your listener a chance to argue with you!

However, if I say to you, "This love is a jagged piece of glass." Oh, yeah! Your right brain is in its element now! All of the associations you have, both physical and emotional, with a jagged piece of glass suddenly become attached to the notion of love. Your right brain is now ready for whatever I want to blame on that horrible, painful, dangerous love thing. Your emotions are engaged while, at the same time, your rational, critical left brain has been disabled. It can't process that phrase at all.

Engage your listener's right brain. Don't let him argue with you. Stay away from the analytical left brain by using right brain language.

The right brain language game

Surprising images, unusual comparisons and juxtapositions, unexpected associations, and intuitive connections are all part of the language your right brain speaks fluently. Don't be afraid to experiment, to try out ideas, and explore hunches. Here's a game that will give your right brain a chance to start talking.

Read Shortcut 15 for more ways to give your left brain the boot!

Use the list of words in Shortcut 42. Choose eight words that attract your emotional attention and write them in a list on a piece of paper. Next to it make another list of eight words including the following:

> Two colors (one light, one dark)
> One kind of weather
> One kind of physical activity
> One thing that is either cold or hot
> One sound of any kind
> One word that describes what something feels like to the touch
> One word that describes a taste

Now, choosing words that are across from each other in your two lists, make up short phrases that include both words. Feel free to be creative, add words, change the order, but the phrase must include both words, one from each list. When you've matched up all eight words from each list into phrases, choose any phrase and write a verse or chorus lyric that includes it. This is a great exercise for loosening the hold your left brain can sometimes impose on your thoughts. Give your right brain a good workout with this game whenever you feel the need to stretch yourself. Vary the word categories in your second list to keep the game fresh.

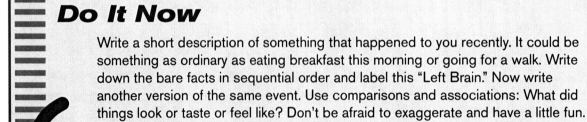

Do It Now

Write a short description of something that happened to you recently. It could be something as ordinary as eating breakfast this morning or going for a walk. Write down the bare facts in sequential order and label this "Left Brain." Now write another version of the same event. Use comparisons and associations: What did things look or taste or feel like? Don't be afraid to exaggerate and have a little fun. Entertain yourself! Label this "Right Brain." Try doing this exercise and the right brain language game frequently. Keep a journal and do one of these every day.

Shortcut #60

Use Poetic Language and Still Make Sense

Use a combination of evocative and direct language.

Your song lyric has two big tasks to accomplish.

- It has to evoke emotion through the use of vivid language, fresh images, and intriguing ideas.

- It has to ensure that listeners understand what's happening to the characters as the situation develops.

Achieving a balance between these two can be a challenge. Push the explanations too hard and your song comes across sounding flat; push the poetic language too far and listeners can't follow what's happening. Try using some of the following techniques to blend the two so that you accomplish both of your lyric goals.

➤ **Write explanatory lines that incorporate vivid language**
In songs, you can "sneak around" someone's defenses, or "run recklessly" over their feelings. Both of these phrases are explanatory yet colorful; they use vibrant language to get their point across. This is a useful technique for preserving a poetic, evocative quality while still conveying the information your listeners need in order to understand what's happening.

Create a blend of poetic language and explanation.

➤ **Come right out and tell us**
Rob Thomas's hit song, "Ever the Same" is a great example of poetic imagery used effectively. He knows he has to keep the listener with him. So, just in case his verse imagery of wounded soldiers in the moonlight is too obscure, he comes right out and says, "I'm telling you now ..." then he goes into a series of very direct, unambiguous statements that communicate his message.

Don't be afraid to mix poetry with conversational or explanatory statements. Not only does it create a safety net for your listener, it provides an opportunity to add contrast and grab attention.

➤ **Give us enough time to follow you**
If you're comparing your love to the wind in one line and visiting a dungeon of despair two or three words later, your listeners may have trouble keeping up with you. Give them time to process an image—to find an appropriate mental picture to go with the word. If you give them more than one image, they'll have to make a choice. (Is love flying free or is it imprisoned in a dungeon?) Song lyrics move along quickly. If your listeners are puzzling over something, they've probably missed a few lines and then you've lost them.

Try to spend at least two lines on an image. Set it up with related images that reinforce it or create a context. In the second verse of "Ever the Same,"

Rob Thomas writes a poetic description of a once carefree love using images from nature. He describes standing in the wind and feeling free like flowing water. Then he adds a second line that continues to describe how the water flows in the warmth of the sun. Listeners have plenty of time to picture the images and let them evoke the qualities of light and freedom the writer wants to suggest.

➤ **Use a "palette" of related and contrasting images**

Organize your song images into a palette of related groups.

Images are the driving force behind many of today's great lyrics. However, just throwing *any* old images at your listener will undercut the strength of *all* of them. Think of your images in terms of an artist's palette. Your palette includes a range of colors (images), sorted into broad groups that are generally related in some way. For instance, if you're writing a song that includes modern, urban imagery—sidewalks and city streets—be careful about suddenly tossing in a dragon and a book of magic spells unless you have a specific reason for doing so and you make that clear to listeners.

Consider keeping to a single group of images within a verse. If you're using images from nature in your verse—wind, ocean, rain, sun, moon—stay within this natural palette throughout that verse. While contrasting images can be very effective, make sure you give your listeners enough time to make the switch. If you're taking them from nature images to a crowded city street, keep them in each place for a few lines so they have a chance to catch up with you and get involved before making another change.

Do It Now

1. Look through several hit song lyrics to see how they mix poetic, evocative phrases with explanatory ones to make sure listeners understand what's happening. In those lyrics that feature a lot of imagery look for palettes of images. Write down all the images in the song and see if you can sort them into broad groups.

2. Write or rewrite a lyric of your own so that it uses a mix of evocative language with phrases that explain what's going on in the situation.

See "Shortcut Resources" on page 261 for information on where to find current music charts, hit songs, lyrics, and legal downloads.

Shortcut #61

Let the Details Do the Talking

Details pull listeners into your song.

"Hello, *National Enquirer?* This is "the details" calling!"

You can bet the *Enquirer* will take *that* call. The details love to talk, they tell the whole story, the inside scoop, complete with emotions. Best of all, they pull the reader right into the scene.

Now, we're not talking about just any details. The ones we're interested in—let's call them the "telling details"—are the little things that convey a whole lot of information. Here are a few. See if you can fill in the rest of the story after hearing just the telling details.

- A phone call, a shout of excitement, the key to a new house, bare walls and a carpet, a bottle of champagne.

- A Billie Holiday song playing softly, the circle of light from a single lamp, a letter creased from being folded and unfolded many times, the word "sorry."

- A photograph in a special frame, warm embers in a fireplace, a wedding ring on a hand that's not as supple as it once was, a card that reads, "40 wonderful years!"

- A limousine, an expensive dress with a torn shoulder strap, an unsteady walk, a frozen smile, the harsh, stabbing light of flashbulbs, the black glass of a tinted window, a pale reflection.

- Bright sunlight and blue sky, a shoreline, a lone figure walking with slumped shoulders and head down.

Make up a list of details like these and write a song based on it.

A short string of telling details can give listeners all they need in order to understand what's going on in the song. Let them fill in what you *don't* say. By letting listeners do some of the work for themselves, you draw them in and get them actively involved. Just be sure you give them enough details, before turning them loose!

Let listeners fill in what you don't say.

Supporting details

Each of the groups of details in the list above includes the obvious ones; all you have to do is connect the dots. But, there are a few details that are seemingly unrelated to the storyline—the embers of a fire, dim lamplight, popping flashbulbs. These help increase the effectiveness of your lyric by adding atmosphere, involving the senses, and underscoring the emotional tone of the situation. Don't forget to put these in; you get to use everything in the scene to help you communicate the situation.

In the final group of details, I included a sunny day—the opposite of what the walking figure seems to suggest—to add contrast and increase the feeling of despondency. Try playing with the details: use contrast, try some opposites. Feel free to experiment until you've got the right amount and the right mix to convey your theme.

Gathering the details

For more ideas on capturing the details, see Shortcut 67.

To pull together the details for your lyric, choose a situation you'd like to write about. Imagine yourself in the situation; really get inside it. Make a list of images, sounds, and feelings that occur to you as you imagine yourself inside the scene. Don't just look for the big things; take note of the small points as well.

Not every hit song uses details to convey the situation; however, certain genres, like Country and Rap, tend to lean on them more than others. Check out songs like the following to get the inside scoop from the telling details.

Genre	Title	Performer
R&B/Soul	"No Scrubs"	TLC
Pop	"New Shoes"	Paolo Nutini
Country	"Mud On the Tires"	Brad Paisley
Rock	"Paralyzer"	Finger Eleven

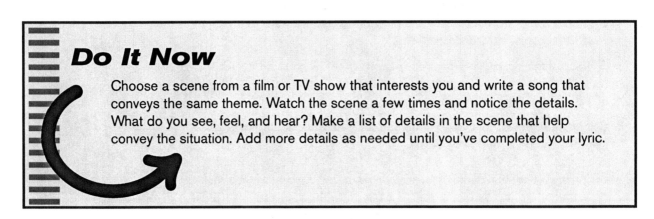

Do It Now

Choose a scene from a film or TV show that interests you and write a song that conveys the same theme. Watch the scene a few times and notice the details. What do you see, feel, and hear? Make a list of details in the scene that help convey the situation. Add more details as needed until you've completed your lyric.

Shortcut #62

Take Us Where the Action Is

Give your lyric motion, energy, and activity.

When we watch a good movie, it's all about action. The characters kiss, fight, shoot, climb, embrace, shout, and make love. Hearts break, tears flow, crooks sneak, heroes fly. There's plenty of *motion* along with the *emotion*. As a songwriter, adding some of this activity to your songs can encourage people to plop down in a chair, turn up the sound, and listen.

Four ways to add action to your song

➢ **Replace abstract or general statements with action**
When you have a statement in your song like "I remember how it was," try replacing it with an action. Your listeners don't remember how it was; they weren't there. Show them the action. What did the other person do? What did the singer do? A more effective line might be: "I remember when you held me close through the long nights." In Rob Thomas' "Ever the Same," when he wants to say, "I'll be there for you when times are hard," he describes an action: "Just let me hold you while you're falling apart." This gives listeners a specific image, drawing them deeper into the story.

➢ **Action words and images create a sense of energy**
When you're working on a song that's focused on the singer's emotions, not triggered by specific events that can be shown, use action words to describe the emotions. Natasha Bedingfield's "Unwritten" is a good example. The song is about an idea: growing up, standing on the brink of adult life. The songwriters create a sense of action within this thoughtful song by using words that suggest motion and activity: "staring," "open up," "reaching," "taste it," "release," "speak," "drench," "live." These motion-filled words add energy and urgency to what might otherwise be a quiet, rather dull, interior monologue.

➢ **Use action-based examples in a concept song**
"Live Like You Were Dying," recorded by Tim McGraw, is a powerful concept song. The theme is: Enjoy and appreciate life to the fullest while you can. The writers could have taken a preachy approach, telling us that life is short and we should value every moment. But they know it won't be as effective as showing the actions a man would take if he knew he were dying: He goes skydiving, mountain climbing, and bull riding. He expresses his appreciation for friends and loved ones by being kinder and offering forgiveness. These are all action-based examples. By using these concrete, action-based examples, the writers created a series of interesting, energetic images that draw listeners into the song and convince them of the concept without ever preaching.

Keep things moving! Use action to add energy and interest.

> **Run the film**
>
> Some songs actually follow the characters as if they were in a film; you might even think of these songs as "mini-movies." In Fantasia's "Truth Is" listeners see her encounter a former boyfriend, and watch her react to a photograph of his new love. Even small details are pictured: he pays for lunch as he promises to keep in touch. All of this, of course, leads straight to the chorus where the singer's thoughts and feelings are revealed in an interior monologue ("I was thinking to myself ..."). The actions described in the verses offer listeners a "movie" to watch while the choruses give direct access to the singer's emotions. This combination of "camera work" and inner monologue creates an effective balance that provides the audience with plenty to feel and to see.

Do It Now

1. Look through hit song lyrics for examples of the techniques listed here. Look for action words and scenes.

2. Write a verse and chorus using any of the action-based techniques above or rewrite a lyric, replacing abstract ideas with concrete actions or action words.

See "Shortcut Resources" on page 261 for information on where to find current music charts, hit songs, lyrics, and legal downloads.

Shortcut #63

Three Tips for Using Rhyme Effectively

Make rhyme your ally—know <u>why</u> you are rhyming.

When we think of song lyrics, we automatically think about rhymes. After all, rhyming played a central role in our very first experience with songs: *Mary had a little lamb whose fleece was white as SNOW. And everywhere that Mary went the lamb was sure to GO.* This deeply embedded link between songs and rhyming remains with us when, years later, we decide to write songs of our own. The link is so powerful that a songwriter may bend a line out of shape or change what she intended to say just to include a rhyme.

If you understand why we use rhymes and how to create an effect with them, then you can make a conscious decision to rhyme. This puts *you* in control rather than letting *rhyme* control you.

> **Rhyme is a memory aid**
> Rhyme is used as a memory aid in dozens of quick-recall formulas such as *Thirty days hath September / April, June, and November.* A lot of us would be writing checks dated April 31st if we hadn't memorized that little rhyme at some point! Advertisers, too, understand the recall power of rhyme and add it to jingles to increase the chance you'll remember their product name.
>
> *Rhyming Tip:* If you use a rhyme within your hook line or make your hook the second line of a pair of rhyming lines, you increase the chance that listeners will remember it.

Use these tips to make rhyming work for you!

> **Rhymes offer a sense of completion and release**
> A rhyme consists of two lines: a *setup* line and a *completion* line. The setup line gives us the first word of a rhyming pair and the second line completes it, delivering the rhyme itself. The anticipation, then arrival, of the second line creates a feeling of tension followed by release. Once we hear *A B C D E F G*, we're expecting something that rhymes with "G." When we get to *L M N O P,* we can breathe a sigh of relief, our expectation has been fulfilled by the completion line. However, if we hear *L M N O … X,* we're surprised; the tension remains, waiting to be released. This can get the listener's attention but if left unresolved it could become uncomfortable.
>
> *Rhyming Tip:* Fulfill the listener's expectation but with a twist. Extend a rhyming line by a couple of words or syllables so the rhyme occurs later than anticipated, thus delaying the sense of release. This adds a fresh feel to what might otherwise be a predictable rhyme. Here's an example:
>
> Predictable …
> *You reach for something to hold*
> *But all that you touch is cold.*

Less predictable …
You reach for something to hold
But all that your hands uncover is cold.

> **Rhymes add emphasis**
> A rhyming word draws attention to itself; it's doing something besides just being a word. It's echoing an earlier word and has added weight because it releases tension. Be sure the rhyming word is one you want your listeners to notice. If you're shuffling the words in your completion line just to create a rhyme, chances are your rhyming word will not be the important one.
>
> *Rhyming Tip:* Write your completion line first, then go back and write the setup line.

Break the tyranny of rhyme!

We have associated rhyming with song lyrics from such an early age that it's difficult for most of us to write a lyric without rhyming. There are hit songs that don't rhyme in places where we expect them to or barely rhyme at all. Dido's "White Flag" is a great example. In today's hits, rhyme is often used in creative ways that break our nursery rhyme expectation. Or it's de-emphasized to allow non-rhyming but important words to get more attention.

To break the tyranny of rhyme, practice writing lyrics that don't rhyme at all. It's harder than it sounds! Use a hit song melody or a melody of your own and write a new lyric. Don't make any effort to rhyme any of the lines. Instead, write what you feel. Use images to get your message across. Experiment with other Shortcuts that interest you. If a rhyme happens to occur, you can keep it but don't go looking for one. Get used to giving yourself a choice. To rhyme or not to rhyme, that's *your* decision.

Give yourself a choice: to rhyme or not to rhyme!

Do It Now

1. Listen to hit songs and notice how the rhyming words draw your attention, add emphasis, and complete a setup line.

2. Play with some rhyming pairs of lines. Test these effects for yourself. For instance, end a completion line with a strong word you want to emphasize; then create a setup line that leads into it. Just for comparison, try ending your completion line with a weaker word, one that isn't important to listeners.

3. Try the exercise in the last paragraph of this Shortcut. Practice writing without rhyming.

See "Shortcut Resources" on page 261 for information on where to find current music charts, hit songs, lyrics, and legal downloads.

Shortcut #64

Maintain Believability
While You Rhyme

Make sense even when you're making rhymes.

People don't talk to each other in rhyme. When we're in an intimate moment or going through an emotional crisis, we don't break into a big, hook-filled lyric in which the ends of lines have words that sound the same! Yet, many of today's hit songs manage to maintain a demanding rhyme scheme while conveying a believable emotional moment. Now *that's* a challenge!

A spontaneous feel is essential in today's big hit songs. Listeners want to believe the singer just thought of the things he's saying, and that the emotions are real and occurring right now. Rhyming works against that response; it just isn't something that happens naturally. However, rhyme can create useful effects, so you want to keep it around. *The solution: keep your rhyming words low-key and the surrounding lyric conversational.*

See Shortcut 63 for tips on creating effects with rhyme.

Keep it conversational

In Avril Lavigne's "My Happy Ending," she rhymes the words "pretending" and "ending" in the last two lines of the chorus. This is the payoff of the chorus and it includes the title line of the song. Giving it a strong, attention-grabbing rhyme is a good idea but *this* rhyme is a familiar one. It could sound predictable, and self-consciously "rhyme-y" if it weren't for the conversational, honest language that surrounds it. Both lines use the natural word order anyone would use when speaking these phrases. The second line includes a slang phrase—"So much for …"—that adds a casual, tossed-off feel. Together the naturalness and casual tone balance the crafted, self-conscious quality of the rhyme, making the lines sound believable. If you can look at a pair of rhyming lines in a song of your own and say, "That's the way I would say it; it just happens to rhyme," then you're in good shape!

That's the way I would say it; it just happens to rhyme!

Vowel rhymes

In the big hit songs of earlier eras, careful rhyming was a must. Audiences waited to hear what clever rhyme Cole Porter or Oscar Hammerstein II would come up with. At that time, in that style, two rhyming words had to share the same vowel sound followed by the same consonant sound, so-called *perfect rhymes* like "fat" and "cat" or "love" and "above." But … no longer! When writing for today's mainstream music genres—Pop, Country, R&B/Soul, and Rock—look for *vowel rhymes*, sometimes called "near rhymes" or "assonance." These are words in which the emphasized vowel sound is the same but the consonants that follow are different. Here are a few examples:

find / time	most / closed
love / enough	night / life
play / mistake	met / sent
now / house	cover / another
do / cool	spoken / open

In today's hit songs, singers hold out the vowel sounds and de-emphasize the consonant sounds that follow, allowing you, the songwriter, to "cheat" on the final consonants of a rhyme.

When you use vowel rhymes, you have access to a far wider choice of rhyming words than you do when you limit yourself to perfect rhymes. It's easier to maintain a conversational tone and the rhyme doesn't draw as much attention to itself, encouraging the casual, believable feel of today's songs. A perfect rhyme, however, might still be used to add extra emphasis to a hook line. Check out Keith Urban's "Somebody Like You" for example.

Working with tight rhyme schemes

A rhyme scheme that includes multiple rhymes that occur close together can be effective, but be careful! Sometimes a couple of lines like this will just fall into place as you're writing a first verse; a smooth, conversational series of rhymes no songwriter in their right mind would turn down! You're ecstatic. But, uh oh. Now you have to do it again in your second verse. (Yes, you do. Listeners are expecting it and you can't let them down.) You'll need to write another, parallel series of rhyming lines that's just as smooth and makes just as much sense as the lines in your first verse. Try writing many versions—it could be ten, twenty, or even thirty—until you find a combination of words, rhymes, ideas, and phrases that are as good as the inspired lines in your first verse. Take a look at the verses in Natasha Bedingfield's "Unwritten" to see how something like this is handled in a hit song.

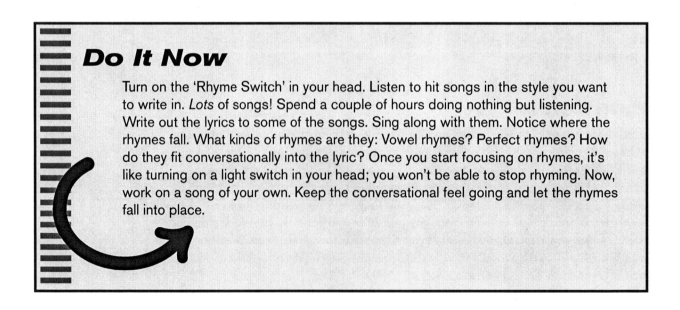

Do It Now

Turn on the 'Rhyme Switch' in your head. Listen to hit songs in the style you want to write in. *Lots* of songs! Spend a couple of hours doing nothing but listening. Write out the lyrics to some of the songs. Sing along with them. Notice where the rhymes fall. What kinds of rhymes are they: Vowel rhymes? Perfect rhymes? How do they fit conversationally into the lyric? Once you start focusing on rhymes, it's like turning on a light switch in your head; you won't be able to stop rhyming. Now, work on a song of your own. Keep the conversational feel going and let the rhymes fall into place.

Shortcut #65

Use a Variety of Phrase Lengths and Rhyme Patterns

Avoid the "Greeting Card Syndrome" in your lyrics.

You've decided to spend an afternoon working on a lyric. Good! You sit down with a blank page and begin. What comes out are nice four-line verses with rhyming words in predictable places and an even, seesaw feel to the line lengths. Every verse has a regular "tum-ta-tum-ta-tum-ta-tum" rhythm. Somehow the emotion you set out to communicate is not really coming through. Instead, you are reminded of birthdays and graduations. Why? Because what you are writing is a greeting card poem, not a song! Your lyric is suffering from *Greeting Card Syndrome*.

Experience the difference for yourself

You've probably heard the phrase "a poem is not a lyric." Put it this way—in today's market, *a greeting card poem is not a lyric*. The simple, repeated rhythm patterns and regular line lengths of greeting card verses create a cozy, homey feel that works well for sentimental cards but not for the intimate, emotional revelations of today's song lyrics. Equally important, these conventional greeting card patterns just don't support the unpredictable melodies that are characteristic of contemporary hit songs.

Greeting card poems won't work with today's hit melodies.

To get a feel for the difference between greeting card poems and hit song lyrics, *read* a few of today's lyrics. You can find them in fake books, song folios, or online at legal lyric sites like Yahoo! Music (www.music.yahoo.com/lyrics). Try a Rock genre lyric like "It's Not My Time" (3 Doors Down) or a Pop lyric like "Ever the Same" (Rob Thomas). You'll see the variety of line lengths and the unpredictable rhythm and rhyme patterns that are used. Without their melodies, it's sometimes difficult to see the patterns at all. These lyrics were most likely written to a melody.

Write lyrics that "sing" to today's melodies

When writing lyrics "on the page"—writing a lyric without a melody—everyone has a tendency to fall into the basic nursery rhyme patterns we heard as children—*Roses are red, violets are blue / Sugar is sweet and so are you!* The "tum-ta-ta-tum/tum-ta-ta-tum" rhythm pattern and regular line lengths feel so natural, and are so firmly rooted in our memory, that they drown out everything else. To write lyrics with the kind of variety and unpredictability you hear in today's hit songs, it helps to have a melody in mind as you write. It may not be the melody you end up using, but it will act as a guide to help you write a lyric that "sings."

Write your lyric to a melody!

➤ **Play the "melody swap" game**
You can play this game with a collaborator or another songwriter. Each of you writes a melody and records a simple version of it. You don't need a whole song, a verse and chorus will do. Now, swap melodies and write a lyric using the other person's melody as a guide. Using someone else's melody helps you break out of old habits and discover new patterns. Use the pattern of line lengths and word rhymes in your first verse to write the second verse. Repeat the chorus and add a bridge with a contrasting line length and rhyme pattern to finish your song.

➤ **Use a ghost song melody to practice writing lyrics that "sing"**
If you don't have a collaborator or songwriting friend who can provide a melody, try using a hit song melody temporarily. Choose a recent hit song you like and practice writing lyrics to the melody. For a step-by-step guide that will show you how to do this, read Shortcut 73.

➤ **Be prepared to rewrite your lyric**
If you have no choice but to write your lyrics without a melody, keep your options open. Be prepared to rewrite to fit a collaborator's melody. If you want to take your lyric further without a melody, try adding a couple syllables or words to lengthen a line or extend a thought past the end of one line into the next. Consider breaking some of your lines into shorter phrases and adding some rhymes within lines. All of these suggestions are characteristic of contemporary lyrics.

Do It Now

Choose a hit song to use as a ghost song. Follow the step-by-step instructions in Shortcut 73 to practice writing a lyric that "sings." IMPORTANT: Be sure you don't use *any* of the ghost song lyric in your own song. The ghost song lyrics are protected by copyright!

See "Shortcut Resources" on page 261 for information on where to find current music charts, hit songs, lyrics, and legal downloads.

Shortcut #66

Balance "You" and Your Listeners

You may write your song for one person,
but many are listening.

Many songs, hits and otherwise, feature a character called "you." The lyric focuses on something the singer says or wants to say to "you": "I love you." "You hurt me." "I want you." "I'm leaving you." The overall sense is of an intimate, honest moment of communication. Of course, a few hundred thousand people might be listening in, but the song acts as if they're not there.

Actually, a hit songwriter is *very* aware of those thousands of ears. She has to ensure that listeners have enough information to be able to understand what has brought the singer and "you" to this crisis point. The difficulty is that in a real conversation, especially in an emotionally-charged situation, the speaker is not likely to recap the facts for the benefit of an unseen audience! However, a hit songwriter has to find a way to do just that in a song lyric.

Hit songs invite listeners inside an intimate situation by giving them the important background details they need to know. For instance, Beyoncé's "Irreplaceable" does a great job of describing exactly what led up to the confrontation in the song, even as the action is taking place. When physical appearance or actions are important, hit songs offer descriptive details that allow listeners to picture the scene. What could be more intimate than John Mayer's "Your Body Is a Wonderland"? He sings as if he and his lover are completely alone, while at the same time he vividly describes the scene for listeners.

Hit songs invite listeners inside a private moment.

How to keep your listeners in the loop

As a songwriter, you're often writing about something that happened to you. Frequently it's in the context of a relationship—a special moment, an insight, or a break up. If your lyric is addressed to the other person in the relationship ("you") it can be very easy to get caught up in personal incidents and emotions. When this happens, the needs of listeners have a lower priority. And that's the way it should be … at least for the first draft. Until you have your lyric idea roughed out, it's important to follow the inspiration and emotions that are driving your song. *Then* go back and start thinking about your listeners.

First, write what you feel, then rewrite for the rest of us!

Put a copy of your rough draft to one side so you can refer back to it; it will be there to remind you of your initial inspiration. Then, look through the lyric for places where you've assumed some knowledge that your listeners don't have. Use images, telling details, and action words to communicate that information. Here are some questions listeners may have:

- What led up to this situation?
- Who is involved?
- What motivates him or her?

• Why is the singer saying these things?
• Why does he or she feel this way?

If physical appearance or action is important to understanding the situation, be sure to include descriptive phrases.

You don't need to go deeply into the specifics of your particular situation—that might be *too* much information. However, you *do* need to give listeners enough imagery and insights to allow them to picture what's going on and feel what the singer is feeling. Read Shortcut 71 for more suggestions on how to communicate effectively with listeners. A song that really engages an audience is one that invites them to participate in an intimate or revealing moment. Don't keep them on the outside while you carry on a fascinating exchange with "you." Let them in!

Do It Now

1. Check out hit song lyrics in which the singer addresses "you." Notice how the songwriter communicates information we need to know in order to understand what's happening in the song.

2. Write or rewrite a lyric of your own that's addressed to "you." Include information about a) something "you" did that created the situation in the song, or b) how the singer feels about "you" and why.

See "Shortcut Resources" on page 261 for information on where to find current music charts, hit songs, lyrics, and legal downloads.

Shortcut #67

How to Never Write Another Cliché

Put yourself in the scene and use what you find.

A *cliché* is a phrase that once expressed an important truth or feeling, but through overuse has lost its emotional impact. Clichés are tempting to use because they do express something true—they never would have been used by so many writers, songwriters, and poets if they didn't. The problem is we've been exposed to them so often, we don't hear them anymore. A cliché is like an empty space in your song.

Here are a few examples of clichés:

> *Our love is like a fairy tale.*
> *You're always there for me.*
> *Love is blind.*

Each of these lines is trying to communicate something about a relationship but we've heard them so often, they have lost any real meaning.

Treat a cliché as a starting point

If you write a cliché like "love is blind" don't stop there. This is a starting point not an ending point for your lyric. Ask yourself: Why do I want to say that? What is it about this relationship that suggests blindness? Then ask yourself: What are some other ways to express blindness? What happens if I explore images and feelings related to blindness, for example, darkness and light?

Write down the related images and phrases that come to you:

> *Blind = darkness, confusion, no way forward, stumbling.*

Try plugging these words into the cliché or using them to develop the cliché phrase, adding more interest and clarity: *I'm stumbling through this love of ours.*

Try a twist on the cliché or extend it to say something new: "Love is blind" could become "love is a blind alley," which could lead you to a different set of images.

Treat that familiar phrase as a starting point.

Don't write someone else's song

Clichés are often the first things that come to mind when you think about a theme. That's because other people have said those things so often when dealing with that same theme. Think of it this way: *When you write a cliché, you are actually writing someone else's song!*

You may be writing clichés because you're not really clear on what *you* want to say. Spend some time writing down your feelings and thoughts. Don't aim for a lyric; just get your ideas down. Then look for those concepts that are original and might offer listeners a fresh insight or new slant on the theme.

Immerse yourself in the feeling or situation

Imagine the situation as vividly as you can. Be there! Live it!

Clichés happen when you remain on the surface emotionally, when you write about a situation or character or event without really feeling it. Put yourself in the middle of the situation you're writing about. Don't talk *about* it; be *in* it. Imagine it as vividly as you can. Be there! Notice the small details, the sights and smells and sounds. Put those details into your song so your listeners can live it with you. When you write a song about something that happened to you in the past or something you hope will happen in the future, imagine yourself in those situations as if you are there *right now*. Tell your listeners how it feels, show them what is important, even if it's something very small.

Be emotionally present. Be observant. Be fearless. Be honest. And you will never write another cliché. You will never write someone else's song.

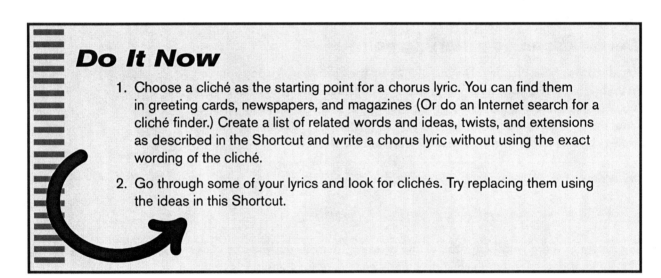

Do It Now

1. Choose a cliché as the starting point for a chorus lyric. You can find them in greeting cards, newspapers, and magazines (Or do an Internet search for a cliché finder.) Create a list of related words and ideas, twists, and extensions as described in the Shortcut and write a chorus lyric without using the exact wording of the cliché.

2. Go through some of your lyrics and look for clichés. Try replacing them using the ideas in this Shortcut.

Shortcut #68

Make Your Characters Believable

Use authentic language to convey your characters.

As a songwriter, you are part scriptwriter, part novelist, and part film director. Each of these creates a world that draws in the audience by making them believe the characters that live in that world are real. If you're sitting through an entire movie thinking about how well the actors are faking foreign accents, the director has failed to do his job; you were never captured and pulled inside the film. The same holds true for songs. If you're thinking about what great vocal cords the singer has, the songwriter has failed to capture your imagination and emotions by making her characters believable.

Keep your language honest, authentic, and expressive

Scriptwriters have both images and dialogue to help create their characters; songwriters have only the voice and words of the singer. Make certain that those words sound authentic while supporting the situation and theme of your song.

For example, in Avril Lavigne's "My Happy Ending," she opens with a line that includes the idiomatic phrase, "It's not like we're dead." The tone and style of the language is confrontational, youthful, and edgy. It establishes the singer's character and creates believability right at the beginning of the song. A line like this invites the audience to identify with the singer.

Brad Paisley's "Mud On the Tires" features a very different type of character. In this lyric, the singer asks polite questions, his manner is charming and indirect. References to "trotline" and the time of the sunset tell listeners that he enjoys being outdoors and is a keen observer of nature. Without making listeners aware of it, the songwriter has painted a vivid, believable picture of the lead character using language and imagery.

The language you use makes your character believable.

Here are a few tips for using language that conveys your character's believability to your audience.

- Use language that's appropriate to the singer's age and background.

- Keep the language conversational. Use the word order most people would use in casual conversation.

- Give us information about the character by showing us how they speak. For example, are they argumentative, deferential, aggrieved, or sarcastic?

Singer-songwriters: pay attention to believability, too

If you're a singer-songwriter, you may feel that because you *are* a real person, whatever you write will be believable. However, it's not that easy. You have a unique problem. While you need to be honest about who you are, listeners don't need or want to know about every single aspect of your personality and life. Choose those aspects that add up to an interesting, unique "persona." Be sure those parts you do choose are honest and express a real and important part of you. Look for a lyric style that fits your persona. A romantic or moody image might lean more toward a poetic style of language, whereas a youthful, edgy persona may be more direct and confrontational. Whichever you choose, make certain to maintain a conversational word order in your lines to add realism and believability to the persona.

Should you use slang?

There's a difference between being conversational and using slang. Slang is often short-lived and may be limited to a particular group. It's impossible to say which slang phrases may cross over into general usage and become conversational. Unless you're writing for a specific group (for example, Hip-Hop and Rap), slang can be a drawback. It can cause confusion in listeners who don't know the meaning of the slang or it may give your song a dated feel after just a few months.

Slang could give your song a dated sound.

If you want to keep the slang phrase in your song and still continue to pitch it to artists, be prepared to re-record those lines and update them every year. A good general rule is to keep your language conversational within the genre in which you're working and avoid using phrases that are faddish.

Do It Now

1. Listen to hit songs in the genre you're interested in. Notice how language is used to convey characters and situations. What kind of vocabulary does the singer use? How does he or she address other characters in the song or the listener? What does the language in the song tell us about the characters?

2. Try writing a verse and chorus in the voice of a character. Use vocabulary and speaking style to convey information about the character to your listeners.

See "Shortcut Resources" on page 261 for information on where to find current music charts, hit songs, lyrics, and legal downloads.

Shortcut #69

Two Songs Are Not Always Better Than One!

Keep your song on track ... a single track.

When two songs try to cram into the space where only one should be, things can get confusing. Listeners become frustrated very quickly when they invest their emotions in a situation only to be diverted onto another track in a later verse. And, as a songwriter, if you're going to treat a situation with any real depth, there won't be room within the limited lyric "real estate" of a single song to handle more than one.

Here's an example of a verse that's got enough ideas to launch two songs ... or more!

> *You're telling me lies.*
> *I see how you look away*
> *When I ask you where you stayed last night.*
> *I'm too weak to be what you need, I know.*
> *The demons of my past have got a grip on me.*
> *I'm on my knees praying that everything*
> *Will turn out all right.*

On the surface it appears that this is a single situation, but look closer, it's actually two situations. The first three lines focus on a suspicion of infidelity; the last four lines have to do with something that happened in the past and how it's affecting the current relationship.

Keep your song on a single track

Here are four tips for keeping your song focused on a single theme.

> ➤ **Give it the two-song test: Ask the questions**
> How do you know if you've got two songs? If your lyric suggests questions that change *substantially* during the song, you've probably got two songs. In the above example, the questions suggested by the first three lines are: *Why did the other person lie? Is he or she being unfaithful? What will the singer do about it?* Your listeners are primed and ready to go with that situation. Then the lyric suddenly switches gears, focusing on the singer's past and the demons that drive him or her. Now there's a new set of questions for listeners to ask: *What demons? Why does the singer feel so weak and helpless? What will the singer do about this?*

Is your song trying to answer too many questions?

There's no hope of answering all these questions in any depth in the space of one song. Each of these two emotional situations deserves and can support an entire song. Try separating your two themes, removing the lines that belong to one of them, and saving them for another song.

> **To stay on track, use the questions the title asks**
> Use the questions suggested by the title (see Shortcut 44) to lead you into and through your song. Remember, the title will be repeated several times during your song, and all your lines should support it. Many of your lyric lines will be answering the questions suggested by your title, which will help to keep the song tightly focused. Yes, more questions are likely to come up as the song progresses. Just make sure they're closely related to or result from your original title questions.

> **Stick to your theme**
> Don't be pulled off track by a brilliant lyric line that suddenly occurs to you from out of the blue. One line doesn't make a song great, but it *can* pull your song off track, reducing its effectiveness. When you get a line like this, check to see if it introduces a new set of questions. If it does, put it aside and use it to start a new song.

Real life is messy. Songs aren't.

> **You don't have to tell us everything!**
> Many times a song is based on personal experience. Just because it happened in real life doesn't mean you have to tell every single detail. *Real life is messy. Songs aren't.* Pick and choose the incidents and ideas that are essential to the situation. You'll write a hundred more songs! Save your extra ideas for those.

Do It Now

1. Look through the lyrics of hit songs you like and notice how the song remains focused on a single situation or set of questions.

2. Write a verse and chorus using a title line and the questions it suggests. Remain focused on a single situation or theme as you write.

See "Shortcut Resources" on page 261 for information on where to find current music charts, hit songs, lyrics, and legal downloads.

Shortcut #70

Take Your Creativity for a Walk

Stay focused and use everything your inspiration gives you.

It's a wonderful feeling to just abandon yourself and let inspiration and creativity carry you through your song. But consider this: Your inspired muse may be working on two or three songs at the same time! Once you open the floodgates, once you turn on the "creativity switch," inspiration comes flowing out and it may have *a lot* of different things it wants to say. That's just fine as long as you realize what's happening. It's so easy to get excited about all those lines that are arriving magically! You start stuffing them all into the song you're working on, stretching the song's theme to include one line then another. Pretty soon, you've got a lot of great one-liners but your song has lost focus and that means it has lost emotional impact as well.

Give your creativity some guidelines

So how can you let your creativity flow and still give your song a tight thematic focus? You actually have more control over your creativity than you might think. Try giving it some direction; let it know where you want it to go. It's like taking a dog for a walk; the dog wants to rush here and there, checking stuff out, while you would prefer that it walk beside you so you can get where you're going. You have to put some kind of leash on the dog with just enough lead so you can give it a gentle tug and say, "No. We're going *this* way." But not so restrictive that it plops its butt down in the middle of the street and won't move. Here are a couple of suggestions for giving your creativity some guidance.

Let your creativity flow but give it some guidance.

➤ **Start with your song title.** Write down two or three questions that the title suggests. Keep coming back to those questions to remind yourself—and your creativity—where you are headed.

➤ **Rough out a development path.** Read Shortcut 53 to find out how to work up a development path for your song. Keep your notes brief; you want to suggest a direction while leaving room for exploration.

Like a stubborn puppy, your creativity might refuse to cooperate at first. Try some of the suggestions in Shortcut 15 for getting your creative right brain going. Keep the "sandbox" attitude suggested in Shortcut 17. Gradually, you'll see a change. Be firm. Remember, *you're* the boss.

Use the two-song approach

Even after you've given your inspiration some idea of where you want it to go, it will still give you a few rough gems that don't fit the song on which you're working. If a line doesn't fit your development path or answer your title questions, write it down on a separate sheet of paper. It belongs in a different song. There's no "Law of Creativity" that says you can only work on one song at a time!

After a while, when you feel you're losing touch with the emotions in the song you're currently working on, put it to one side. You can come back later with a fresh perspective. In the meantime, take a look at the lines you've written down on the other sheet of paper. Maybe there's a song there you'd like to begin developing. Sometimes, when you're not looking, a whole song can start to take shape! Again, try using the title questions or a development path to help you sort out which lines belong in the song. Save the others for later and start the process over again.

Keep two songs going. When you need a break from one, work on the other.

Do It Now

This exercise will not only help you create raw material for *two songs*, it will help you "unstick" yourself from the idea that you can only work on one song at a time.

Pick a short phrase you'd like to use as a title (Title #1). Use Shortcut 44 to come up with the questions the title asks. Now create a second title (Title #2). Write it at the top of a separate page. Find the questions for that title and write them down beneath it. Put Title #2 aside and tell yourself you'll work on it later.

Now, let your creativity play with the answers to the questions for Title #1. Try a few lines using images and examples; write down everything that comes to you. Take a break then come back. Take a look at Title #2. Write a few lines that answer the questions for that title.

Glance at Title #1 and jot down a line that might work then return to Title #2. Go back and forth as often as you like. Work on one title as long as ideas are coming to you. When you get stuck, work on the other. If a strong line suddenly occurs to you, check to see *which* title it belongs to and *where* in the song it belongs.

Shortcut #71

The Communication Checklist

Be "other-directed." Keep listeners involved and interested.

Here's a story I wrote. It's called "I Fell For You."

> *Sometimes I don't feel like getting up in the morning. The sun is shining. It's Wednesday. I put on my clothes and combed my hair and went out with my friends. You were there. The music was loud. We danced all night. He was the kind of guy I could fall for, yes I could. He said, "Goodnight" and I thought, "I'll never see you again." It's another day. I've got to go to work. I hate my job.*

Did you enjoy that story? Did you get involved emotionally? Be honest with me now. It's okay, I can take it, even though it's about my latest breakup and I'm passionately attached to it and I wrote it from the deepest, most vulnerable places of my heart and it tells it exactly like it was, I promise you. Let me tell you more about it … oh, you don't want to hear?

Self-involved vs. other-directed

From my point of view, it felt good to write that story because I got to relive it. If there are blank spots, I can fill them in because I was there. However, you, the reader, are missing a lot of information. You don't know why I did what I did or how it felt. I didn't bother to make my story consistent or coherent. I didn't give you a picture of the people or places I was talking about. If you're not interested in hearing more, I can't really blame you, can I? I only wrote it for myself.

There are two ways to approach writing a song:

- The first way: *What do I want to say?*
- The second way: *What do I want to tell you?*

Self-involved or other-directed, it's your choice.

These sound like the same question but they're different in one important way: the first is *self-involved;* the second is *other-directed.* If I'm just talking to myself (What do I want to say?), I can say anything I want to. But, if I want to tell my story to someone else (What do I want to tell *you?*) I'll need to express it in a way that's understandable, interesting, and relevant to you. If I don't bother to do that, why should you bother listening to me?

To attract listeners and keep them interested a song needs to be well organized, deliver information in a way listeners can understand, and provide support for the actions and emotions of the characters.

Use the "Communication Checklist" to see if your songs are self-involved or other-directed.

COMMUNICATION CHECKLIST

1. **Did you introduce the characters?**
    Make sure listeners know who is involved in the situation. Some small detail that offers an insight into a person or a brief physical description can bring the characters to life for your listeners.

2. **Did you set the scene?**
    Where does the action take place? If you "saw her face in a crowded place," then say so. Details can be effective; choose the ones that are relevant. If the sleet-grey sky echoed your emotions, that's good information.

3. **Are your time frames organized?**
    A lyric may shift from the past (What happened.) to the present (How I feel about that.) to the future (What I think will happen.). Try keeping these organized into groups of lines. Spend at least a pair of lines or a whole verse in one time frame. Listeners don't have a time machine that can make quick trips for every line.

4. **Does your situation develop?**
    You know what happened but listeners have no clue. You don't have to tell them every single thing. Like a good storyteller, choose the relevant information, the important details that convey the larger picture, and put them in some kind of order that listeners can follow.

5. **Did you stick to your theme?**
    You have very limited space in which to get your message across—just a couple of verses, a chorus, and a bridge. Make every line lead toward and support your theme. If you go off on a side trip, listeners have no choice but to follow. Then, getting them back on track takes precious time.

6. **Are your pronouns consistent?**
    To make sure listeners understand who is doing what to whom, keep your pronouns consistent. She is always she, I am always I, and you are you. If "you" refers to a specific person, be cautious about using it in a broader sense, as in idiomatic phrases like "you never can tell."

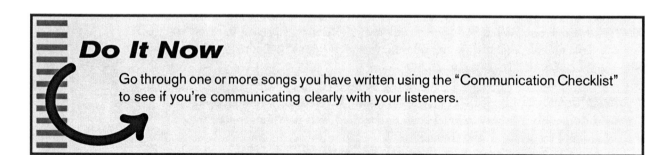

Do It Now

Go through one or more songs you have written using the "Communication Checklist" to see if you're communicating clearly with your listeners.

Shortcut #72

Ten Ways to Turn a Ho-hum Lyric Into a Powerhouse

Go from lackluster to blockbuster!

So, your song is done! In your opinion, it's a knockout. You've got a powerful theme and you feel plenty of emotion every time you sing what you've written.

But wait … why are you getting only a lukewarm response from listeners? Are they insensitive? Less than bright? Maybe not. If they could put it into words, listeners might tell you they feel like they're standing *outside* your song, trying to look in through a fogged-up window. They know something's going on but they can't see things clearly enough to tell what it is, so they're not able to get emotionally involved.

You, the songwriter, have to be the listeners' eyes and ears. Open up the window; invite your listeners *inside* the song by giving them plenty of context, visual details, and vivid examples. Here are ten ways you can give your lyric transparency and emotional impact.

Be your listeners' eyes and ears.

1. **Be sure your listeners have enough information**
   Many songs are based on personal experience. It's a great source of material, the only drawback is that while *you* know all the details of what happened —the context, the background, and the people involved—your listeners know nothing at all. You need to choose those incidents and details that convey the whole story in a limited number of lines. Go through your lyric to make sure you've included enough information to convey the characters and incidents in your situation clearly. See Shortcut 52 and 53 for tips on how to do that.

2. **Answer the questions suggested by the title**
   A strong title suggests questions that need to be answered within the body of the song. Check your title questions and be certain you've answered them in your lyric. Also, check that you didn't introduce elements into the lyric that raise unanswered questions. Read Shortcut 44 "Answer the Questions the Title Asks" to find out more.

3. **Use vivid, specific language**
   Use images, details, action words, and specific examples to convey the situation and emotions in your song. For instance, if you have a line like "you walked away and left me here," try telling us *how* the person walked away. How about "you sailed away" or "you skipped out" or "you crept off." A simple word substitution like this can add interest and information that helps open up the foggy window so we can see inside. For more on using this kind of language, see Shortcut 62.

Don't forget to include the details.

4. **Avoid generalizations and abstract statements**

If you make a general statement like "life has no meaning," you're missing an opportunity! Just telling us isn't going to make us feel it, no matter how true the statement might be. Try substituting an image with its associated emotions, ideas, sensations, and experiences. Shortcuts 57 and 58 can provide you with insights and practice in replacing general statements with specific images and examples.

Use images to make us see and feel it!

5. **Make sure your "key lines" say something important**

Check "the lines they always hear" to make sure you aren't throwing them away. These key lines are your chance to lead the listener deeper into your story. To find out more about key lines, read Shortcut 56.

6. **Check for natural flow of language**

Make your lines flow in a way that sounds conversational. Avoid using an awkward or unnatural word order to accommodate a rhyme (see Shortcut 64). Listeners notice these awkward moments. If something sounds wrong or unnatural, they'll start to distrust the singer and pull away from the song. Rework any lines that are there just for the rhyme. While you're at it, check for "filler" words that are there to keep the rhythm going—words like "just" and "then." Find a way to write the line so that *every* word is working hard to convey information.

Imagine you're telling, not singing, your story.

7. **Create forward momentum**

Keep your song moving forward by continually adding information and developing the situation. If you sketched out your song before you started (see Shortcut 47), take another look at your sketch to make certain you kept things moving according to plan. If you didn't sketch out your song beforehand, do it now. Look for any holes that need to be filled in, anything you could add that would deepen our understanding of the characters at a critical point. Conversely, look for anything you could take out that would help to pick up the pace.

8. **Stay true to the character of the singer**

Make sure the lyric is consistent with the character the singer is portraying. Keep the language appropriate for the genre, character, and story of the song. Shortcut 68 has useful tips that will help make your characters believable. This applies to singer-songwriters, too! You are the lead character in your own song.

9. **Mix poetic lines with direct statements**

If your lyric leans heavily on poetic language, listeners may miss some crucial information. Use as much creative imagery and associative language as you wish, but try throwing in a few direct statements to communicate those important points that listeners must have in order to understand what's happening. Shortcut 60 can show you how to use this technique.

10. **Beat what you already have**

If you have *any doubts at all* about a line or a section of your song, see if you can write something better—something stronger, clearer, more vivid.

Just put the lines you've written to one side and see if you can beat what you have.

You're not throwing anything away; it's important to acknowledge the work you've done. If you can't beat what you've already got, then use it. But if you don't *try* to beat it, you'll never know what you might have come up with. It's worth the investment of time to find out. Make new lists of related and contrasting words (see Shortcut 45). Write two or three new verses; try a new bridge using some of the images and words from your lists. If the new lines or verses are more effective than the ones you already have, replace the old ones with the new lines.

Try to beat what you have!

Do It Now

Go through one of your song lyrics and apply the techniques in this Shortcut. See if you can add more impact, originality, and memorability to your lyric.

Shortcut #73

Write Your Lyric to a Ghost Song Melody

Write a lyric that sings and strengthen your skills with this exercise.

In this Shortcut, you'll find out how to expand and strengthen your lyric writing skills by "collaborating" with the best songwriters in the business. You're going to practice writing a new lyric to an existing hit song melody, replacing the original lyric with one of your own. Remember, the lyric and melody of the hit song are protected by copyright. This is an exercise; do not use any of the hit song melody or lyric in any song of your own.

When you use a hit song melody to write your lyric, you accomplish several things at once:

- You write a lyric that "sings"—it has rhythmic and phrasing interest because it was written to a melody, not "on the page."

- You can concentrate solely on your lyric because song structure and melody are temporarily taken care of by the ghost song.

- You get a feel for how your lyric sounds when it's sung to a hit melody. It can change your expectations for your lyrics and open up a new way of hearing them.

- You embed some of the techniques that give hit song lyrics a contemporary sound, getting a feel for the variety of line lengths and rhythm patterns that characterize today's music. No more greeting card verses for you!

How to write an original lyric to a ghost song melody

1. **Choose a ghost song in the genre you want to write in**
   Listen to hit songs in the genre you're interested in or choose a song from the Song List on page 265. A good ghost song has a clearly defined structure and uses the song title in the chorus.

2. **Determine the song structure**
   Write down the complete lyric of the ghost song while becoming familiar with the melody. Create an outline of the song's structure by making a note of where the chorus, verse, pre-chorus, and bridge sections are. You're going to be using this structure for your own lyric; if you aren't sure what the structure is, then try a different ghost song.

For more on song structure, see Part Three of this book.

3. **Look for the song title**
   Find the song title; it's often in the first or last line of the chorus. (In a Verse /

Verse / Bridge / Verse structure, it's in the refrain line.) Now write a new title that you can comfortably sing in the same place as the ghost song title. You don't have to match the original syllable for syllable, just let it feel natural. Take your time finding a strong title that *you* want to work with; make it your own, rather than something that's related to the ghost song title in any way. Use Shortcuts 40 through 42 for tips on creating a solid title.

4. **Create your raw material**
   Come up with two or three questions suggested by your title. Then, make a list of words, phrases, and images that are related to your title and a separate list of contrasting words. See Shortcuts 44 and 46 for more on these ideas.

5. **Write a chorus lyric to the ghost song melody**
   Now, sing or hum the chorus melody of the ghost song and begin to work on your chorus lyric. (If you're not comfortable singing, just speak the rhythm of the notes and don't worry about the pitches.) Your title is already in place (see Step 3), so fill in around it. Try answering one of the title questions you came up with. Work in a few of the related images and phrases from your list. The content of this lyric comes from you; don't look to the ghost song for lyric ideas.

6. **Write verse and bridge lyrics to the ghost song melody**
   Now that you have your chorus, develop your idea further for your verses. Use Shortcut 47, along with your title questions and raw material, to get a rough idea of what each verse will be about. Then work with the ghost song melody to rough out your first, and then your second verses. If the ghost song has a bridge, follow the same procedure.

Vocalize your lyric as you work

As you work on your lyric, sing your words to the ghost song melody. *It's important to vocalize your lyric.* The point of the exercise is to write to a melody, not work out your lyric on paper. (You can keep track of lines that you like by writing them down.) If you can't sing the pitches of the original melody, just talk-sing your way through while preserving the rhythm of the melody.

By the time you finish your chorus you'll probably know the ghost song melody well enough to sing it without playing the original track. You can work on your own without the distraction of the original lyric by just turning off the music. Continue to sing the melody while tapping your foot to keep the tempo close to the original. If you still need to hear the original song, try playing the hit song at a low level. If you play keyboard or guitar, buy the sheet music and play it yourself.

(!) *The lyric and melody of the hit song are protected by copyright. This exercise is for practice only.*

Do It Now

Use the steps in this Shortcut to write a new lyric to a hit song melody.

See "Shortcut Resources" on page 261 for information on where to find current music charts, hit songs, lyrics, and legal downloads.

PART FIVE

Shortcuts to Hit Melodies

As a songwriter, one of the most exciting, valuable,

and eye-opening skills you'll ever learn

is how to analyze hit melodies!

It will open up a world of fresh ideas

and help you stay "up to the minute"

with new trends in hit songwriting ...

Shortcut #74

Study Hit Melodies: Just Count to 4!!!

Look inside the inner workings of hit song melodies.

I don't want you to believe a single thing I tell you about melody! That's right; I want you to doubt everything I say in the melody Shortcuts in this section. I want you to test everything. Check out hit song melodies for yourself. Discover new ideas on your own. How do you do that? By analyzing the melodies that make hit songs so compelling and unforgettable.

Useful!

It's easier than you might think. There's only one indispensable skill you *must* have in order to understand contemporary melody. Read notes? *No.* Play piano or guitar? *No.* To analyze a hit song melody all you have to be able to do is *count to 4.* After you get to 4, you start over again at 1. That's all there is to it.

First ... find Beat 1

One of the most prominent features of hit songs is a steady, regular beat that can be arranged easily into groups called "measures" or "bars." The most common grouping is four beats. In a song based on four beats per measure, every measure of the song will have four steady, regular beats. You can recognize these groups because the first beat of the group, Beat 1, is emphasized. All hit songs work hard to ensure the listener knows where Beat 1 is. It's the strongest beat of every bar; it's emphasized by the instruments (especially the drums) and often by the melody. If listeners lose track of Beat 1, they will lose touch with the rhythm of the song, so hit songwriters and producers make sure that doesn't happen!

Most songs feature 4 beats per measure.

Beat 1 is the strongest beat.

Start with something easy

Here's how you would count a simple song like the "Alphabet Song," a nursery rhyme everybody knows (it has the same melody as "Twinkle, Twinkle, Little Star"). You can feel the beat emphasis as you sing: "A B C D / E F G ..." The letters fall on the four regular beats with letters A and E falling on Beat 1 of each measure.

Measure 1

Beat 1	Beat 2	Beat 3	Beat 4
A	B	C	D

Measure 2

Beat 1	Beat 2	Beat 3	Beat 4
E	F	G	(pause)

Tap your foot in a steady rhythm and keep track of the beat number on your fingers, as you sing your way through the rest of the song. Notice that on "L M N O" there are *two* notes per beat. Song melodies can add notes or stretch out notes, weaving in and around the four beats of each measure. However, *you* must tap your foot in a steady, regular rhythm. Practice on more nursery rhymes like "One, Two, Buckle My Shoe" and "Pop! Goes the Weasel," until you can tap a steady rhythm with your foot, keep track of Beat 1, and notice what the melody is doing. This is a skill you're going to be using frequently in the melody writing Shortcuts so it's a good idea to become comfortable with it on these simple songs.

Now try counting a few hits

Listen to some of the hit songs listed below and count groups of four beats starting with Beat 1. I've given you a few hints with each song. Once you can count along with some of these songs, try some of your own favorite hit songs.

Practice on easy songs then move on to hits.

"1 2 3 4" (Feist) — Just follow her lyric to get started!

"All I Have to Do Is Dream" (The Everly Brothers) — Start counting on the first "Dream …"

"Black Horse and the Cherry Tree" (KT Tunstall) — On the radio version, Tunstall counts "2, 3, 4" at the beginning of the song. That'll get you started. In the chorus, Beat 1 is on the first "no" of each line.

"Who Needs Pictures" (Brad Paisley) — The instruments on the intro emphasize Beat 1. The word "old" is the first lyric that lands on it.

If you think you've lost track of Beat 1, stop counting and listen for a while until you find it, then start counting again. There are some hit songs that use three or six beats per measure—Kelly Clarkson's "Breakaway" is an example—but these are in the minority. Stick with four beats per measure for now.

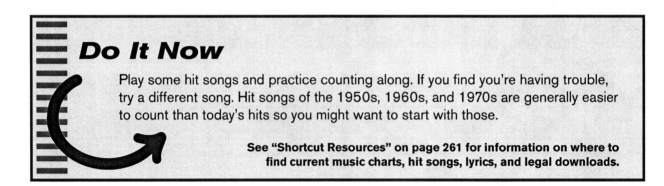

Do It Now

Play some hit songs and practice counting along. If you find you're having trouble, try a different song. Hit songs of the 1950s, 1960s, and 1970s are generally easier to count than today's hits so you might want to start with those.

See "Shortcut Resources" on page 261 for information on where to find current music charts, hit songs, lyrics, and legal downloads.

Shortcut #75

"Phrase-ology": The Hit Songwriter's Secret Weapon

Know how to recognize and use melodic phrases.

Just as commas and periods are used to group the words on this page into easy-to-understand phrases so, too, the notes of a melody are grouped into short phrases, creating an organized, memorable experience for listeners. Melodic phrases are the key to today's hit song melodies. Start thinking about melody, not just in terms of verse and chorus sections, but in shorter bits—a single line and sometimes even half a line.

In fact, the easiest way to understand melodic phrases is to compare them with word phrases. A word phrase is simply a group of words that expresses an idea; a melodic phrase is a group of notes that expresses a musical idea. Word phrases are often separated by a short pause or comma. Melodic phrases are often separated by a rest, or pause.

Melodic phrases are like word phrases.

For a simple example of phrasing, sing the nursery rhyme "Twinkle, Twinkle Little Star." The melodic phrases begin and end with the word phrases, so they're easy to find. After you've done that, sing the melody of this nursery rhyme without the words —use a nonsense syllable like "da-da-da"—and see if you can feel where the melodic phrases begin and end.

A melodic phrase feels complete in itself

You can become more familiar with phrases by trying a little experiment: Sing "Twinkle, Twinkle Little Star" again without words, and stop singing in the middle of the first line—say, after the first five notes. You'll hear an incomplete melodic phrase. (The lyric phrase is similarly incomplete: "Twinkle, twinkle, lit …") Even without the lyric, you can tell when you sing those first five notes that the musical phrase feels incomplete; the melody wants to get to those next two notes to finish the musical idea.

Most of the time songwriters agree on where a melodic phrase begins and ends, though not always. It really is a question of "feel." It's up to you whether a phrase feels complete or not, though it's often fairly obvious. If this concept of melodic phrases is new to you, spend some time getting familiar with songs that have clear and obvious melodic phrases. Listen to American standards like "I've Got the World on a String" or early Rock hits such as "Wake Up, Little Susie" for practice identifying melodic phrases. There's a list of songs in the "Do It Now" section of this Shortcut.

Does it feel like the beginning and end of a musical idea? If so, it's a phrase.

Some of the things you can do
with melodic phrases

I want you to be aware of melodic phrases so that you can manipulate them. Thinking about, working with, and reworking melodic phrases can make the difference between a ho-hum song and a hit song. No kidding! Here are a few of the things you can do with melodic phrases to increase the impact, freshness, and memorability of your melody. I've included the Shortcuts where you'll find more information.

$\Rightarrow$

*Things you can
do with phrases.*

- Make a predictable or dated melody sound contemporary and fresh (Shortcut 100).

- Use phrase repetition and variation to create a memorable melody (Shortcut 78).

- Mix long and short phrases to add contrast and interest (Shortcut 90).

- Shift the starting beats of phrases to turn hum-drum repetition into a hypnotic flow (Shortcut 91).

- Create a melody with forward momentum by eliminating the pauses between phrases (Shortcut 92).

Start writing with "phrase-ology" on your very next song. Give your melodies shape, momentum, and contrast. It's an indispensable tool for writing today's hits!

Do It Now

Here's a list of hit songs you can use to get some practice recognizing melodic phrases. In the first group, the melodic phrases almost always match the lyric phrases and many phrases will be about the same length. In the second group, there are a variety of phrase lengths and pauses in some unpredictable places. Remember, melodic phrases can be a matter of opinion. I just want you to become aware and start to listen for them. You're going to be using them.

Group 1: Start with these songs: "Michael Row the Boat Ashore" or any traditional Folk or Blues song, "All I Have to Do Is Dream" (The Everly Brothers) or any early Pop or Rock song, "I Fall To Pieces" (Patsy Cline) or any traditional country song.

Group 2: (WARNING: These are harder!): "Bless the Broken Road" (Rascal Flatts) or any current Country hit; "First Time" (Lifehouse) or any contemporary Hot AC/Pop hit song; "Like You'll Never See Me Again" (Alicia Keys) or any current Urban, R&B/Soul hit song.

See "Shortcut Resources" on page 261 for information on where to find current music charts, hit songs, lyrics, and legal downloads.

Shortcut #76

Raw Material: Use the Rhythm and Pitch of Speech

Use your spoken lyric to launch your melody.

Every time you open your mouth to speak, you start singing a melody! Don't believe me? Just try saying the following line out loud without any pitch or rhythm—the main ingredients of melody—in your voice: "What happened? I was only gone for a minute."

It probably came out something like this: "What-hap-pened-I-was-on-ly-gone-for-a-min-ute." But this line *has* pitch and rhythm! Though not a very natural sounding line, it has a single-note, steady-beat sort of melody. The truth is, *you can never remove all the melody from your voice because you can't speak without it!* When we speak we use pitch, rhythm, pace, and volume, just as we do when singing a melody. The only difference is, in a song, these elements are exaggerated.

Every time you speak, you sing a melody!

We use melody to communicate emotion when we speak

Sometimes the melody of speech can communicate as much information as the words themselves. Try this: say the phrase "Oh, no?" as if you are asking a simple question. Now try saying "Oh no." with a sarcastic, disbelieving, "you've got to be kidding" tone. It's an entirely different melody with a downward motion in a lower note range. Just by changing the melody of speech you gave the same words an entirely different meaning.

Now, say the same phrase—"Oh no!"—as if you're feeling anxious and frightened. Put some urgency into it; really mean it! Say it again with even *more* feeling! Notice the difference in the melody? The words are pitched higher and the pace is faster than in the other two examples. In fact, the more emotion you put into a spoken phrase, the more the melodic elements like pitch and rhythm are exaggerated. As you increase the emotion in your voice, the line between speaking and singing becomes harder to distinguish.

The more emotion you put into your voice, the more the spoken melody is exaggerated.

Start a chorus melody from a lyric

You can begin the process of creating a melody for your lyric simply by speaking it and then exaggerating the melodic elements—pitch, rhythm, pace, and volume. Start with your chorus lyric first. Choruses generally have more emotional energy than verses. As we saw with the "Oh, no!" phrase, when there's more emotional urgency, the melody of speech tends to be naturally exaggerated.

Speak the first line (Line 1) of your chorus lyric with as much emotion as you can put into it. Do this two or three times until you begin to hear the natural rhythm and pitch. For instance, as you add emotion to a lyric like "I can't go on without you," you'll notice that certain words become emphasized, such as "I CAN'T go on with-OUT you." These emphasized words also begin to rise in pitch. Try exaggerating these pitches by jumping up to a higher note or stretching the note out, holding it longer … or both. Play around with your Line 1 lyric until you find a melody you feel you can work with that's not too far from your original spoken line.

As you sing your melody, begin tapping your foot or strumming a rhythm (not a chord) on a guitar. If you've got a music software program with rhythm loops or a keyboard with built-in drum patterns, try using one of those. Sing Line 1 a few times until you feel comfortable with it. Then see what happens if you repeat this same melody with your Line 2 lyric. If that doesn't work, then look for the melody embedded in the spoken lyric of Line 2 just as you did with Line 1. Remember to put plenty of emotion into your voice when you speak the line.

This melody is likely to sound somewhat predictable, but remember, this is just your raw material. Once you have your chorus melody roughed out, start playing with the Shortcuts in the melody section of this book. Try shifting the starting point of your lines. How about adding a couple of words so that a line extends longer than we expect? Throw a pause into the middle of a line or take one out. You can try all of these and still hold onto the natural pitch, rhythm, and emphasis of your spoken lyric!

Work up a verse melody

To achieve the conversational tone of many of today's verses, try speaking your verse lyric in an honest, relaxed way. Think about the meaning of the words as you say them. Repeat the verse lyric a couple of times with the intention of communicating it clearly. Now, keeping the pauses that occur naturally, try exaggerating the little ups and downs of pitch in your speaking voice. Look for rhythm patterns you can repeat. Play with the phrases until you find a blend of direct speaking and rhythmic phrasing that you like. It's all up to your taste and what you feel works. Just remember to keep that conversational tone in your voice. This will keep the verse from overtaking your big emotional chorus melody.

What next?

Find out more about using the natural melody of speech in Shortcut 84.

Don't get married to your rough melody too early—you're going to be making changes—but you should make a recording of it to use as a reference. Your initial "spoken word melody" is important; it's the one that most closely parallels the emotion you hear in your own lyric. It's easy to lose touch with that original starting point. A recording will recall that emotion for you if you feel you're drifting away. Record both your rough melody idea *and* a spoken word version.

Use your handheld digital or cassette recorder to get a rough idea recorded. While you sing, keep time by clapping your hands, using a metronome or rhythm loop, or strumming an acoustic guitar while damping the strings. Remember, this is your raw material, not the finished melody. Don't worry about chords or accompaniment for now. You just need to have a recording of your initial idea as a reference.

Do It Now

1. Start noticing the natural rhythm and melody of speech all around you. Television shows and films with big dramatic scenes are good places to begin "tuning in."

2. Listen to hit songs in your genre and notice how the melodies reflect the natural emotional content of the lyric. Try speaking the chorus and verse lyrics with plenty of emotion and see how the song's melody reflects what you came up with.

3. Rough out a verse and chorus melody with lyrics based on the method in this shortcut.

See "Shortcut Resources" on page 261 for information on where to find current music charts, hit songs, lyrics, and legal downloads.

Shortcut #77

Raw Material: Write Your Melody First

Create a melody without a lyric.

In Shortcut 76, I showed you how to use the rhythm and pitch of a spoken lyric to help you create the raw material for a melody. But what if you're writing melody first and you don't have a lyric? It can still be useful to keep in mind the natural sound of the spoken word.

How verse and chorus melodies work

Generally, verse lyrics explain what's going on. They tend to be conversational and informative in tone compared to the chorus. So, when writing your verse melody, imagine the singer talking in an honest, direct tone of voice. Because you don't have a lyric yet, you don't know *exactly* what's going to be said but you can aim for a general emotional tone. Is the singer sad, happy, relieved, or despairing? What emotion do you want your melody to convey? As you work on your verse melody, try keeping it in a low or limited note range to give your chorus a chance to build.

When you get to your chorus, remember that the lyric is likely to become more emotional. The more emotional we are when speaking, the more the melodic elements of speech are exaggerated, so exaggerate those same elements in your melody. Try a wider and higher note range, and stronger rhythmic emphasis. Stretch out some notes and use interval jumps to allow the melody to become the focus of the song during the chorus. Try to build on the emotional tone you set up in the verse.

Define the song structure by using contrast in your melody.

Make certain that your sections are clearly defined

When writing a song melody without a lyric, one of the biggest problems composers run into is lack of structure—where's the chorus? Where's the verse? Define your sections clearly by using plenty of contrast in your melody. Shortcuts 80 and 81 can give you some ideas for creating contrast with note range and pace. Use the layout sheets in Shortcut 29 to help you sketch out the structure of your song. Don't leave it to the lyric writer; it's the melody that defines the song form!

Do It Now

Select one of the layouts in Shortcut 29 and write a verse and chorus melody using the techniques in this Shortcut.

Shortcut #78

Repetition With Variation Keeps Your Melody Fresh

Do it, do it again, go away, then come back ... for melodies.

Just think about how good it feels to leave your everyday life behind and go away on vacation. The funny thing is, after ten days or so, you're ready to head back home again, back to your own comfortable bed and familiar surroundings.

The same principle is at work in songwriting. When you create a melody line then repeat it, it becomes familiar, like being at home. If you then go away to a different melody line, it feels like a vacation; it's something new and exciting. Then, when you return to the "home" melody, it feels good to be back on familiar ground.

Let's call it the "Vacation Rule." It sounds simple but it really works for listeners! It looks like this: Do it, do it again, go away, then come back. This seems to be just the right mix of familiar and new.

The Vacation Rule

Try writing a short melody using the Vacation Rule.

Try the Vacation Rule!

> Line 1 – Create a short melodic phrase—any five or six notes will do.
> Line 2 – Repeat Line 1.
> Line 3 – Go to a different phrase with different notes.
> Line 4 – Now, return to your first phrase.

You can hear the Vacation Rule in many hit song melodies. There's a good example in the chorus of Daughtry's huge hit, "It's Not Over." The first line introduces the melody ("It's not over ..."), the second line repeats it, the third goes away ("This love is killing me ..."), and then the melody returns to the opening phrase for the fourth line ("It's not over.").

Once you set up your first line, repeat it and go away, you have a Vacation Rule situation. You can then build some interesting variations.

➤ **Variation #1**
> Line 1 – Create a short melodic phrase.
> Line 2 – Repeat Line 1.
> Line 3 – Now go to a new phrase.
> Line 4 – Return to the Line 1 phrase
> Line 5 – Repeat Line 1.
> Line 6 – Now go to another new phrase with new notes and rhythm.

There are many variations. Set them up with a repeat of your opening line.

There's a good example of this variation in the verse of "Every Breath You Take"

(The Police). Although this song isn't a current hit, it's become a staple of radio, and still sounds fresh.

> **Variation #2**
> Line 1 – Create a short melodic phrase.
> Line 2 – Repeat Line 1.
> Line 3 – Now go to a new phrase.
> Line 4 – Repeat Line 3.
> Line 5 – Return to the Line 1 phrase.
> Line 6 – Repeat line 1.
> Line 7 – Now go to a different phrase with new notes and rhythm to
>   wrap up the section.

You can repeat the rhythm of a phrase and change the note pitches! See Shortcut 88 for more info.

Check out the chorus of Rascal Flatts' "What Hurts the Most" to hear an example of this variation.

Although you're going to repeat your opening *melody* line, you don't need to repeat the *lyric*. Try writing a new lyric for your second line while your melody repeats as in the Rascal Flatts song. The repetition of the melody gives listeners something familiar while the lyric adds new information.

The Vacation Rule is a tool

The Vacation Rule is a broad, general pattern and there's plenty of room for creativity, so don't limit yourself to these variations. Use this Shortcut to suggest ideas rather than telling you what your melody *should* do. Play around with the Vacation Rule pattern and notice how it's used in various hit songs you like.

Do It Now

1. Listen to some of the songs mentioned in this Shortcut. Notice how the melody follows the Vacation Rule pattern or a variation. Listen to hit songs in your genre and look for other variations on this pattern.

2. Try writing a verse or chorus using the Vacation Rule.

See "Shortcut Resources" on page 261 for information on where to find current music charts, hit songs, lyrics, and legal downloads.

Shortcut #79

Tension & Release: Add Energy and Dynamics to Your Song

Build anticipation and suspense in your melody, then release it.

From Bach to Beethoven to Brad Paisley, the engine that drives the emotional enjoyment of music is the melodic interplay of *tension and release*. Listeners love the roller coaster created by a song that builds anticipation and increases tension until finally releasing the pent up energy with an explosive *whooooosh!*

What is melodic tension and release?

One of the simplest examples of tension and release is the word "amen" sung at the end of a hymn. If you sing only the first syllable ("ah") and don't finish the word, you'll remain in a slightly uncomfortable state of suspense. Things are unfinished; you're anticipating something that doesn't happen. When a song sustains and even builds on that feeling throughout an entire verse or pre-chorus, the sense of resolution, when it does happen, is exaggerated.

How do tension and release work in a song?

In a hit song, listeners hear the same chorus melody at least three or four times, often more. All this repetition should become boring, yet, in hit songs, listeners look forward to hearing the chorus again and again; they'd be disappointed if they didn't! Why? Because the chorus is where the tension that's been built up in the previous section finally reaches a climax and is released. *Whooooosh!* The success of the chorus depends, in part, on how much energy and anticipation is built up by the melody that leads into it. A good songwriter winds up that melody like a pitcher winds up before throwing a fastball. Then delivers the goods!

Build tension and release it in your melody. Listeners love it!

Four ways to add tension and release to your melody

➢ **Pitch**
  A gradual upward motion in your melody can build a sense of anticipation. It may last over the entire verse or might take place over a quick two-line pre-chorus or both. A descending motion in your melody line, on the other hand, tends to resolve and release energy. This doesn't mean that *every* line must be a series of rising or descending notes—that would be predictable. If the highest note of a line is higher than the highest note of previous lines, the listener will feel that the entire melody is ascending. The same holds true for a descending melody. A line with a note that is lower than a previous line's lowest note will be perceived as a descending melody.

In Natasha Bedingfield's "Unwritten" the pre-chorus melody slowly rises, creating *tension* beginning with the phrase "staring at the blank page ..." The rising motion slowly builds *anticipation*, which lasts a full six lines and is finally *released* in the opening line of the chorus. This is an excellent use of a slow build and big release to create a dynamic roller coaster effect for the listener.

> **Pace**
> Packing a lot of notes into a small space creates tension and suspense, especially when delivered with a choppy feel. Fewer notes and a smooth delivery tend to release energy. A good example: Jason Mraz's "Remedy (I Won't Worry)." The densely packed notes and choppy rhythms of the verse and pre-chorus wind up the song as tight as a spring, which suddenly uncoils on the first smoothly, soaring line of the chorus ("I won't worry my life away"). Shortcut 81 can give you more information on creating contrast in pace.

> **Beat emphasis**
> Emphasizing the *strong beats* (Beat 1 or Beat 3) makes listeners feel settled and comfortable; they *expect* these beats to be emphasized. To create tension, emphasize the *weak beats* (Beat 2 or Beat 4) or the *upbeats* (the "and" in between beats) which will create a feeling of uncertainty in listeners. In "You're Beautiful," James Blunt emphasizes weak beats and upbeats throughout the verse creating a sense of insecurity and unresolved tension. The chorus then shifts, emphasizing strong beats, releasing the uncertainty and creating resolution. Read Shortcut 89 to find out more about using strong beats, weak beats, and upbeats to create an effect.

> **Repetition and variation**
> Repetition of melodic rhythm patterns or note pitches builds tension that can be released by moving on to something different. Check out Toby Keith's "Love Me If You Can" to hear repetition used to subtly build tension in the pre-chorus, starting with "My father gave me ..." Shortcut 88 can give you more information on using repetition of melodic rhythm patterns.

Do It Now

1. Check out some of the hit songs mentioned in this Shortcut and listen to the various ways in which melody is used to create tension and release it. Listen to hit songs in the genre you'd like to write in and see if you can find more examples.

2. Write a melody using one of the suggestions in this Shortcut.

See "Shortcut Resources" on page 261 for information on where to find current music charts, hit songs, lyrics, and legal downloads.

Shortcut #80

Be an Attention Hog:
Use Contrast in Note Range

Try this ear-catching technique to get attention.

I want you to be an attention hog! Not just a little piggy, a HOG!!! Grab all the attention you can and point it right at your great song. You want people to hear you, right? Then, make them listen! This is no time to be shy!

One of the best ways to get attention is to use contrast. As you learned in Shortcut 22, if you speak in a soft voice and then suddenly begin shouting, you'll get attention. But if you continue to shout, people will eventually stop listening. It's the combination of both loud *and* soft that works. Humans notice change and ignore that which remains constant. Use change to make them notice *you*.

When it comes to grabbing attention, the real powerhouse is melody. And the most obvious "notice me" melodic device is contrast in note range. Simply put, if your verse is in a low note range and your chorus is in a high note range, you'll create the kind of change that listeners notice.

Create contrast in note range

Low versus high note range is the simplest form of melodic contrast. There are many ways to create it. Here are a few suggestions:

➤ **Try an interval jump up at the top of your chorus.** For a startling effect use an abrupt shift in note range. Check out "First Time" by Lifehouse, or P!nk's "Who Knew" and notice how a quick change of note range at the beginning of the chorus grabs attention.

➤ **Use an ascending phrase to lead us to the new note range.** Move your melody gradually up (or down) to a new note range, creating tension and anticipation. You can hear this technique in "I Drove All Night" (Celine Dion) or, in the Rock genre, "Paralyzer" by Finger Eleven.

Both abrupt shifts and gradual builds will work.

➤ **Gradually return to the original note range.** Again "I Drove All Night" provides a good example, as does Ashlee Simpson's "Pieces of Me." In both of these songs the chorus melody, after reaching a peak, returns at the end to the note range of the verse.

➤ **Shift abruptly back to the verse note range.** Just as you can grab attention with an interval jump at the top of your chorus, you can use the same ear-catching technique at the end of your chorus going into Verse 2. U2's "Vertigo" has a powerhouse chorus that keeps climbing higher before plunging abruptly back down to the verse range. Seether's "Rise Above This" also drops the note range between the end of the chorus and top of Verse 2. Talk about contrast!

Here's a fun idea to try!

➢ **Try using the same melody one octave higher.** In Lifehouse's "First Time," the chorus and pre-chorus have the same melody, but the chorus is one octave higher, giving it plenty of emotional urgency and creating contrast with the pre-chorus. This is a great example of what a change in note range alone can do. Try this trick in one of your own songs!

➢ **Use a subtle change in note range.** The R&B/Soul genre (and other Urban genres like Hip-Hop, Rap, and Urban Dance) tends to create contrast using pace rather than big changes in note range, but you can still hear subtle shifts in note range. Alicia Keys' "Like You'll Never See Me Again" is a great example. In this song, the *overall* note range of the verse is lower than the *overall* note range of the chorus. Notice where the high notes and low notes generally land in the verse and compare that with the high and low notes of the chorus. This will give a good idea of where the note range is settling in.

See Shortcut 24 for more on this song form.

➢ **Use contrast in note range between verse and bridge.** You can give the Verse / Verse / Bridge / Verse song form plenty of hit appeal by creating a lot of contrast between the note ranges of the verse and bridge. Listen to Keith Urban's big Country hit, "Somebody Like You" to hear this. (The bridge begins with the lyric "I want to feel the sunshine …") With it's soaring melody and high notes building to a peak, this bridge is so huge and catchy it could be a chorus. It doesn't include the song's title, however, and the verses do, putting this song clearly in the Verse / Verse / Bridge / Verse category. Big bridge melodies with a lot of contrast have helped to put this song form back on the hit song charts, especially in the Country genre.

Do It Now

1. Songs from various genres use different amounts and types of contrast in note range. Check out the genre you're interested in and notice how contrast in note range is created between sections.

2. Try adding more contrast in note range to a song of your own.

See "Shortcut Resources" on page 261 for information on where to find current music charts, hit songs, lyrics, and legal downloads.

Shortcut #81

Contrast in Pace
Keeps Listeners Tuned In

Use note length and note pace to add variety and interest.

Afastpacedbreathlesslyric
Canbeexcitingforawhileanddrawlistenersintoyoursong
Butitgetsoldfastsobecareful
You'lllloseyouraudienceifyoukeepitupfortoolong
Youreallycan'texpectotherstodosomething
Youdon'tevenlikedoingyourself.Imeanhowmuchfunisthis?

I'm feeling overwhelmed!

Did you read all of that or did you give up halfway through, or earlier? After a line or two, did it seem like it was just too much work to try to sort out individual words? Did you figure you'd skip it and pick up the gist of it later? If so, then you know how listeners feel when you give them a busy, fast-paced melody and lyric that lasts for more than a few lines. It's interesting for a while, but it takes a lot of mental effort to sort things out. Listeners soon get tired, the notes and words begin to run together, the song fades into the deep, dark recesses of consciousness, and … you've lost them.

On the other hand, there's …

the … slooooooow … ballad … with … waaaaaaaaaaay … toooooooooo … many … pauses … and … not … enough … ac … tion … to …sustain … (yawn) … innnnterest.

Now I'm bored!

This is where contrast in *pace* comes to the rescue!

What does "pace" mean?

Pace refers to the rate at which something happens, in this case, the rate at which words and notes are delivered to the listener. This does *not* refer to the underlying tempo or rhythm of your song; a steady underlying groove is essential in today's hit songs. Pace refers only to words and notes. A fast-paced verse may have two or three notes or words per beat, a slow-paced chorus may hold a note or word through several beats.

Pace refers to the rate at which notes and words are delivered to the listener.

"Remedy (I Won't Worry)" by Jason Mraz is a good example of a hit song with a lot of contrast in pace. The verse and pre-chorus feature fast-paced notes and words; there's plenty of action here! The machine-gun speed of the delivery makes some serious demands on listeners; there are three to four words and notes per beat. By the time the big, slow-paced chorus begins (starting with the words "I won't worry …"), listeners definitely need a break! Notice that the underlying song *tempo* and groove never vary, just the pace of the words.

A change of pace gets attention!

It's been proven in hit song after hit song: Varying the pace between sections of your song creates interest and keeps listeners tuned in. To keep your audience interested and involved, a fast-paced, wordy verse like the one at the beginning of this Shortcut might be followed by a medium-paced pre-chorus and a slow-paced chorus. Here's how that would look:

Try varying the pace to grab and hold attention.

VERSE:
Here'safastpacedverse
Withfourlinesofimages
Andamelodythatmatches
Thepaceofthewords.

PRE-CHORUS:
Here's a pre-chorus that slows the pace
Giving listeners some variety and leading to...

CHORUS:
A ... chorus ... with plenty ...
Of room ... to catch ... a breath, yes ...
A ... chorus ... with plenty ... of space.

Add a change of pace to your song

To create contrast in the pace of your song begin by setting a steady beat. Tap your foot at the tempo (speed) you want, or, better yet, use a rhythm loop, drum machine, or metronome to provide a steady beat.

- Try writing a verse melody with two to three notes per beat. Then, write a chorus with notes that stretch out over two to four beats. (You can create a rough lyric—sometimes called a "dummy" lyric—to give yourself something to sing, or use nonsense syllables like "da" or "la.")

- Consider writing a transitional section, a pre-chorus, with a medium pace, say, one word per beat.

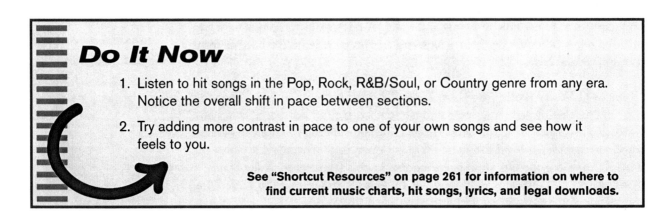

Do It Now

1. Listen to hit songs in the Pop, Rock, R&B/Soul, or Country genre from any era. Notice the overall shift in pace between sections.

2. Try adding more contrast in pace to one of your own songs and see how it feels to you.

See "Shortcut Resources" on page 261 for information on where to find current music charts, hit songs, lyrics, and legal downloads.

Shortcut #82

Make Your Melody Shout,
"THIS is the CHORUS!"

Melodic contrast and a little flashiness
will ensure your chorus gets noticed.

These days, the majority of hit songs on the charts in all genres are in the Verse / Chorus song format. Some of them have pre-choruses that set up the chorus, some don't. But they all have big, beautiful, can't-get-'em-out-of-your-head, hook-driven choruses! You want to be sure *your* chorus gets noticed. Here are three techniques you can use to make your chorus *STAND OUT!*

> **Raise your chorus to a higher note range than your verses**
> Moving your chorus melody to a higher note range implies a heightened state of emotional intensity. When we get upset, angry, or anxious, our voices tend to rise both in pitch and volume. So, if your chorus has greater emotional intensity than your verses—as Pop and Rock choruses usually do—then going to a higher note range may be a good choice for you.

> **Slow the pace of notes and words in your chorus**
> A successful chorus often takes the emphasis off words and puts it on melody. Consider stretching out and sustaining some of the notes in your chorus. Hold out a word while changing notes. Use fewer words, ones that sum up the essence of your theme. These techniques will place more emphasis on melody/emotion and take it off of words/explanation. Save explanations for your verses. Make your choruses all about feeling the emotion at the heart of your song.

> **Use melodic twists to surprise your listeners**
> This is a great idea to try after you've done the other two. It can make the difference between a chorus that sounds predictable and one that sounds fresh and exciting.

For a melodic twist in your chorus:

• Try an "interval jump"—skip a few notes going up or down. Do it on an important word of the lyric to shine a spotlight on it. If you feel daring, try two jumps in a row. Read Shortcut 93 for more on using this technique to surprise your listeners and underscore key words in your lyric.

• Extend a line longer than expected by adding a couple of extra words and notes instead of a pause at the end of the line. Run the phrase right up to the following line to create forward momentum.

• If you're using a series of long phrases, try replacing one with two short, repeated phrases. No need to repeat the lyric, just the melody notes. Keep the lyric moving along.

Read about Verse / Chorus song forms in Shortcuts 25 & 26.

You can find out more about these ideas in Shortcuts 90 thru 93.

• Add a pause in the middle of a phrase, then, either speed up the rest of the line to catch up or just let it run longer than expected.

• Move your entire chorus earlier or later by a beat. Just start singing one beat earlier or later. Avoid starting every phrase on the first beat of the measure.

Do It Now

1. Listen to hit songs in the genre you're interested in and look for the chorus melody techniques listed in this Shortcut.

2. Try one or several of these techniques in one of your own choruses.

See "Shortcut Resources" on page 261 for information on where to find current music charts, hit songs, lyrics, and legal downloads.

Shortcut #83

The *Tao* of Undeniable Hook Writing

*Use this path to get your hooks headed
in the hit song direction.*

Publishers are fond of saying things like, "What I'm looking for is a hit song with an undeniable hook." As if you haven't already figured that out. It's what *everyone* in the music industry is looking for! Just what is a "hook" and why is it so important?

A hook is a phrase, both melody and lyric, that does three things:

- It catches the listener's attention.

- It sums up a memorable emotional experience.

- It's easy to recall and stays with the listener after the song is over.

There will be other interesting, appealing lines in your chorus—as many as you can put into it—but the hook is the one that stands out, making a lasting impression on listeners. A good hook is, therefore, worth seeking.

There's no formula for writing undeniable hooks. If there were, every songwriter would be writing killer hooks all day and all night. But there are things you can do to get your hook into the "undeniable" ballpark. Try some of these suggestions. They can help bring you closer to your goal. They are not rules; they are a *tao*, a "way." Follow it in peace and creativity.

Follow the Tao, the Way of Hook Writing.

The *Tao* of Undeniable Hook Writing

道 *Emphasize the hook's key words with your melody.*
Use your melody to underscore the important words in your hook lyric. Place the key words on the highest notes or notes that are held longer. In Rascal Flatts' "What Hurts the Most" the word "hurts" and the word "most" are clearly the ones the audience is meant to hear and feel.

道 *Seek attention by using contrast.*
An interval jump—skipping over notes upward or downward—can provide contrast in note range that gets attention. In Daughtry's "It's Not Over" the leap up to the first syllable of "over" makes listeners take notice. Read Shortcut 93 to find out more about using interval jumps.

道 *Use repetition with a twist.*
Although repetition can help listeners remember a line, too much of the same thing can become boring. Try this simple twist: Rather than simply repeating your hook, consider repeating the melody while changing the lyric. To hear this idea, listen to "Complicated" by Avril Lavigne. The

second line of the chorus repeats the hook melody but changes the lyric. Imagine what this chorus would sound like with a repeat of the entire hook melody *and* lyric!

道 *Syncopation can give your hook melody a distinctive sound.*
A great hook is both easy to remember *and* fresh, giving it the "catchy but different" quality that listeners love. How can you make your hook both familiar and distinctive at the same time? Try this: Write a predictable-sounding melodic hook (I dare you!), then play with the rhythm of the melody.

- Add a pause in an unexpected place.

- Move a note so it emphasizes an upbeat.

- Shift the starting point of your whole phrase a beat later or earlier.

The Fray's "Over My Head (Cable Car)" is a great example of the last technique. If you sing the hook "Over my head" starting the word "over" on Beat 1, it sounds very predictable. By slipping the phrase earlier just a little bit so that the second syllable (o-VER) lands on Beat 1, the whole phrase sounds fresh and interesting. Shortcuts 89 and 91 can show you how to use these ideas.

道 *A hook does not exist in isolation.*
To give your hook more impact, try building anticipation as you lead up to it. If your chorus opens with the hook, use a pre-chorus to build tension as in Nickelback's "Someday" or Celine Dion's "I Drove All Night." For more insight into building anticipation, read Shortcut 86.

A hook does not exist in isolation.

道 *Let your melody soar, then come to rest on the hook.*
Try the reverse of the previous technique. Place your hook at the end of a high-energy chorus, allowing the intensity to drop down to an intimate, melodic resolve on your hook lyric. Take a listen to Brad Paisley's "Mud on the Tires" or P!nk's "Who Knew" to hear how this is handled.

Do It Now

1. Listen to some of the hit songs mentioned in this Shortcut. Notice how the hook is constructed. Look for the techniques listed above. Can you spot any others?

2. Revisit a hook in one of your own songs or write a chorus featuring a hook using the techniques of the *tao* of hook writing.

See "Shortcut Resources" on page 261 for information on where to find current music charts, hit songs, lyrics, and legal downloads.

Shortcut #84

Give Your "Key Lines" a Melody That Speaks to Us

Use the rhythm and pitch of speech to underscore important lines.

In Shortcut 76 "Raw Material: Use the Rhythm and Pitch of Speech," I showed you how you can use the natural melody of the spoken word to help you create the raw material for a strong melody. However, you can do even more with the melody of speech; it's an important ally that can be used to give the "key lines" in your song added emotional punch and clarity.

Melody in everyday speech

We don't speak in a monotone. Every phrase of every sentence has a series of pitches. When we ask a question, the pitches usually rise. ("Don't you think so?" "Are you going somewhere?") When making a statement, the pitches usually descend at the end of the phrase, indicating finality. ("I knew that." "Don't bother me.") In general, rising melodies in speech indicate uncertainty, hope, vulnerability, or yearning; descending melodies convey decision, confidence, sorrow, or resignation. Of course, this is an oversimplification—and you want to be careful about being too literal in your songwriting—but these natural spoken melodies can be useful when you want to underscore the emotional content of a key line in your song.

Rising melody = uncertainty optimism vulnerability yearning

Descending melody = finality confidence sorrow resignation

Why the natural melody of speech is important

Let's say you've got an important lyric line, for example a hook, like this one: "What am I gonna do about you?" Written on the page like this, there are a couple of ways the phrase could be interpreted: 1) the writer might actually be wondering what to do about this person or, 2) it could be a rhetorical question, one that isn't really looking for an answer—"I'm frustrated, fed up with you, I gotta do something about you." Other lyric lines will help to establish a context, but your melody could also give us a big clue. If this is a real question looking for an answer, if the singer is genuinely uncertain about what to do, a rising melody line could do the trick. On the other hand, if the singer is simply expressing frustration or making a comment on the situation, then a melody with a descending direction could be more effective.

Depending on the direction of the spoken pitches, the phrase takes on two different emotional shadings: the first one suggesting that the speaker is in a more vulnerable, uncertain emotional state than the second. *If this lyric line is important to the meaning of your song, especially if it's your hook, be sure to choose a melody that supports the right interpretation.*

Melody can help convey the meaning of a line.

Rhythm, pauses, and emphasis are important, too

Word emphasis, pauses between words, and rhythm—all melodic elements of speech—also contribute to the emotional impact of lyric lines and are just as important as pitch.

For instance, if you're writing a song with the hook line, "I'm leaving you. It's over," you want to be sure your audience clearly understands the meaning and gets the full impact of the emotion in this line. Start by finding the natural melody within the spoken line; try speaking it with plenty of feeling: "I'm leaving you. It's over!" Do this a few more times and really say it like you mean it. Notice which words and syllables are emphasized, where the pauses are, and the general trend of the pitches.

Most people would say, "I'm LEAV-ing you. (pause) It's O-ver." with a downward trend in the pitches of the notes. This conveys a sense of finality and reinforces the emotional meaning of the line. Now, try saying this line while emphasizing different syllables and dropping out the pause, like this: "I'm lea-VING you it's o-VER." Say the line a couple of times and try adding a lot of emotion! Not only does it not work, it becomes funny! If someone said something like this to you, would you take them seriously? No way! Neither will your listeners.

Make your key lines speak to us emotionally

To find out more about key lines, read Shortcut 56.

The key lines in your song are the ones listeners always hear. Obviously the most important key line is the hook, often the first line of your chorus. Other key lines include the payoff and lead-in lines of your chorus and the first line of your verses. You can make certain these lines convey the emotion you intend and give them extra memorability by exaggerating the natural spoken pitch and rhythm of the lyric. To hear the natural melody of speech used in hit song choruses, check out Rihanna's "Take a Bow," Daughtry's "It's Not Over," and Dierks Bentley's "What Was I Thinkin'."

Do It Now

1. Listen to hit songs and pick out the important lines in the chorus, the ones you really notice. Check to see how the melody underscores the emotional message of the lyric by mimicking the emphasis, rhythm and pitch of speech.

2. Look at the chorus or refrain line in one of your own songs. Is the melody giving your lyric as much emotional support as it could? Try speaking the important lines in your chorus with plenty of feeling. Now exaggerate the melody in your spoken lines and try creating a chorus melody from there.

See "Shortcut Resources" on page 261 for information on where to find current music charts, hit songs, lyrics, and legal downloads.

Shortcut #85

Verse Melody Strategies That Work

The verse melody plays a vital role.
Is it working as well as it should?

Your chorus melody has a big EGO! It better have—it's got to make sure that people pay plenty of attention to it. Your verse melody, on the other hand, is somewhat shy. "Don't notice me," it says, "You're supposed to look at my friend, the chorus."

Don't tell your egomaniac chorus, but the verse melody plays several essential roles in your song. It's the first real part of the song we hear. It introduces us to the emotional tone of the song. It carries us like a freight train rolling inevitably towards the chorus or refrain line. It provides the contrast that allows the chorus to soar. Perhaps most important of all, it underscores your verse lyric making sure we hear every word so when the chorus rolls in, we have a clear framework for it. Here are three strategies for approaching your verse melody that will put it to work for you:

Strategy #1:
Keep the verse melody conversational

In the Verse / Chorus form in all genres, the chorus carries the emotional weight of the song while the verses are more conversational, conveying the information that supports the emotions in the chorus. Try speaking your verse lyric in a conversational tone then exaggerate the natural rhythm and pitch of speech to begin your verse melody. Listen to P!nk's "Who Knew" or Phil Vassar's "In a Real Love" to hear good examples of this type of verse melody.

Read Shortcut 76 to learn more about using spoken words to create your melody.

If you're writing your melody without a lyric, you can still evoke the intimate, relaxed tone of ordinary speech. Before you start writing, spend some time listening to the natural cadences of everyday speech with its pauses and subtle melodies. Write down a few lines to use as a guide even if you don't plan on turning them into a lyric. There's more information on how to do this in Shortcut 77.

Strategy #2: Use melodic repetition
to keep the focus on the lyrics

Because verses are used to convey important information that's needed to develop the song and set up the chorus, keep the listener's attention focused on the lyric rather than the melody. Try building your verse melody around just two or three melodic phrases and repeat them. Using repetition will ensure your listener isn't distracted by a busy, over-demanding melody. You'll hear this type of verse in Toby Keith's "Love Me If You Can" and "Ever the Same" by Rob Thomas.

For tips on using melodic repetition, see Shortcut 78.

Strategy #3: Make your refrain line memorable

The Verse / Verse / Bridge / Verse song structure doesn't have a chorus, instead it has a refrain line that appears in the same place in each verse. Although it's part of the verse melody, the refrain has to be memorable! Use Strategies #1 and #2 for the rest of your verse melody, but give your refrain line extra punch with a surprise twist or strong, emphasized word. In Keith Urban's Country hit "Somebody Like You," the first three lines of the verse melody are conversational, have a solid, steady rhythm and a fair amount of repetition. Then, there's a long pause that sets up the refrain line "I wanna love somebody ..." and for good measure, part of the refrain line is repeated. You can't miss it!

Do It Now

1. Listen to the verse melodies of hit songs in the genre you want to write in. Notice how they keep the focus on the lyric by using repetition and a conversational style. Look at how the melody of the verse sets up the chorus.

2. Write a verse melody using any of the above strategies. If you don't have a lyric, you can use a "dummy" lyric. A dummy lyric is one that exists simply to provide something for you to sing while working on your melody. It can be nonsense syllables or any phrases you make up. You're going to replace all of these temporary lyrics with completely new ones once your melody is written.

See "Shortcut Resources" on page 261 for information on where to find current music charts, hit songs, lyrics, and legal downloads.

Shortcut #86

Pump Up Your Pre-Chorus

Use it to deliver an ace of a chorus.

Great tennis players have perfected the art of the serve, learning to deliver the ball just where they want it. Obviously it takes power and accuracy, but it takes something else as well, something you might not notice: the perfect little toss of the ball into the air before slamming it home. That little toss sets up an entire sequence of powerful events. Think of your pre-chorus as the toss that puts your song right where you want it so you can slam your chorus over the net for an ace!

The pre-chorus sets us up for the chorus

A pre-chorus can make us feel like we're hanging suspended, holding a breath before the big *whoooooshing* exhale of the chorus. Or it can build momentum, stepping up the energy from a conversational verse to a big, emotional chorus. No matter how you handle your pre-chorus, there is one thing it must do— create anticipation, making the listener feel like something important is about to happen. *The chorus is coming!*

➤ **Use a series of short, repeated phrases.** This type of repetition can add tension, winding up the song before delivering the chorus. Rascal Flatts uses this technique in the powerful pre-chorus of "What Hurts the Most." Keith Urban does a subtler version of the same thing in "You'll Think of Me" by adding a gentle push of energy on the line that kicks off the chorus.

➤ **Use a rising note phrase.** Build a feeling of anticipation in listeners with a series of ascending pitches leading into the chorus. Listen to Natasha Bedingfield's "Unwritten" to hear a strong rising line that jumps straight to the chorus. Daniel Powter's "Bad Day" also sets up the chorus with a powerful pre-chorus that ends with a strong upward moving line. He adds extra tension by holding the final note before releasing into the chorus. This is a well-used device that can sound a little dated if not handled carefully; try jumping into the chorus without holding the note too long.

Find out more about tension and release in Shortcut 79.

Here's a twist on the rising note phrase: In Dierks Bentley's "What Was I Thinkin'," there are two short phrases just before the chorus; the first is a descending phrase followed by a perfect little rising phrase just before the chorus kicks in.

➤ **Pick up the pace by using more notes or words per beat.** Eliminating pauses and picking up the pace of the notes and words can create a sense of increasing energy. You can hear this in Alicia Keys' "Like You'll Never See Me Again" on the line "… take for granted the time you may have here with me" and the following line. A very effective send-off for the chorus!

Keep the pre-chorus energy going and going and going ...

The one thing you don't want your pre-chorus to do is let the song's energy drop. Releasing the tension too soon or writing a predictable pre-chorus can reduce the impact of your chorus.

- If your pre-chorus feels predictable, consider shortening it. Launch into your chorus early, before it's expected. If you have a four-line pre-chorus, try cutting it in half and going to your chorus after only two lines. Sometimes the pre-chorus is just a single line that follows the end of the verse. It may be as short as half a line. Check out Nickelback's "Someday" to hear a single line ("Nothing's wrong just as long ...") that kicks off the chorus with plenty of energy.

- Avoid releasing the tension too soon. Try staying away from the "home" chord of your song (the I chord of I, IV, V). Read Shortcut 107 to find out about "home" and "leading" chords.

Lead-in lines use the same techniques

There are plenty of hit songs that don't have a separate pre-chorus section. Instead, they may use the last line or last few notes of the verse to set up the chorus. Don't feel you have to write a separate pre-chorus section to use these strategies.

Of course a pre-chorus can't guarantee an ace if the chorus doesn't follow through with strength. However, a well-built pre-chorus can create anticipation, giving the opening lines of your chorus a better chance of scoring with listeners!

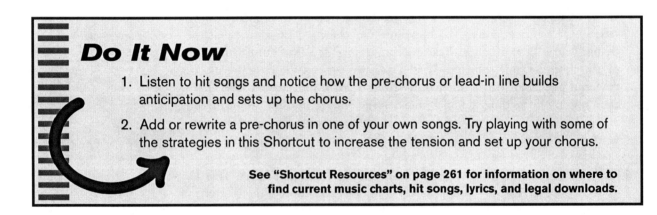

Do It Now

1. Listen to hit songs and notice how the pre-chorus or lead-in line builds anticipation and sets up the chorus.

2. Add or rewrite a pre-chorus in one of your own songs. Try playing with some of the strategies in this Shortcut to increase the tension and set up your chorus.

See "Shortcut Resources" on page 261 for information on where to find current music charts, hit songs, lyrics, and legal downloads.

Shortcut #87

Build a Big, Beautiful Contemporary Bridge

Throw your listeners a curve they'll love.

I've heard a few songwriters say that bridges are old-fashioned and they don't use them in their songs. I have two responses to that: 1) Many of today's biggest mainstream hits feature powerful, well-crafted bridge sections, and 2) maybe *you're* just writing old-fashioned bridges!

Today's bridges offer an opportunity to add a peak emotional moment to your song, create dynamic contrast, and make a left turn that adds a surprising, ear-catching twist to your melody. What self-respecting songwriter would want to pass up an opportunity like that?!!

The bridge keeps your listeners involved in your song. There's a very good reason why bridges occur about two-thirds of the way through a song; by that point, listeners have heard the verse and chorus melodies a couple of times and they're ready for something new. If your song has been building dynamically from verse to chorus, then, like a roller coaster after the first couple of big hills, it's time for a curve! It's up to your bridge to deliver it.

Use your bridge to create a peak moment and a surprising twist.

Two examples of bridges that deliver the goods

Like a verse or chorus, a bridge melody can build and release tension. In Trace Adkins' Country hit "You're Gonna Miss This," the bridge (starting with the line "Five years later …") maintains the energy level of the preceding chorus. It stays in the same high note range and keeps the forward momentum going until the final line when it releases tension in a descending phrase and resolves in an intimate moment that reinforces the song's theme in a unique way. The beginning of the final chorus stays at the same intimate level, then *boom* you're back up to the full-powered chorus level again. A great attention-grabbing moment and a wonderful, unexpected twist!

In Rob Thomas' "Ever the Same" you can hear the opposite dynamic. The bridge (beginning with the line "You may need me there…") starts out with a conversational feel, maintaining it until the very last line when the melody leaps up an octave and launches into the final chorus with plenty of energy.

Both of these approaches create a moment that surprises listeners, catching them off-guard, and setting them up for the final, pull-all-the-stops-out sections of your song.

Four secrets to writing hot, contemporary bridge melodies

➢ **Raise the energy.** To build or maintain energy after a big chorus, keep your bridge in the same note range as your chorus or move it even higher!

➢ **Go intimate.** *Take the opposite approach:* If you have a big, dramatic chorus, try an intimate bridge to create contrast. Use a lower note range than the chorus and maintain energy by using repeated, short phrases to create tension.

➢ **Build tension.** If your chorus melody has a lot of interval leaps, try a bridge that revolves around a few adjacent notes in any note range. Restraining the note range builds tension that you can release in the final choruses.

➢ **Add contrast.** Change the melodic rhythm patterns to add contrast. If your chorus has long, smooth phrases, try short, choppy ones in your bridge.

The Verse / Verse / Bridge / Verse song form

In this song structure there's no chorus. Instead two verses are followed by a bridge, then another verse. To compete with today's big, hook-driven choruses, you've got to give your bridge melody plenty of emotional punch. To hear a wonderful example, check out the two bridges in "Every Breath You Take" (The Police) or the big, blockbuster bridge in Keith Urban's Country hit "Somebody Like You." Because verses in today's hit songs are generally conversational and low-key in tone, you can create a lot of contrast by writing a bridge melody with big interval leaps, strong melodic rhythm patterns, and a wide note range. You can hear all of these ideas in Urban's "Somebody Like You." The bridge begins with the line "I wanna feel the sunshine ..." Not that you could miss it!

Do It Now

1. Listen to bridges in today's hit songs. Look for ways that the melody sustains energy, creates contrast, and keeps the momentum of the song moving forward. Notice how it develops out of the prior section and leads into the section that follows.

2. Write or rewrite a bridge in one of your own songs using one of the bullet-point scenarios given in this Shortcut.

See "Shortcut Resources" on page 261 for information on where to find current music charts, hit songs, lyrics, and legal downloads.

Shortcut #88

Melodic Rhythm Patterns: The Key to Catchy Melodies

Here's the big secret to writing interesting, memorable melodies.

Melodic rhythm patterns are at the heart of every hit song melody ever written! So of course, we all sit around thinking about them, right? We have lively discussions with other songwriters about the melodic rhythm patterns in the latest hit songs, right? Wrong. Most of us are not even aware of melodic rhythm patterns. Sure, we've picked up the concept unconsciously from the songs we've been listening to all our lives. We use them by habit or instinct. *But we don't think about them, or make choices based on using melodic rhythm patterns in the most effective way.*

Here's how you can use this powerful tool to make your melodies easy to remember, give them shape, organization, and listener appeal.

What is a melodic rhythm pattern?

Basically, a melody consists of a series of notes. That sounds easy enough. The hard part is ... if you want to appeal to listeners, you can't use just any old series of notes. For instance, if you sit down at a piano and play a scale, that's a series of notes, but it won't interest listeners very much. A steady string of rising and falling pitches is predictable and boring.

So, how can you turn a scale into an interesting melody? You could change the pitch of the notes by going down instead of up, or part of the way up, then down, but you'll still have a steady string of notes. *It lacks rhythmic interest.* A melody consists of both pitch *and* rhythm; you can work with either one to improve your melody. So, instead of changing the pitches, focus on changing the rhythm.

A melody is a series of notes with pitch and rhythm.

Try this: Play or sing a steady, rising line of eight notes—a scale. Now do it again and hold the first two notes longer, then speed up the next three notes, then hold the last three notes longer, like this:

Long Long Short Short Short Long Long Long

You've changed the *rhythm* of the notes but not the pitches. It's not a killer melody yet, but definitely more interesting. Now, sing the same series of notes but add a pause after the first short note, like this:

Long Long Short Pause Short Short Long Long Long

The rhythm of a melodic phrase is the pattern of long notes, short notes & pauses.

Now you've got something that might be the basis of an interesting melody. Change the pitch of the last note—try gong down instead of up— and you've got a start on what sounds like a song melody instead of a scale.

The trick to writing interesting, easy-to-remember melodies

Of course that was a very simple example but it illustrates the concept of melodic rhythm. Don't make the mistake of thinking that melody consists only of pitch. The rhythm of the notes—the pattern of long notes, short notes, and pauses—plays a crucial role. Without it, melodies wander aimlessly or turn into predictable scales. Together pitch *and* rhythm can make your song catchy, fresh, and unforgettable.

To show you how pitch and rhythm work together to make a memorable melody, I want you to take a well-known standard—"America the Beautiful"—and sing the melody without words, just use a nonsense syllable such as "da" or "la." Removing the lyrics will help you focus on what the melody is doing.

Sing the first line of "America the Beautiful" ("Oh, beautiful for spacious skies …") using "da-da-da" instead of the lyrics. Listen for the rhythm of the melody—where the notes are long or short.

The first two notes of this melody are long followed by two short notes.

Long Long Short Short

Try this! Repeat a rhythm pattern but change the pitches!

This is the first melodic phrase of the song and it introduces you to a featured, repeated *rhythmic pattern* of the melody. The next four notes of the melody repeat this same rhythmic pattern but notice how the pitch of the two short notes is lower this time. If you "da-da" through the rest of this song, you'll hear the "Long Long Short Short" rhythmic pattern over and over with different note pitches. This is the big secret to writing interesting, easy-to-remember melodies: *Repeat a melodic rhythm pattern while changing the pitches!*

It's everywhere!

This idea of repeating the rhythm of a melodic phrase while changing the pitches can be found in every successful piece of popular music from Beethoven's "Fifth Symphony" (*da-da-da-DA, da-da-da-DA*) to today's top ten hits. This is not an exaggeration; it's everywhere once you start looking for it. For instance, try the "da-da" technique on "Every Breath You Take" by The Police.

> *Line 1:* Short Short Long Long Long
> *Line 2:* Repeat pitches and rhythm pattern of line 1.
> *Line 3:* Short Short Short Long Long. Repeat with different pitches.
> *Line 4:* Repeat Line 3 rhythm pattern with different pitches.

There are only two rhythm patterns in this verse! That means there's plenty of repetition keeping the melody focused and memorable. Varying the pitches keeps it interesting.

To hear another way this technique can be used, check out "Bless the Broken Road" by Rascal Flatts. In the chorus (beginning with "Ev-er-y long lost dream …"), each line consists of the same melodic rhythm pattern:

Short Short Short Long Long Long

The short notes are repeated with the same rhythm and pitch on every line of the chorus. The long notes retain the same rhythm but *change pitch*. This gives the chorus a tight structure and makes it very easy to remember without ever being boring.

What melodic rhythm patterns can do for you

Few things turn off a listener faster than a melody that sounds disorganized, aimlessly wandering this way and that. Whether it's an uptempo song or a slow ballad, if your melody doesn't use at least some repeated melodic rhythm patterns, it will lack the focused, structured quality that listeners like to hear.

When you have a melody that feels unfocused, check your melodic rhythm patterns. Consider using no more than three to four melodic rhythm patterns per verse or chorus section.

- Try repeating a pattern with different pitches before moving on to the next pattern.
- Alternate two patterns before changing to a third.
- As in "Bless the Broken Road," try starting each line with the same pattern, then varying the end of the line.
- Repeat a short pattern in the same line, as in Line 3 of "Every Breath You Take."

Give your song tight structure and focus with repeated melodic rhythm patterns.

This is a powerful Shortcut to writing hit song melodies. If it's a new technique for you, study hit song melodies, especially big hook-driven choruses, to see how melodic rhythm patterns are used. The more you study, the easier it will be for you to acquire this skill.

Do It Now

1. Choose a hit song you like in a genre you want to write in. Sing the melody using the "da-da-da" technique. Notice the rhythm patterns of the notes. Do your hear any repetition of rhythmic phrases? (Hint: the chorus is the most likely place to find good examples.) Find places where the pitches change while the rhythm remains the same

2. Take a melody of your own and check for melodic rhythm patterns. If needed, use some of the suggestions in this Shortcut to organize and focus your melody.

See "Shortcut Resources" on page 261 for information on where to find current music charts, hit songs, lyrics, and legal downloads.

Shortcut #89

Use Syncopation to Add Rhythmic *Zing!*

Emphasize a mix of strong beats, weak beats, and upbeats.

Say a publisher tells you your song has a "nice melody." Chances are she won't be offering you a contract for that one! Nice melodies may not finish last but they don't often go to No. 1 on the charts either. The phrase "nice melody" has *blaaaaaaaaah* written all over it. It may mean "workmanlike but predictable," "mediocre but familiar"—you get the idea. Often, it just means that nothing about your melody shouts "Hey, fresh and exciting here!"

How do you get "fresh and exciting" into your melody? In the previous Shortcut, you saw how the rhythm patterns of your melody add focus and memorability to your song. But memorable is not the same as fresh and exciting! A nursery rhyme is memorable but it certainly isn't exciting. Once again, we turn to rhythm to provide us with the answer. To add a fresh, catchy, exciting twist to your melody, use *syncopation*.

Understanding syncopation: Strong beats and weak beats

See Shortcut 74 to learn how to count beats per measure.

Most hit songs have four evenly-spaced beats per measure. All four are emphasized, but Beat 1 and Beat 3 receive more emphasis than the Beats 2 and 4. The former (1 and 3) are called "strong beats" and the latter (2 and 4) are called "weak beats." If your melody emphasizes the strong beats, it's doing what listeners expect it to do and it has a predictable feel. *Syncopation occurs when a weak beat is emphasized.* That's what listeners *don't* expect. It surprises them and shakes them up. Here are a few syncopation tricks you can use to add rhythmic *zing* to your melody and wake up a snoozing listener.

Strong = 1 & 3. Weak = 2 & 4.

- Begin a phrase on a weak beat instead of a strong one.

- Put your highest or lowest note on a weak beat.

- Accent a note that falls on a weak beat by putting an important word on it and holding it.

Upbeats: Now things really start jumping!

Upbeats on and.

As you count the four steady, emphasized beats in each measure, try adding an "and" between them: "1 and 2 and 3 and 4 and." The "and" is called the "upbeat." These are extremely weak beats. Emphasizing *these* beats is a real rhythmic surprise! You can mix in notes that fall on upbeats to give your melody plenty of fresh twists. However, beware: emphasizing too many upbeats may cause your listener to lose track of the down beats! Use them for seasoning.

• Try any of the techniques listed for emphasizing weak beats on the upbeats.

Pauses

Pauses are as important as notes! An unexpected pause can create a sense of surprise and unpredictability in your melody. To hear this for yourself, sing "Mary Had a Little Lamb" and add a short pause just before the word "lamb." Notice how different this familiar melody sounds when you do that. Here are a few ways you can play with pauses.

• Add a short pause in the middle of a melodic phrase. If you want to preserve the original length of the line, speed up the next word or two.

• Try putting a pause on any strong beat (Beat 1 or 3) and work the rest of your phrase around it.

• If you have a pause of two to three beats at the end of every line, your melody will tend to sound predictable because your *pauses* are predictable. Try extending some of your lines by a couple of notes (and words) to fill in one of the pauses.

Shortcut 92 has more tips on using upbeats and pauses.

Do It Now

1. Choose a hit song that you like in a genre you want to write in. Count along and notice which beats are emphasized. Where do the strongest notes and words fall?

2. Take a melody of your own and check the rhythmic syncopation of your melody by counting along and noticing where your phrases begin and which beats are emphasized. If you are emphasizing strong beats primarily, try any of the techniques above to add rhythmic interest.

See "Shortcut Resources" on page 261 for information on where to find current music charts, hit songs, lyrics, and legal downloads.

Shortcut #90

Mix It Up With Long and Short Phrases

Use a variety of phrase lengths to keep things interesting.

Get rid of that predictable drone!

Have you ever had the experience of listening to someone drone on and on and on? Your attention drifts. You start to feel sleepy. You don't register a word they're saying because everything runs together into one long sentence. The problem could be that it *is* one long sentence. The speaker is not using a variety of phrase lengths to break up thoughts into coherent bits and keep things interesting. Great writers and speechmakers know about this phrasing trick and use it. From Shakespeare to Abraham Lincoln to Martin Luther King Jr., the speeches we remember are the ones that can be broken up into sound bites, or phrases, with each phrase defined by a pause: "To be (pause) or not to be (pause) that is the question." The most effective and memorable speeches use a mix of phrase lengths, like this:

> *Four score and seven years ago* (LONG)
>
> *Our fathers brought forth on this continent* (LONGER)
>
> *A new nation* (SHORT)
>
> *Conceived in Liberty* (IN BETWEEN)

Listen for phrase lengths in hit songs

Today's hit songwriters have figured out that breaking up phrases into a variety of lengths keeps listeners interested. Often the phrases will be organized into patterns—such as two short phrases, then a long one—that will be repeated.

Shortcut 74 can show you how to count beats or you can just do it by feel.

To study phrase lengths in today's hits, you can count along and figure out exactly how long the phrases are, but often it's easier to just listen and try to sort things out by ear. Here are two hit songs that use a mix of phrase lengths. I've included a few notes to help you get going. Listen to the songs and see if you can recognize the phrase lengths.

"Who Needs Pictures" (Brad Paisley)
> Country melodies tend to keep a low profile, always striving to sound conversational and natural. But don't be fooled, there's plenty going on in terms of phrase lengths. In this beautiful hit song by Brad Paisley, he starts the verse with a long phrase ("There's an old Kodak camera …") and follows it with a shorter one. Line 3 is the same length as Line 1. Line 4 consists of two short phrases, setting up the chorus section. The chorus starts off with two short phrases followed by a long one. He repeats this pattern then wraps up the chorus with a payoff line ("Who needs pictures …").

"Breakaway" (Kelly Clarkson)

Here's a great example of a Pop hit that mixes long and short phrases. The verse starts with two short phrases ("Grew up ... / And when the rain ...") followed by a long phrase ("I'd just stare ..."), then the pattern is repeated with one more long phrase added ("I could breakaway ..."), leading right into the chorus. The chorus starts with two long phrases followed by three short ones and then a long one. This pattern is then repeated. This song is in 3/4 time, meaning it has three steady beats per measure, unusual for a hit song. (If you're interested in writing with this feel, this is a great song to use as a ghost song. See Shortcut 2 to find out more about ghost songs.)

Try using a variety of phrase lengths

If your chorus melody consists of a series of four lines, all of the same length, your listeners may start drifting away. Keep them interested and guessing what will happen next by using a variety of phrase lengths.

- Try breaking up long lines by adding a pause, creating two shorter phrases.

- Add extra words and notes at the end of a phrase, filling a pause and creating an unexpectedly long line.

- Organize your phrases into patterns, such as two short and one long. Repeat the pattern with a different lyric.

Do It Now

1. Listen to the songs mentioned in the Shortcut and other contemporary hit songs. Notice the variety and organization of phrase lengths that are being used.

2. Check out the phrase lengths in some of your own songs. If you find that your verse or chorus features phrases that are all the same length, try using the suggestions in the Shortcut to add more variety.

See "Shortcut Resources" on page 261 for information on where to find current music charts, hit songs, lyrics, and legal downloads.

Shortcut #91

Start Your Phrases on a Variety of Beats

A small shift in your starting point can make a big difference.

What if you were invited to a dinner party and the host put a plate of plain, warmed-over spaghetti in front of you. You could eat it, but you'd be pretty disappointed. Now, imagine you are the host and your listeners are your guests. If you serve them a plate of warmed-over spaghetti, they may not even stick around for dinner. They'll go looking for someplace where the food is fresher and more interesting.

Sometimes songwriters serve up a melody that sounds like something from the 1970s that's been sitting in the fridge for awhile. You really can't expect listeners to hang around for that. However, when a melody sounds predictable or dated there's often a simple fix that can take care of the problem. Let me show you how adding a little variety to the starting points of your melody lines can spice things up.

Find the starting points of your melodic phrases

Phrases start on the first emphasized note or word.

A melodic phrase begins with the first emphasized word or note in a phrase. If the first emphasized note or word lands on Beat 1, then that melodic phrase starts on Beat 1. Pick-up notes don't count; these are the one or two quick notes that lead up to the emphasized note, often used for words such as "and" and "but." Sometimes a pick-up can be longer than one word—"But if I …" "Can't you …" "Oh, baby …" If these words are sung quickly and the following word or note is emphasized then they are pick-up notes.

In many classic Pop songs from the 1960s and '70s, you'll hear a series of melodic phrases that start on the same beat, often a strong beat (Beat 1 or Beat 3). To hear a song with phrases that begin on Beat 1, listen to a classic hit like "Joy To the World" (Three Dog Night) or "Walk This Way" (Aerosmith). You'll need to count along to figure out where the melodic phrases begin. If you haven't done this before, you may need to listen to the song several times. It's not easy to count the beats *and* listen at the same time to what the melody is doing. See Shortcut 74, "Study Hit Melodies: Just Count to 4!!!" for practice.

Today's hit songs start phrases on a variety of beats

In today's melodies in *all* genres, songwriters use a greater variety of starting points for phrases than they did in previous decades. By varying the beat on which melodic phrases begin, contemporary melodies keep listeners on their toes with interesting beat emphasis and an element of unpredictability. To hear phrases with a variety of start points, listen to the following two songs and count the beats.

"Who Knew" (P!nk)

P!nk's hit song, "Who Knew," uses a variety of phrase start points to make this fairly simple melody sound fresh and surprising. The first two lines begin on Beat 2 ("You took my hand ... You promised me ..."), followed by two short phrases that begin on Beat 4 ("Uh huh. That's right."). The opening lines of the chorus begin on Beat 1 ("someone ..." "three years" etc.), then the melody features a series of phrases that begin on Beat 3. ("I know ... better ...") Write out the lyrics and see if you can identify the phrase starts.

"For a Moment Like This" (Kelly Clarkson)

Here, a rather conventional sounding pop ballad melody is given a fresh twist just by starting phrases on unusual beats. The verse opens with three lines that begin on Beat 2 ("What if I ..." "Would you ..." "Almost the feeling ..."), followed by two lines that begin on Beat 1. The real surprise happens when the chorus melody begins early, on Beat 3 ("MO-ment like this ..."), letting the final word of the phrase ("this") land on Beat 1. It turns the beat around in a way that listeners love, even though they can't say exactly what's happening.

Experiment with starting points for phrases

Play one of your own song melodies and count the beats. Notice where your melodic phrases begin. If most of your phrases are starting on or near the same beat, especially Beat 1, try some of these ideas to add a fresh feel.

➤ **Shift a melodic phrase later by one beat**

To start a phrase later, just add a pause at the beginning. This will change where the notes fall in relation to the underlying beat. Different notes will be emphasized. See if you like what happens. If you don't like the sound, move the phrase back where it was.

Try shifting the starting points of your phrases. You can do it!

➤ **Shift a melodic phrase earlier by one beat**

This is a little more difficult than moving a phrase later. If your phrase starts on Beat 1, you'll need to count the beats in the measure before it and start singing when you reach Beat 4 of the previous measure. Sing the new phrase a few times until it feels comfortable. Again, if you don't like it, just move the phrase back where it was.

➤ **Emphasize upbeats instead of downbeats**

When the emphasized notes of a melody tend to fall on the downbeats (Beats 1, 2, 3, and 4), it creates a predictable, familiar feel. (Many nursery rhymes, such as "Twinkle, Twinkle Little Star," do this.) You can shift a phrase half a beat later and start it on an upbeat (the "and" between the downbeats). Here's a variation: You can add a short pause in the *middle* of your phrase, creating two shorter phrases. By adding a short pause, your new second phrase will most likely start on an upbeat. Play with these ideas and see what happens.

Read Shortcut 89 for more ideas on using upbeats.

➢ **Shift repeated phrases to start on different beats**

If you have a pair or a series of repeated phrases, try starting a repeat on a different beat. To hear this technique, check out Beyoncé's "Irreplaceable." The opening phrase ("You must not know 'bout me") begins just after Beat 1. The repeat starts just after Beat 4! To achieve this effect, the writers simply eliminated a pause at the end of the first phrase and went straight into the second phrase earlier than expected. Sliding a repeat earlier like this catches the listener off guard and creates plenty of interest! If you want to write for today's R&B/Soul genre, you'll want to learn how to use little rhythmic twists like this.

Do It Now

1. Check out today's hit songs in the genre you're interested in. Count the beats and notice where the phrases start. Different genres use more or less variety in their phrase starts. R&B/Soul and Pop use a lot; Country and Rock use less.

2. Using a melody of your own, try shifting the start time of a phrase or two to add a fresh twist to your melody.

   See "Shortcut Resources" on page 261 for information on where to find current music charts, hit songs, lyrics, and legal downloads.

Shortcut #92

Create Forward Momentum in Your Melody

Eliminate pauses and use weak beats to keep your melody moving.

There's one thing you can say for certain about today's hit songs: Once they start rolling, there's no stopping 'em! Like an express train, they rarely pull into a station long enough for a listener to hop off. Today's audiences love the feeling of being swept along at top speed, falling forward into the next verse or chorus. Radio loves the "express train" effect because listeners will ride the song all the way to the end where the commercials are waiting with open arms.

Write a melody that rolls forward like an express train!

Give your melody forward momentum

To build forward momentum into your melody, you need to suggest the idea that there is *always something happening or just about to happen in your melody*. There are two clever tricks that will help you create this effect in your melodies.

➤ **Eliminate pauses, especially at the ends of lines**
Today's hit song melodies have very few long pauses. When pauses are used, they're rarely longer than two beats. The only exception is an instrumental break between song sections—between verse and chorus, for instance. Some songs, like Seether's "Rise Above This," even eliminate these pauses, plowing ahead from section to section without stopping for breath.

This is in contrast to the melodic style of previous decades in which long pauses often followed each line. To hear the difference, listen to 1980s-era hits like Glenn Frey's "The Heat Is On" or Berlin's "Take My Breath Away" with its six to ten beat pauses between lines. Then check out more recent hits like "Better as a Memory" (Kenny Chesney), "Everything" (Michael Bublé), "The Pretender" (Foo Fighters), or "Be Without You" (Mary J. Blige). In each of these songs, almost all of the pauses are two beats or less except for section breaks, giving these melodies a sense of continuous motion and energy that appeals to today's listeners. The express train doesn't stop often in today's big hits!

Read Shortcut 74 if you need to learn how to count beats.

➤ **Emphasize weak beats and upbeats**
The second trick has to do with beat emphasis. When the important words and notes of a phrase land on the strong beats (Beats 1 and 3), it gives your listeners a grounded, solid feeling. They like this feeling of groundedness but after awhile it starts to feel a little predictable, a little bit *stuck*. When you emphasize weak beats (Beats 2 and 4) or upbeats (the "and" between beats), you *unstick* your melody, creating an unsettled, floating feeling—a sense that things are in motion and ungrounded. Mixing strong and weak beat emphasis

gives your listeners the best of both worlds; they know where solid ground is, but the melody takes on a feeling of momentum and change.

Many of today's biggest hits mix strong and weak beat emphasis to create forward momentum. Matchbox Twenty's "How Far We've Come" is a great example. The verse lines all begin on a weak beat (Beat 2). The regular rhythm of the words gives the weak and strong beats equal emphasis. The chorus starts on the strongest beat, Beat 1 ("I believe the world ..."), shifts to Beat 3 ("Oh, well ..."), then starts the hook/title lines on Beat 2 ("Let's see how far we've come ...") while eliminating all but the briefest of pauses. The result is a rolling juggernaut of a melody!

For more insight into using beat emphasis, read Shortcut 89.

Use either one or both of these techniques—shifting beat emphasis and eliminating pauses—to add momentum and interest to your melodies. If you're not familiar with these ideas, spend some time studying hit song melodies—counting the beats and learning to recognize where the emphasized notes fall. It takes practice to be able to count beats *and* listen for beat emphasis. Try using recent hit songs as ghost songs to help you embed these ideas, so you don't have to think about them when you're writing. Shortcut 102 can show you how.

Do It Now

1. Listen to some of the songs mentioned in this Shortcut or find others you like. Count along with each song and notice where and how long the pauses are in the melody. Then go back and study where the beat emphasis is. Notice when the beat emphasis shifts from strong beats to weak or upbeats. Where do the melodic phrases begin? Where do the important words fall? Notice how these melodies affect you as a listener.

2. Check your own songs for pauses and beat emphasis. Try eliminating pauses longer than three beats. Extend your lyric/melody line to fill the space or start the following phrase earlier. Try shifting some of your accented words and notes from a strong beat to a weak beat or upbeat to add interest and momentum.

See "Shortcut Resources" on page 261 for information on where to find current music charts, hit songs, lyrics, and legal downloads.

Shortcut #93

Get Attention and Express Emotion With an Interval Jump

Hear what a leap between notes can do for your melody!

Ballet dancers do it. Pole-vaulters do it. Olympic gold medal ice skaters seem to defy gravity while doing it. There's something about a soaring leap or dazzling jump that's very appealing. Maybe it's just the idea of starting in one place, landing in another, and skipping all the tedious steps in between!

In music, a leap like that is called an "interval jump." It's a very simple idea; it just means skipping over a few notes. You can start on a low note and land on a high one or vice versa. You can make the jump, then slowly return to your starting point, or end as quickly as you began. Whichever you choose, if you do it right, the effect can be much greater than you might expect from such a simple concept.

Go ahead and jump! Skip over a few notes!

➤ **Use an interval jump to draw attention**

If someone is speaking in a normal, conversational pitch range and suddenly shifts to a higher note range, it gets your attention A change in vocal pitch generally indicates a change in emotion; your brain tells you to check it out. In a song melody, a pitch jump up or down will accomplish the same thing. That's why you often hear an interval leap at the beginning of a chorus section; it gets the listener's attention just when you want to convey something important.

In "First Time" by Lifehouse, there's an interval jump of more than an octave between the last note of the pre-chorus and first note of the chorus, drawing attention to the all-important first line of the chorus. U2 saves the effect for the *end* of the chorus in "Vertigo," jumping several notes higher for the word "feel," thereby pointing your attention toward this key word.

➤ **Add emphasis to key words**

Often, when we want to emphasize a word or syllable, we speak it in a higher or lower pitch range than normal. Exaggerating this idea in your melody can suggest a likely place for an interval jump. In "You're Beautiful," James Blunt uses a big interval leap to punch up the important word in the opening lines of the chorus and give it a highly emotional yet natural feel. "You're BEAUT-iful, you're BEAUT-iful …" Try speaking this short phrase with a lot of emotion and you'll notice how your voice wants to rise on the same syllables.

For more on using emotion in spoken words to create melody, see Shortcut 84.

➤ **Create a feeling of motion and energy**

Leaping up and down over a series of notes can convey a sense of activity and movement. You can hear this technique in the opening lines of the chorus in Phil Vassar's Country hit "In a Real Love." He sings a series of short, high notes ("With a little bit of …"), then drops to a quick low note, goes back up to the high, short notes and down again. The low notes underscore the words "live," "learn," "fuss," and "fight," effectively conveying the ups and downs of real love.

Matchbox Twenty used a series of interval jumps very effectively in their Pop hit "Unwell." The back and forth leaps of the chorus melody contribute to a sensation of unbalance, dizziness, and lack of solid ground, just the right feeling to underscore the lyric's message. The technique can also be used to build energy. Listen to the lines that lead up to the chorus in Alicia Keys' "Like You'll Never See Me Again" to hear this idea.

Play with a series of interval jumps!

➤ **Evoke a sense of vulnerability**
Sometimes a higher voice can suggest a child's voice, one that is helpless, naïve, or vulnerable. Check out "Apologize" by OneRepublic. On the words "too late" at the top of the chorus, the melody features an interval leap up of five notes and a change of voice from a conversational tone to a softer high sound, adding a touch of yearning even as the singer tells us it's too late to save the relationship.

➤ **Write the money note**
When writing interval leaps, keep in mind the singer's range and the ways a note can be delivered. There are singers with the skill to deliver a big interval jump with power, emotion, and control. These singers like to display their chops and their fans love to hear them do it. The moment that really sells the song "My Heart Will Go On" is the octave jump on the word "wherever." A singer of Celine Dion's ability turns this huge leap into an emotional rush!

Give them the money note!

Do It Now

1. Listen to hit songs in your genre. Look for interval jumps and notice how they are used.

2. Try adding interval jumps to a song of your own. Using the suggestions above, look for appropriate places in your song where they would underscore the lyric or emotion.

See "Shortcut Resources" on page 261 for information on where to find current music charts, hit songs, lyrics, and legal downloads.

Shortcut #94

The Fake: Set Up an Expectation Then Break It

Use a time-tested football strategy.

Listeners love a mix of the familiar and the unexpected. Just like a fan at a football game, they know all the plays, they just don't know which one will happen next. And when the quarterback pulls off something surprising, they go crazy!!!

As a songwriter, you're in the quarterback position; you're the one calling the plays. When you set up the other team (and the fans) to expect one thing then deliver another, you have a good chance of scoring a touchdown.

You're the quarterback!

Play Strategy #1: Vary the third line

Like any fake play, you'll need to set it up by making listeners expect that a particular thing is likely to happen. One successful strategy is to establish a strong melodic line at the top of the chorus, repeat it so it's firmly established, then start to repeat it a third time but do something different after the first few notes.

You can hear solid examples of this play strategy in the choruses of Daughtry's "It's Not Over" and Avril Lavigne's "My Happy Ending." In Lavigne's chorus, the third line ("And all of the memories …") starts out as if it's going to be a repeat of the first two lines. Listeners are feeling comfortably smug, "knowing" what's coming next. But the rhythm of the notes soon shifts and the interval jump in the melody repeats several times instead of just twice, as in the opening lines. Listeners are drawn back in just as the song reaches the payoff lines of the chorus. Touchdown! A beautiful fake out.

Play Strategy #2: Vary the repeat of a series

This is a variation on the strategy I just described. Here, the songwriter sets up an expectation by writing a set of repeating phrases, and then making it appear as if the entire set will be repeated. In the 1970s and '80s that's just what would have happened, so this is a strong expectation that's been reinforced over the years by many hit songs.

In Beyoncé's "Irreplaceable," there's an effective fake play based on this expectation. The first four phrases of the chorus have a nice symmetrical feel: the melody of the first phrase is sung twice ("You must not know 'bout me"), then the second phrase melody is sung twice. Next the song goes right back to the opening phrase which is sung twice—a clear indication that the songwriter is planning to repeat all four of the opening phrases! The following line is a repeat as expected but the line after that one ("so don't you ever …") is a complete surprise! The unexpected detour draws attention and gives the end of the chorus added punch, a big plus if the last line of the chorus is the only place where the title appears, as is the case in this song!

Play Strategy #3: Vary the last line

See Shortcut 90 for more on varying your phrase lengths.

Like the all-American, red-blooded songs that they are, Country melodies are not about to miss out on a football-inspired Shortcut like this one. You can hear an interesting fake in Rascal Flatts' "Bless the Broken Road," where the chorus consists of a whole series of short phrases, leading listeners to expect a payoff line that is also short. Instead, the payoff line (beginning with "God blessed the broken road ...") is substantially longer than expected, drawing attention and setting up the all-important title/hook line.

Do It Now

Write a chorus melody that uses one of the play strategies listed in this Shortcut to create and then break an expectation.

Shortcut #95

Be Unforgettable: Organize Your Melodic Rhythm Patterns

Add structure, focus, and memorability to your melodies.

There's an electronic game I like to play called *Simon*. The game beeps out a random series of pitches and the player has to play them back, the same pitches in the same order. Once there are nine or ten in the series, it's tough to remember them! A missed pitch triggers an ugly *blaaatt* sound.

Most people, when they put on a music CD or turn on the radio, are not looking to play a round of *Simon*. But if you write a melody that wanders through any old random series of pitches and you expect listeners to remember it, that's just what you're asking them to do. *Blaaatt!*

No more random melodies!!

You can make your melodies easier to remember and more interesting than a *Simon* game by getting rid of that random quality. The opposite of a random series is a series of repeated, well-organized patterns. In this case, repeated melodic rhythm patterns: the pattern of long and short notes that makes up a melodic phrase.

The key to writing a memorable, catchy melody

One of the most memorable melodies in the history of pop music is "Over the Rainbow," written by Harold Arlen and E.Y. Harburg. It doesn't have a big, repeated chorus with an in-your-face hook; it doesn't even have a lot of lyric repetition, just the title line. So why is it so easy to remember this melody? Because it consists of exactly *two melodic rhythm patterns and one held note*.

Shortcut 88 can tell you more about melodic rhythm patterns.

Pattern 1: an interval jump consisting of two long notes ("Some-where …")

Pattern 2: a five-note phrase with the rhythm Long Short Short Long Long ("… o-ver the rain-bow")

The next line of the song begins with Pattern 1. The *pitches* are not the same as in the first line but the phrase has *the same melodic rhythm*, two long notes. This phrase is followed by a long, held note ("high").

Here's how these two melodic rhythm patterns and one held note are organized in the verse of "Over the Rainbow":

    Pattern 1 / Pattern 2
    Pattern 1 / Held note
    Pattern 1 / Pattern 2
    Pattern 2 / Held note

Two rhythm patterns and a held note! This melody is a poster child for memorable and catchy! *The repetition and organization of rhythm patterns make the melody easy to remember, the changes in pitch and lyrics keep it interesting.*

Melodic rhythm patterns in contemporary hit songs

So if this is such a good idea, are we still using it in today's hit songs? You bet we are! Take a look at a No. 1 hit like Avril Lavigne's "Complicated." On first listen, the melody seems to be ... complicated; yet it's memorable, it sticks with you. That didn't happen by accident. There are just three melodic rhythm patterns used in the chorus of this song and they are carefully organized. The chorus begins with Pattern 1 ("Why'd you ... complicated"), followed by Pattern 2 ("I see the way you"). Pattern 3 is a series of interval jumps beginning with the phrase "You fall ..."). Here's how the chorus is organized.

Pattern 1 / Pattern 2
Pattern 1 / Pattern 2
Pattern 3 / Pattern 2
Pattern 1

Add more memorability to your melodies

Now, listen to one of your own songs; see how many melodic rhythm patterns you can identify in your verse or chorus melody and notice how they are organized. To make it easier, sing or play your melody without the lyric. Remember, the note pitches can change; it's the pattern of long and short notes you're looking for.

A memorable melody uses a small number of melodic rhythm patterns.

If you've got more than four different patterns in a section, your melody may not have enough repetition to stick in the listener's mind. Consider eliminating one or two patterns while repeating others. Organize your patterns—try repeating your first and second patterns at least once during the section. If you have two rhythm patterns that are similar, alter one of them to create more contrast so listeners can distinguish them.

Some melodies have too much repetition and a predictable organization. Ah, but this can be great raw material for a hot melody! Try adding interest by changing the note pitches and lyrics while preserving the melodic rhythm. Switch the order of your patterns to surprise your listeners.

Do It Now

1. Thinking about melodic rhythm separately from pitch and lyrics might be a new idea for you. Familiarize yourself with it by looking for melodic rhythm patterns in hit songs. See how many repeated patterns you can find in a chorus or a verse. How often were the patterns repeated and how were they organized? Did the songwriter change the pitches and lyrics?

2. Try writing a chorus melody using only three rhythm patterns. Remember to vary the note pitches and lyrics to keep your melody interesting.

See "Shortcut Resources" on page 261 for information on where to find current music charts, hit songs, lyrics, and legal downloads.

Shortcut #96

Get Rid of That Predictable Resolve

Break an expectation in the most predictable spot.

When you reach the end of your chorus, do you find yourself writing the same kind of melody in song after song? You're not alone. It's tough to find creative, fresh ways of wrapping up the last line of a chorus. After all, it's been done a lot of times in a lot of songs. How do you find something that hasn't been done to death already? Compounding the problem is the fact that listeners know where this line is going: Like a horse headed for the barn at the end of a long ride, that final line is going *home*.

The end of the chorus wants to go home.

What is a resolving line?

In music theory there are elaborate definitions for words like "resolve" and "resolving line." For our purposes in this book, assume it means exactly what it says. When you resolve a melody, you let go of all the tension, heave a big sigh of relief, take your shoes off, sit down in a comfy chair, and say something like "It's good to be home." The melody is done; it's not going anywhere, at least not for a few beats or measures.

Because resolving a melody releases the tension, it's not something you generally want to do in the middle of your chorus, but it does feel natural and inevitable at the end of a chorus. This is where your lyric pays off as well, making the resolving line one of the most important lines in your song. You want it to sound fresh and interesting.

Resolving lines release tension.

NOTE: A verse that is heading into a chorus ends with a lead-in line, not a resolving line. See Shortcut 86 for more on lead-in lines. However, if you're using the Verse / Verse / Bridge / Verse song form and the last line of your verse is your refrain line, it *will* be a resolving line.

Freshen up your resolves

So how do you get around the problem of those familiar, predictable resolves? If you know where the line is going, how can you give it a surprising twist?

➢ **Set it up with a pause**
Add a pause just before your resolve to increase anticipation. Your listeners *know* what's coming but *when* will it come? Dierks Bentley's "What Was I Thinkin'" drops in a big pause right in the middle of the resolve line. "I know what I was feelin' "—Waaaaaait for it!—"but what was I thinkin'?" Listeners all know what's coming but making them wait builds tension and strengthens the resolve when it finally arrives.

Try some of these solutions for freshening up the last line of your chorus.

> **Make the last line of your chorus longer than expected**
> Extend the resolving line by an extra word or even a whole phrase. In other words, make the horse trot a few extra steps before reaching the barn door. The chorus of Rascal Flatts' "Bless the Broken Road" consists of six short lines, leading listeners to expect yet another to wrap up the section. Instead, there's a long final line that adds weight to the end of the chorus as the lyric pays off ("God blessed the broken road …").

> **Get to the resolve early**
> In P!nk's "Who Knew" she sings the two-word title on the last line of the chorus. Even though the melody resolves firmly to the home note, listeners still feel like they're left suspended; it seems to have ended too soon. The song does a neat trick to accomplish this. It sets up a series of phrases starting with "I know better …" and starts to repeat that series ("… and ever"), but stops cold with the resolving line ("who knew"). In Shortcut 94 you can read more about creating and breaking expectations with a series of phrases.

> **Just for fun, try something totally surprising**
> Before deciding on your resolve, take a few minutes to play with some unusual solutions. U2's "Vertigo" resolves the chorus with a rising, energy-producing line that's completely unexpected, creating—what else? A sense of vertigo!

Do It Now

1. Check out recent hit songs and listen to the final line of the chorus. Notice how the song resolves that line while keeping it interesting.

2. Choose a song of your own and check to see if you can strengthen the final line of your chorus using any of the techniques listed in this Shortcut.

See "Shortcut Resources" on page 261 for information on where to find current music charts, hit songs, lyrics, and legal downloads.

Shortcut #97

Write Your Melody
Without a Chord Progression

Put that guitar down! Move away from the piano!

So, you want to write a song. What's the first thing you do? You pick up your guitar or sit down at a keyboard, right? It's what you've always done. And every professional songwriter you've ever seen is pictured sitting at a keyboard or strumming a guitar.

Maybe it's time to rethink that picture. If you're playing a piano or guitar while writing a song, what you're probably doing is writing a chord progression with a melody attached to it. A lot of your attention is focused on the chord progression, rather than the melody. Most listeners, however, are more focused on the melody; you're never going to hear a listener say, "Wow, what a great chord progression! I've *got* to hear that song again!" Try writing your melody without a chord progression and add the chords later.

Write a melody without chords

Step 1: Although you're going to work without any chord accompaniment, it's a good idea to choose a tempo and rhythmic feel for your song. Keep time by tapping your foot, clapping or using a metronome. If you have a software program or keyboard with rhythm loops, choose one you like and set it to play. Make sure it's a loop that doesn't include chords or a bass line; all you want is percussion.

Step 2: Choose a title for your song and develop the raw material for a lyric using Shortcuts 41 through 45. Start with the chorus, using your title as the opening line. Use the pitch and rhythm of your spoken title to get you started on a melody (see Shortcut 76).

Try this 4-step process for writing a melody and adding chords later.

Step 3: Work on your chorus melody, adding lyric phrases from your raw material, repeating your title melody, and playing with new melodic patterns until you have something that feels like it might work. Record this—a handheld cassette or digital recorder will work fine—then continue on to the verse, making sure there's plenty of contrast in note range and pace between chorus and verse melodies.

Step 4: Once you've roughed out a verse and chorus melody, record it in a song form: start with the verse, then chorus, verse, and chorus. Once you have a rough idea of your melody recorded in a fixed form, you can play it back and start working out the chords for it. Then use some of the melody shortcuts to rewrite and strengthen it.

Shortcut #98

Go From Inspiration to Finished Melody

The melody that "just occurs" to you is a starting place, not an end.

Melodies just happen, don't they? The melody that occurs to you while you're writing a lyric or wakes you up in the middle of the night seems so right and complete, you're tempted to feel it would be foolish to tamper with pure inspiration. Frequently, however, these melodies sound predictable. They lack contrast, interesting twists, and a contemporary sound. What your inspiration has given you is *an idea* with the potential to be a strong melody.

A melody that "just comes to you" is an idea, a starting point.

Here are some strategies that will help you get your melody from the "idea" stage to a more developed state. These suggestions will preserve your original, inspired melody while developing those crucial areas where today's hit songs need extra punch.

1. **Identify and strengthen the song structure**
   Initial melody ideas often lack contrast between sections and tend to have a lot of section repetition. Check your melody to determine the structure. If you have a string of similar-sounding sections, you can add variety and interest by moving one section to a higher note range or changing the pace of the notes (not the underlying rhythm or tempo of the song). If you suspect your melodic idea is a verse section, try writing a chorus to alternate with it.

2. **Add emphasis to the "key lines"**
   Shortcuts 56 and 84 highlighted the key lines in a song's lyric and melody. These are the lines that listeners notice first. Give your melody an extra boost at these points.

The first line of the chorus: Be sure to draw attention to this line by creating contrast or releasing tension. Try an interval jump at the beginning of the line or a change of pace or interesting rhythm pattern in the melody.

The chorus payoff line: This is the last line of the chorus. It's an important lyric line that adds a memorable moment to the song and a sense of completion. Drive it home with your melody. Try a line that resolves in a fresh way. Shortcut 96 can give you some tips on how to do that.

The first line of the verses: This is the line that draws listeners in. Aim for a conversational, intimate feel in your melody. Often this line provides contrast with the more urgent, emotional feel of the chorus. Be sure you have enough distinction between the chorus and verse melodies. Shortcut 85 covers strategies for constructing a solid verse melody.

The pre-chorus or lead-in line to the chorus: Make this line the wind-up to the pitch. Try increasing the tension by picking up the pace of the notes, using an ascending melody line, or a short series of repeated patterns. Find out more about pre-choruses and lead-in lines in Shortcut 86.

In the Verse / Verse / Bridge / Verse song form, the refrain line is a key line. You can treat it like the payoff line of a chorus. It's going to be a resolving line, so check out Shortcut 96 for ideas on how to make it a winner. Listen to hit songs in your genre to hear how key lines are underscored with melody.

3. **Add a bridge.**
   Melodic ideas don't usually arrive complete with a bridge. Try adding a bridge after your second chorus. In Shortcut 87 you'll find suggestions for building a strong, contemporary bridge!

4. **Check your phrase lengths and rhythm patterns.**
   Go through your melody and check your phrase lengths, phrase starts, and melodic rhythm patterns. If your phrases fall into familiar patterns or emphasize predictable beats try reworking them using Shortcuts 88 through 91.

A word of caution

When a melody "just comes to you," sometimes it's a melody you've heard before, one that's been stored in your memory. Making the changes above will help to enhance the differences, but it may not be enough. If you're worried that you might have inadvertently used an existing melody, play your melody for friends and ask if they recognize it. Continue making changes as suggested above to move it in a more original direction.

Have you heard it before? Change it if you have doubts.

Do It Now

Choose a melody of your own and run it through the steps in this Shortcut. Are you excusing some weaknesses because you're married to the melody that first occurred to you? Try letting go and reworking the melody to give it more structural clarity, strong key lines, and phrasing interest. You can always go back to your original melody if you like it better. The final decision on what works best is always up to you.

Shortcut #99

Four Ways to Give Your Listeners a Breath of Fresh Air!

What to do when your song starts feeling claustrophobic.

Try a little experiment. Just about everyone knows the verse melody of the hit song, "Every Breath You Take" written by Sting and recorded by The Police. It was a huge hit and is still a staple of classic Rock radio.

You don't need to know the lyrics, just hum or "da-da-da" through the melody of the verse. It's the very first section and starts with the title. Go ahead and hum it. Now do it again. And *again*. Is it driving you crazy yet? Are you bored? Simple repetition of a section of a song can make you feel like you're stuck—in a very small room—with no windows.

To avoid that problem, Sting added two wonderful bridge sections with soaring melodies and varied rhythm patterns. (There is no chorus section.) Listen to a recording of this song and notice how the bridge sections allow this song to open up. The wide note range and big interval jumps increase the emotional energy. It seems like the song takes a deep breath before the verse melody returns to that small room once again. This is an excellent example of the feeling of emotional release that can be created by a melody.

Open up your song

If you've got a song that keeps listeners locked up in a small room, try giving them more breathing space in your chorus or bridge by using one or two of the ideas in this list.

Give listeners plenty of breathing room.

- Move a section to a higher or lower note range (Shortcut 80).
- Use interval jumps to break out of a narrow note range (Shortcut 93).
- Create contrast in pace between your sections (Shortcut 81).
- Play with syncopation to add more rhythmic interest (Shortcut 89).

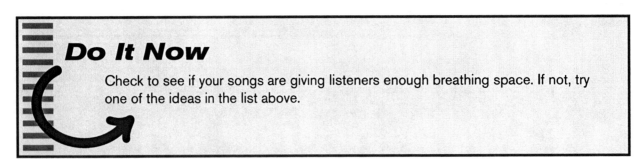

Do It Now

Check to see if your songs are giving listeners enough breathing space. If not, try one of the ideas in the list above.

Shortcut #100

Five Ways to Make a Dated Melody Sound Fresh

Use "phrase-ology" to give that same old melody new life.

If you suspect your melody sounds dated or predictable, congratulations! Why am I congratulating you? First, you've joined the crowd; every working songwriter runs into this problem at some point. Second, you've identified the problem. Good for you! Third, seriously, now the fun begins. This is an opportunity to play with some of the melody writing Shortcuts in this section, specifically the ones that have to do with melodic phrases. You've got the material for a strong, contemporary song; it just needs some reworking.

Before you try the following fixes, go through your melody and locate the melodic phrases. Read Shortcut 75 to learn how to do that.

Ditch that dated melody!

1. **Do you have a *pause* of three to four beats at the end of every line?** This was typical of hit songs in the 1970s and '80s but it isn't done much anymore. Try lengthening one of your lines to fill the pause at the end, add just enough words and notes to fill the space. Run the line right up to the start of the next one. Try this at the ends of various lines to see which feels best to you. You can find more information on phrase lengths in Shortcut 90.

2. **Are all the melodic phrases in a section about the same length?** Again, this is reminiscent of the melodic style of earlier decades and it can create a predictable feel for listeners. *Try this fix:* If the lines are long, replace the third line with two short phrases. Make the phrase half the length of the other lines and repeat it. You may not need to change your lyric; see how the words fall into the new melody and adjust them if needed.

3. **Are your melodic phrases all starting on the same beat?** Today's hit songs mix up the starting points of their melodic phrases. It keeps listeners interested and adds plenty of unpredictability to even the most familiar melody. Try shifting the start time of some of your phrases to surprise your listeners. Start one beat earlier or later, or even a half beat. Shortcut 91 can give you more tips on how to do this.

Try some of these ideas to give your melody a fresh sound.

4. **Is the pace of your phrases too predictable?** A plodding, steady pace can really make your song sound old-fashioned and rob it of emotional impact. Perhaps your lyric is at fault. If you're working with a "greeting card poem," try reworking the lyric to make it sound more conversational (see Shortcut 65). Don't worry about rhyming; just say what you want to say. When you've got a lyric that feels emotionally direct and honest, speak it out loud—with a lot of emotion—and notice where the natural stresses and pauses fall. Now rework your melody to support the new lyric. There's more information on this useful technique in Shortcuts 77 and 84.

5. **Is there enough rhythmic interest within your phrases?** Look at the rhythm of your melody—the pattern of long and short notes. If all of your lines have the same pattern, try varying one or two. Use part of the pattern, then switch to a new pattern. See Shortcuts 88 and 95 for more ideas on updating the rhythmic element of your melody.

Do It Now

Choose a song of your own and try some of the techniques listed above. Record the results; all you need is a vocal with a count-off to establish Beat 1. Give it the "Fresh Ears Test" (Shortcut 115) a couple hours later to see how it feels to you. If you like it, keep it. If you don't, go back to your original melody and try something else.

See "Shortcut Resources" on page 261 for information on where to find current music charts, hit songs, lyrics, and legal downloads.

Shortcut #101

The Melody Rewriting Checklist

Don't leave your melody unfinished.

You wouldn't expect a potter to throw a lump of clay on the pottery wheel, give it a couple of spins and then say, "There! It's done." You'd expect him to mold it, shape it, and work with it until it's a finished product. So why would you accept a blobby, predictable lump of melody? Too many songwriters stop the melody writing process before they've really gotten their melody into shape. Use this rewriting checklist to make sure your melody is a finished product.

Spend some quality time polishing your melody.

REWRITING CHECKLIST

1. **Is your melody clearly conveying the song's structure?**
    Create plenty of contrast in melodic elements such as note range, pace, and phrase length between your sections. When listeners leave the verse and move into the chorus it should be perfectly clear that, like Dorothy and Toto, we're not in Kansas anymore. Try using the first line of each section to emphasize the differences. Check out the Shortcuts that deal with contrast, like Shortcuts 22, 80, and 81, to find out more.

2. **Is your melody underscoring the emotion of the song?**
    Remember, melody communicates emotion. If yours is fighting the lyric, you may be preventing your listener from experiencing the full emotional power of your song. Intensify the impact of your song by creating a melody that exaggerates the natural pitch and rhythm of emotional speech. There's more information on this in Shortcuts 76 and 84.

3. **Do you have a good balance of repetition and variation?**
    Check to see if you're repeating the same pitches, phrase lengths, or melodic rhythm patterns too many times. If you are, try varying one of the lines. You could use the same rhythm pattern but change the pitches to create a mix of familiarity and freshness, extend a phrase or divide it into two shorter ones to add interest. See Shortcuts 88 and 90 to learn more.

4. **Are you using too many phrases? How are they organized?**
    The opposite of too much repetition is too much variation. The problem often lies in a group of disorganized melodic rhythm patterns. Using Shortcut 95, identify the melodic rhythm patterns in your song and write down the order in which they occur. Too many phrases scattered around your song will make your melody sound unfocused, wandering, and complicated.

5. **Do you have enough dynamic energy?**
    Check your melody against current hits in the genre you're interested in. Does your melody build and then release tension in ways that are similar to other hits in that genre? If not, or if the effect is weak, try some of the techniques in Shortcut 79 to pump up the dynamics.

6. **Is there plenty of rhythmic interest?**
   If your melody is plodding along at a predictable, even pace, today's listeners will probably lose interest. Try adding some syncopation: emphasize weak beats or upbeats, add a pause where listeners don't expect one, or eliminate a predictable one. To find out how, read Shortcut 89.

7. **Give it the "Fresh Ears" test**
   Record your melody rewriting ideas then take a break and come back later for a "Fresh Ears" test. (There's more on this in Shortcut 115.) Is your melody memorable and catchy, or too complicated and unfocused? As a listener, would you want to hear it again? Did it stick in your mind? If not, try going back to your original melody and go through the rewriting checklist again.

Don't throw anything away until you've got something you like better!

8. **Beat what you already have**
   Rewriting is never about throwing away what you have. At least not until you have something that beats it! It's hard to let go of a melody line or section until you have something better. Then it's easy! Honor what you've created but don't stop working on your melody before you've explored other possibilities. If you don't find something you like better, then go with what you've got.

Do It Now

Go through one of your melodies and apply the rewriting techniques listed in this Shortcut. Don't forget to record your changes, take a break, and come back to listen with fresh ears.

See "Shortcut Resources" on page 261 for information on where to find current music charts, hit songs, lyrics, and legal downloads.

Shortcut #102

Write a New Melody
Using a Ghost Song as a Guide

Practice writing melodies in a contemporary hit song style.

Throughout the melody section of the book, you've been shown ways in which today's songs make use of syncopation, contrast, rhythm patterns, a variety of phrase lengths, and other creative musical concepts. Talking about them is one thing, to really use them and have them available to you as choices *when you're writing a song* takes some practice. You want to *embed* these melodic concepts through repeated use, so you don't have to stop and think about them while you're writing a song.

The best way to get these techniques "under your skin" is to spend time practicing them. "Learning by doing" is the key to picking up these skills. Here's an excellent exercise for acquiring hit song melody writing skills such as syncopation, contrast, and organized rhythm patterns: Write a new melody to a hit song track using the chords and the ghost song melody as a guide. Remember, the hit song is protected by copyright. Do not use any of the melody or lyric of the hit song in any song of your own. This exercise is for practice in acquiring *techniques and skills* you will use to write original melodies of your own.

Embed these techniques so they're available as choices while you're writing.

Write a new melody to a ghost song

1. **Find a hit song track**
    To do this exercise, you'll need to be able to hear the chords of a hit song without the lyrics or melody. There are a few ways you can do this.

    Karaoke CD and DVDs: You can do this exercise using a karaoke CD or DVD. There are plenty to choose from and many recent hit songs are available. You can find karaoke CDs and DVDs at big online music retailers or order them through your local record store. If you can, try to avoid ones with a lot of background vocals; you're primarily interested in the instrumental track.

    Play the chords yourself on keyboard or guitar: You can play the song yourself. Just look for the chords in fake books or sheet music, both are available through music stores, online sellers, and many libraries. Better yet, use your ears and learn the chords by listening to the track. Try to preserve the tempo and groove of the ghost song. If you have a music software program with a library of drum loops, look for a loop that suggests the tempo and feel of the original hit song recording. Many keyboards have built in rhythm loops and some allow you to simply enter the chord names to create a complete arrangement.

Use a software program: There are some inexpensive music software programs that will provide rhythm and chord arrangements if you enter the chord names. See "Shortcut Resources" on page 261 for some suggestions.

2. **Use the ghost song melody as a guide**
Once the song track is playing, sing the original melody and lyric to a verse and chorus until you feel comfortable. Now you're ready to have some fun. Start changing the ghost song melody by focusing on one aspect at a time.

➢ **Change the pitches:** First, change the pitches of the notes; go up instead of down, start a line on a higher or lower note, or stay on the same note when the hit song melody is moving. You're not aiming to write a great new melody at this point. Just get a feel for changing a pitch while keeping the rhythm and phrasing of the ghost song melody.

➢ **Shorten or lengthen a line:** Drop out the last note or two of a line or add a couple of notes then continue on with the melody. If you add notes, make up a couple of words to sing to them. You can try splitting a long line into two short phrases. Try making up a new lyric for those phrases.

➢ **Play with the rhythm of the melody:** Now, change some of the rhythm patterns in the melody. Hold out a short note or shorten a long note. Try breaking up a long note into several short ones. Turn a series of short notes into a single long note. If the ghost song repeats a rhythm pattern, you repeat your new one. This will preserve the overall organization of the melody.

The lyric and melody of the hit song are protected by copyright. This exercise is for practice only.

➢ **Change the lyric:** You can start changing the lyric at any time. Just begin singing new words of your own as you change the melody. Let your new lyric lead you toward melody ideas.

You're acquiring new skills that will soon feel natural

Using a ghost song track is like putting training wheels on a bicycle until you get the hang of riding it on your own. You're practicing new ideas and techniques that will expand your songwriting skills and open creative doors. Do this exercise with one or two ghost songs. The next time you write an original song, you'll notice a difference!

Do It Now

Choose a hit song to use as a ghost song then follow the steps described in this Shortcut to create a new melody.

See "Shortcut Resources" on page 261 for information on where to find current music charts, hit songs, lyrics, and legal downloads.

Shortcut #103

Write a New Melody to Your Ghost Song Lyric

Use the lyric you wrote to a ghost song and create an original melody.

Before you can jump into this Shortcut, you'll need to create an original lyric to a ghost song melody. If you haven't already done that, check out Shortcut 73 "Write Your Lyric to a Ghost Song Melody."

Once you've written your lyric, you're ready to drop out the ghost melody and write a new one of your own, keeping both the chords and structure of the ghost song. By the time you're done, you'll have experience writing both lyrics and melody in a style that's current and successful. Remember, the melody and lyric of the ghost song are protected by copyright. This is an exercise; you may not use any part of the ghost melody or lyric in a song of your own.

Use your lyric to help you create a new melody

Because you used the ghost song melody to write your lyric, it may be difficult to imagine a different melody with those words. But guess what: *Melodies are not written in stone. They can be changed!* This is one of the most important lessons you'll learn from doing this exercise.

1. **Use the rhythm and pitch of speech to write a new chorus melody**
    In Shortcut 76, you learned how to create the raw material for a melody by exaggerating the rhythm and pitch of spoken words. That's a great way to start a new melody for your lyric.

    Speak the first lyric line of your chorus. Now say it with more emotion. Really mean it! Say it a couple more times. Notice how the pitches move up and down, even if it's just a little bit. Notice where the pauses occur. Try exaggerating the pitches while preserving the pauses and the natural rhythm of your speech. Now try singing this while playing the chords of the ghost song.

    You should be hearing a new melody that *could* work for the first line of your chorus. You may not like it yet but it's a place to start. Remember, at this point, you're creating the *raw material* for your melody. Move on to the second line of your chorus. If the ghost song repeated the first line melody, you may want to do the same. Otherwise, try the same process you used on the first line; explore the melody embedded in your spoken lyric.

    This is the raw material for a melody.

2. **Now use the Shortcuts**
    When you reach the third line of your chorus, you've got something to build on. For instance, if you have repetition in your first two lines, you'll probably

want to vary Line 3. Shortcut 94 can show you how to surprise your listener on this line. Read the Shortcut on writing a chorus melody—Shortcut 82—for more ideas.

3. **Change a line that's too close to the ghost melody**
Once you start working on your new melody, the ghost song melody will begin to fade away. However, if you find yourself writing a line that's similar to the ghost song melody and you can't seem to shake it off, you can make a conscious decision to just do something different. If the ghost melody is an ascending line, you could try a descending one. If the ghost song is hovering around the same note, try an interval jump.

4. **Write the verse and bridge melodies**
You can go through the same process for your verse as you did for the chorus. Since verses tend to be more conversational than choruses, it may be more difficult to hear the pitch and rhythm of the spoken lines. (The more emotional a line is, the more melodic content it has naturally.) You could focus more on "phrase-ology" and less on pitch and rhythm. Shortcut 75 can get you going.

(!) *The lyric and melody of the hit song are protected by copyright. This exercise is for practice only.*

Again, if you have a line that's sticking close to the ghost song melody, make a conscious decision to change it. Move it up or down by a couple of notes, shift the starting point of the line earlier or later (Shortcut 91), or emphasize an upbeat or weak beat (see Shortcut 89).

There's no "right" melody

Always keep one thing in mind: there's no single "right" melody. There are many options and choices open to you and many that will work. Don't lock yourself into something too soon. Feel free to explore and create new solutions to problems.

Do It Now

Use a lyric you've written to a ghost song melody and create a new melody using the method described in this Shortcut.

PART SIX

Shortcuts to Hit Chords & Grooves

To write hit songs, the only musical skill you need

is the ability to play six chords on guitar or keyboard.

That's it! These six chords are the ones that are used

in a majority of today's hit songs.

Understanding the underlying "groove"

will enable you to build on the

rhythmic feel that listeners love ...

Shortcut #104

Chord Basics:
Know the Songwriter Chords

Just six chords, that's all you need!

The majority of today's hit songs use between four and six chords. You can learn to play these "songwriter chords" in less than an hour and start using them in your songs in about the same amount of time. If you're a beginner you may lack finesse but don't let that stop you. If you want to get started writing chords for your songs, you can. Are there ways to dress these chords up and make them sound more sophisticated than just banging away at them? Yes. (Find out more in Shortcut 108.) But in the meantime, with six basic chords, you've got everything you *need* to begin writing solid songs.

The six songwriter chords in the key of C major are:

> C major
> D minor
> E minor
> F major
> G major
> A minor

Play the chords by using the diagrams on the next page.

If you have a keyboard or guitar, you can play these chords right now.

Keyboard players, on the following page you'll see six diagrams of a keyboard with the chord names beside each diagram. Orient yourself by looking for the same pattern of black keys on your keyboard that you see in the diagram—two in one group, three in the other. Put your fingers where the dots are to form each chord. Now, you're playing the songwriter chords in the key of C. ("In the key of C" means that the notes in these chords can all be found in a C major scale. Every major scale has its own set of six songwriter chords. See Shortcut 106 to learn more about scales and keys.)

Guitar players, your set of six songwriter chords is also on the following page. Tune your strings to the standard EADGBE tuning. The low E string is the string on the left side of each diagram. The top fret is the first fret on your guitar. Put your fingers where the dots are.

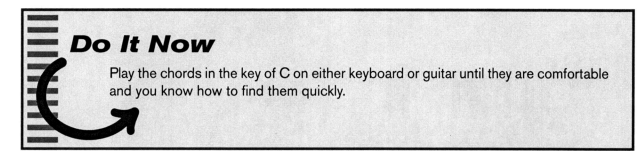

Do It Now

Play the chords in the key of C on either keyboard or guitar until they are comfortable and you know how to find them quickly.

Songwriter Chords in the Key of C

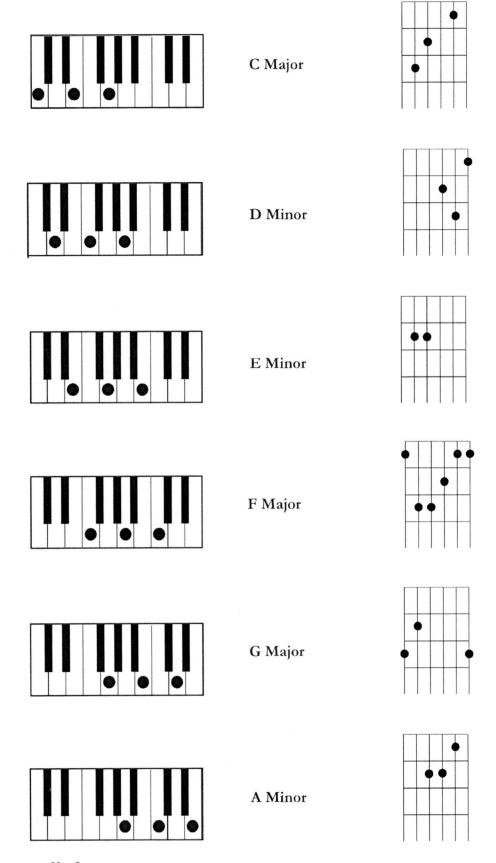

C Major

D Minor

E Minor

F Major

G Major

A Minor

Shortcut #105

Chord Basics: Using the Songwriter Chords

Use four chords to play a mega-hit song now.

Musicians often make jokes about "three-chord songs" but successful songwriters know that many three- and four-chord songs have risen to the top of the charts and stayed there long after their more complicated friends have sunk into elegant, sophisticated history. From Nickelback's "Photograph" to The Fray's "How to Save a Life," four-chord songs have proven to be big hits.

Play a four-chord hit song

Here's how simple a hit song chord progression can be: If you read the previous Shortcut and did the "Do It Now" exercise, you can already play the chords to several hit songs. For example, here's a generic chord progression that's used in many songs, including Santana's hit "Into the Night" and the Red Hot Chili Peppers' "Dani California."

| A minor | G | D minor | A minor |

Listen to recordings of these songs and try playing along, changing chords when the song does.

Play a four-chord hit song!

Move the chords higher or lower

There are many hits that share similar chord progressions and almost all are based on the six songwriter chords. However, these chords may be played a few steps higher or lower. In order to play along using only the chords you learned in the previous Shortcut, you'll need to be able to "transpose" the chords, moving them up or down to match what you hear on the recording.

Most electronic keyboards can transpose chords for you; all you have to do is tell the keyboard whether to move the chords up or down and how much. (Read the manual to find out how to access the Transpose function.) Guitar players can use a *capo* to move chords up, but not down.

To see how this works, transpose your keyboard UP three notes. On the guitar, put your capo on the third fret. Now, play the following chord progression:

C | G | A minor | F

Practice these chords until you feel comfortable, then play along with a recording of one of the hit songs that uses this progression, such as the introduction and verse of "You're Beautiful" by James Blunt. As you listen to the recording, change chords along with it. This is a great exercise, not only for improving your playing skills but also training your ears to listen to chord progressions.

If you want to keep on learning chords and playing more songs, there are plenty of instruction books, DVDs, CDs, and Internet sites where you can learn more. See "Shortcut Resources" on page 261 for some suggestions. Consider taking a few lessons from a live human. Be sure to mention that you want to learn chords. *You don't need to read notes because you're going to be singing the melody line.* Ask to be taught the chords "in a couple of keys" and how to play the chords to a few of your favorite songs.

Do It Now

1. Play along with a recording of any of the songs mentioned in the Shortcut until you feel you can play it without the track.

2. If you really want to stretch yourself, try writing a verse or chorus of your own to these chords. It doesn't have to be great or even very good. Just do it to prove that you can. (Who knows, you may surprise yourself!)

See "Shortcut Resources" on page 261 for information on where to find current music charts, hit songs, lyrics, and legal downloads.

Shortcut #106

Chord Basics: Using Chord Families

Get to know the chords in a couple of keys.

When you sit down at a keyboard to write a song, do you sometimes feel overwhelmed? How do you choose which notes to play? Do you try the "hunt and peck" method until you find something that works? The truth is, there are families of notes and chords, called *keys*, that will help you narrow your choices down to a very manageable few.

Guitar players, you have an advantage over keyboard players; you probably started by learning one or two of these chord families as you played songs. But you may not have learned why, for instance, the chords C, F, and G are found together in one song but don't turn up at all in another song. If you've got access to a keyboard, take a look at it because it's the best way to understand the concept of chord families or *keys*.

Chords belong to groups called keys. A key is based on a scale.

The C scale chord family

We've all heard piano players practicing endless scales. You might even have done it yourself when you were a kid. I did it and hated every minute of it! My fingers never seemed to get any better at it. What I didn't realize was that scales are the doorways to chord families. Once I understood that, my opinion of scales definitely went up! Let me show you how it works.

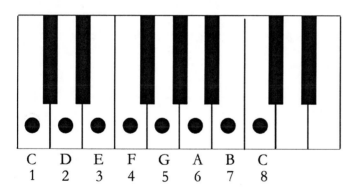

The dots show you the scale of C major. The numbers show you where the scale starts (1) and ends (8). The chords in the key of C major are made up *only* of the notes found in the C major scale. If you look at the first Shortcut in this section, you'll see that the six songwriter chords in the key of C use only the notes in the C scale. You'll also see that each chord is named after one of the first six notes in the C scale: C, D minor, E minor, F, G, A minor.

Chords in the key of C can only use the notes in a C scale!

Now, here's something cool. If you know the G scale, you can now work out the songwriter chords in the key of G, just like you did in the C scale, by counting up the six notes from G: G, A minor, B minor, C, D, E minor. You can then find out how to play these chords by referring to a chord finder or chord book.

How to use these chord families or keys

The scale and its chords are called a *key*. The vast majority of hit songs use the six songwriter chords in a single key, like the key of C. This makes it much easier to find the chords for your song. You don't have to hunt and peck all over the keyboard or guitar neck. Just "audition" each of the six chords in the key you are using until you find the one you want.

Think in terms of chord families to help you with your choices.

If you learn a few keys and their related chords—for instance, the chords in the key of C and G—you can write a song in either of those keys. You could even write a song with a verse in C and a chorus in G! It happens.

Now, when you look at a keyboard, instead of an array of notes, you should start to see a scale and its related songwriter chords. That's all you're interested in. If you play guitar, learn the chords in key groups: the chords in the key of G, chords in the key of F, etc.

Some hit songs do, of course, use one or two chords from outside of their immediate chord family. Think of them as eccentric aunts and uncles. You can get to know them later. For now, the songwriter chords in a couple of keys are the ones you want to get in tight with.

Do It Now

1. Search online or buy a chord finder and learn the songwriter chords in the key of G. (See "Shortcut Resources" on page 261 for recommendations.)

2. Write a song using the chords in the key of C or the key of G. Do it in 20 minutes. Don't worry about whether it's good or bad; just do it.

Shortcut #107

Chord Basics: I, IV, V

Take the chord journey.

Hundreds of hit songs have been built on just three chords, beginning with the traditional Country and Rock songs of the 1950s, right up to the present. In the key of C, the three chords are C, F, and G. These are the chords that are based on the first note, the fourth note, and the fifth note of a C scale. That's why you hear them referred to as the *one, four,* and *five* chords. They're usually written in roman numerals: I, IV, and V.

These three chords can take you far, providing you with a home base, a voyage, and a return ticket! Think of your chord progression as a journey. It's going somewhere and taking you and your listener along for the ride.

Home vs. leading chords: Using I, IV, V

Within a key, there are some chords that want to keep moving; call them "leading chords" because they always want to lead you somewhere else. Other chords feel like they want to stay where they are and not go anywhere; call them the "home chords," because they create a sense of journey's end.

In every key, the I (one) chord is a home chord. It wants to remain right where it is. There's no tension, no need to change. The IV (four) chord is a leading chord; it's unsettled, it wants to keep moving, often toward the V (five) chord. The V chord is another leading chord; it's restless, never holding still. It wants to lead you back to the I chord again. This series—I, IV, V, I—is the most basic chord "journey" you can take. A chord journey can be referred to as a "chord progression."

I = Home base
IV = On the move
V = Return ticket

In your song's chord progression, try teasing the listener by hanging around the leading chords for a while before going home. A hit song might start on the IV chord, move to the V, back to the IV *then* go to the I. There are many different journeys. This is where your taste, your ear, and your knowledge of hit songs comes into play.

Do It Now

Learn the chord progressions to some of your favorite hit songs and study the chord journey. Notice how the journey begins and ends, and where it travels in between.

See "Shortcut Resources" on page 261 for information on where to find current music charts, hit songs, lyrics, and legal downloads.

Shortcut #108

Get the Most Out of
Four- and Five-Chord Progressions!

Make your progressions interesting and contemporary without overwriting.

So, you're the reader who glanced at the previous four Shortcuts and said, "Hey, I already know all this stuff! This is for beginners!" You're right; that was for folks who are not familiar with a musical instrument. You, on the other hand, are a guitar god or a piano wizard and you know a lot of chords in a lot of keys. Surprisingly, *that* may not be a total plus. That's why this Shortcut is just for you.

Current hit songs in all mainstream commercial genres tend to stick to the basic six songwriter chords in a single key and lean heavily on repetition. For accomplished musicians like you there's a real temptation to overwrite. However, in this case, more is *not* better. In big four-chord hits like The Fray's "How To Save a Life," the basic approach works best. Why is that?

The BIG SECRET to using repetitive chord progressions

BIG SECRET!!!

The secret to the success of today's repetitive chord progressions lies in the way the melody relates to them. The chord progression often provides the solid, steady foundation on which a rhythmically interesting melody can be built. Nickelback's "Photograph" and "Far Away" are great examples of rock-steady, repeated four-chord patterns with melodic phrases that begin *in between* the chord changes. This is the trick that keeps these repetitive chord progressions interesting: the melody *doesn't* emphasize the beats on which the chords change. You can hear this technique used in hit after hit.

Add color and life to your chords

In addition to the big trick mentioned above, there are a few more things you can do to bring these four-chord progressions to life.

Bring a simple, repeated chord progression to life with these ideas.

> **Use cluster chords**
> Cluster chords are chords that have more than the standard three notes of a major or minor chord and whose notes tend to be clustered very close together, creating minor or major 2nds within the chord. Use the six songwriter chords but enhance the color or create an atmospheric sound by using "add 2"or a suspended fourth. Chords with extensions, such as a ninth or thirteenth, are sometimes found in the R&B/Soul genre. You won't hear them in Pop or Country, so be careful where you use them.

➤ **Sing the chord extension in the melody line**
In Rascal Flatts' "What Hurts the Most" the opening note of the melody line is the seventh of an F minor seventh chord. As the song progresses, you can hear more instances of extensions in the lead melody line plus cluster chords like D flat add 2. This is a very successful Country crossover hit song that sustains interest and momentum with a four-chord progression.

➤ **Use motion in the root note**
This is an old standby but it's still a winner. An ascending or descending bass line can create a richer sound within a limited chord progression.

➤ **Keep the forward momentum going**
Current hits in all genres tend to avoid resolving the energy until the end of the chorus (if then). When the progression resolves to the root chord, the melody often starts a phrase, keeping the momentum going rather than allowing the song to come to rest.

Don't overwrite!

One of the greatest temptations for players who have mastered an instrument is to "show what you know." When it comes to songwriting, this can get you into a lot of trouble. For instance, if you write a juicy chord progression with a lot of harmonic movement through parallel majors, deceptive resolutions of secondary dominants, and jazz-inflected chord extensions, you may end up losing listeners. They just can't keep up with you. Today it's all about well-organized, repetitive chord progressions with a fresh relationship to the melody. This is a challenging style with a lot of room for creativity. It's worth exploring.

Limit those special chords to one or two per song at most.

Strong, out-of-the-key chord changes are used in today's hits, but be sparing with them. Try to limit yourself to one per song. Check out "You're Gonna Miss This" (Trace Adkins) to hear a four-chord song with a quietly ear-grabbing chord change at a peak moment in the chorus (the C major on "look around"). Daughtry's "Over You" has a catchy chord twist in both the verse and the chorus, but it's the *same one*. When in doubt, keep the chords simple and make the melody do the work!

Do It Now

1. Listen to hit songs in a mainstream genre—Pop, Rock, R&B/Soul, or Country— and check out the chord progressions. Notice how the lead melody line works in and around the chord progression—rhythmically and harmonically—to add interest. If there are any chords outside the key, note where they are and how often they're used.

2. Check the chord progressions in your own songs to see if they need to be updated. See if there are some changes you could make in your melody that would complement and add interest to your chord progression.

See "Shortcut Resources" on page 261 for information on where to find current music charts, hit songs, lyrics, and legal downloads.

Shortcut #109

Become Familiar
With the Chords in Your Genre
It's a long way from Country to R&B/Soul.

Every music genre has a distinctive sound. Rock songs don't sound like Urban-Dance tracks. Country songs don't sound like R&B/Soul songs. While some of this can be accounted for by differences in production (including the underlying drum rhythms), a big contributor to the characteristic sound of a particular genre is the kind of chords that are used in the songs and the way they are used.

Study the way chords are used in your genre

As with melody and lyrics, the best way to learn how chords are used in a particular genre is to look closely at hit songs in that genre. Ask yourself …

- How many different chords are used?

- How many of those are among the six songwriter chords of a single key?

- Is there a key change? Are the chords in the new key contained in the six songwriter chords of the new key?

Chord style and progressions help to define a genre.

- How frequently do the chords change? Once per measure on average? More often than that or less often on average?

- How much repetition is there of two-, three-, or four-chord progressions?

- How many three-note chords are played over a different root note, for example C/G (read as C over G)?

- How many three-note chords (major or minor) are used? For you musicians, how many chords have extensions (ninths or elevenths) or suspensions (sus 4, sus 2) or added notes (add 2)?

Once you have the answers to some of these questions, you'll have a good idea of how chords are used in your genre. Of course every song varies somewhat but if you stray too far away, you'll lose the characteristic sound that appeals to fans of the genre. Country songs rarely use a complex chord like B minor seventh (flat 5) but the R&B/Soul genre *does* use chords like that. Frequently! To hear the difference in chord styles, check out John Legend's "Ordinary People" or Mary J. Blige's "Be Without You" and compare the chords in those songs with any current Country or Rock hit. To give your song a clear stylistic focus, make sure you stay true to the chord choices of your genre.

Learn chord progressions in your genre

Your best teachers are the hit songs in your genre. You can learn the chords by listening to the hit song itself or get them from fake books or sheet music. A fake book is a compilation that includes the lyrics, chords, and lead melody lines of dozens of hit songs. (It does not include a written piano arrangement, only the chord names.) You can buy fake books at online booksellers, music stores, and find them at some libraries. You can buy sheet music online and download it immediately. There are Web sites that offer chords for free but they don't have the publisher's permission to post them. The chords on these sites, especially for the R&B/Soul genre, are vastly oversimplified and often just plain wrong. If you're serious about songwriting, these sites are not recommended.

If you don't know how to play all the chords in a song, look for a "chord finder" online or buy one of the many books, CDs, or DVDs that show you how to play chords. See "Shortcut Resources" on page 261 for some suggestions. Consider taking a few lessons with a music teacher. Just be sure to make it clear that you want to learn the chords *in your genre.*

Do It Now

1. Study the chords in recent hit songs in your genre. (Use the Song List on page 265 for song suggestions by genre.) Compare a few songs in different genres. Answer some of the questions in the list included in this Shortcut.

2. Now, check a few songs of your own to make sure your chords are working to support your genre. If you're a singer-songwriter or band, the chords should be consistent with the genre in which you're working. If you're a songwriter and plan to pitch songs in several genres, make certain that each song is clearly within a specific genre.

See "Shortcut Resources" on page 261 for information on where to find current music charts, hit songs, lyrics, and legal downloads.

Shortcut #110

Base Your Song
On an Existing Chord Progression

You don't have to reinvent the wheel.

If you're writing your song on piano or guitar, you're probably making up a chord progression while you work on your melody and lyrics. That means you're focusing on *three* different song elements at the same time: melody, lyrics, and chords. This can be risky; like juggling chain saws. If any one of them crashes, you're in trouble. To make things easier, how about postponing the process of writing a new chord progression until later (see Shortcut 97) or using an existing progression. Then, you can give all your attention to melody and lyrics. That's one less chain saw!

Write to an existing chord progression

Consider using a chord progression that has a proven track record. There are a few basic chord progressions that have been around for a long time, such as C, A minor, F, G or C, F, C, G. These progressions are called "ice cream changes" because their sound is so sweet and familiar. These and similar generic chord progressions—ones that stick to the six songwriter chords—are not copyrighted. They've been used in many songs. For example, John Mayer's hit "Say" shares its simple C, F, C, G chord progression with the traditional hymn "Amazing Grace."

Freshen up an existing chord progression.

Common chord progressions like these often turn up in early Rock and Country songs, as well as traditional Folk songs, hymns, and songs in the public domain. You can use one of these generic chord progressions as a basis for your song, then change some of the chords to freshen it up.

Write out the chords to a traditional Folk song or any song that uses a standard three- or four-chord progression. Play the chords a few times until you feel comfortable. Try changing the order of the chords or holding a chord for an extra measure. As you get a feel for the chords and where they change, start focusing on melody ideas. Experiment with interesting ways to fit a melody into the chords.

If your common chord progression comes from a copyrighted song, be sure you don't use any of that song's melody or lyric. Stay away from the instrumental arrangement, as well. Any repeated instrumental riffs or hooks are also strictly off limits. The chords are all you're looking for!

Shortcut #111

Choose a Tempo That Supports Your Message

Use tempo to get your listener in sync with your song.

Here's a very short music lesson. It won't take long, that's a promise, and then I'll show you something really cool.

Tempo: what it is

In music, the word *tempo* refers to the speed of the underlying pulse that runs from the beginning to the end of a piece of music.

In classical music, this rate of speed can vary within a piece of music—there are a lot of Italian words that tell an orchestra conductor when to speed up or slow down. But in contemporary mainstream songwriting, it's a very different story! Today's audiences are hooked on an unvarying, regular pulse; they become uncomfortable if the tempo changes during a song. You won't hear a hit song on the current charts that changes the steady, regular pace of the underlying beat. *When it comes to hit song tempo, the rule is: Steady on!*

Use a steady, unchanging pulse. Don't vary the tempo.

Don't confuse the tempo of a song with the rhythm pattern of the drums. Drum patterns can be complex and they can change over the course of a song, *but the underlying, steady pulse never wavers.* Even when the drums pause—for instance to add a moment of dramatic silence—the pulse is still ticking along underneath; it's just silent for a moment. When the drums start up again, they will do so *on the beat.*

Finding the tempo of a song

You can find the tempo of a song by tapping your foot along with the music. Tempo is described in terms of beats per minute or BPM. This phrase means just what it says; if you tap your foot to the regular pulse of a song and count the number of taps that occur within a minute, you come up with the BPM. If you have a metronome, or music software with a metronome built in, it will be easier to track the BPM. Play your song and adjust the metronome until the clicks are playing in time with the underlying, steady beat of the song. The metronome setting will indicate the BPM.

Tempo talks to your body

Okay, that's all the academic music stuff you need to know. Now comes the cool part! You have a natural metronome inside your body; it's your heart. It keeps a steady beat, a tempo that changes depending on your physical and emotional state. Your resting heartbeat is generally between 60 to 80 BPM. This is the rate at which your heart beats when you're relaxed. The rate increases when you're physically active or when you're excited, anxious, elated, angry, or afraid.

Have you noticed that when you're feeling stressed out, playing a piece of music with a slow tempo relaxes and calms you down? That's not just a psychological effect; it's a physical one as well. Your heart rate is gradually slowing down, trying to match the beat of the music. This is called "entrainment" (the synchronization of an internal biological rhythm to an external rhythm). It's how Ambient Chill music chills us out. Of course, it works the other way, too: If you're at rest and a song with a fast tempo starts playing, your heart rate will begin to speed up. You'll start to feel more energetic and alert. That's why a Dance-Pop track like Madonna's "4 Minutes" has a tempo that's much faster—132 BPM—than your resting heartbeat. The track makes you feel energized, it gets your heart moving, and soon the rest of your body feels like dancing along.

Choose the right tempo for your song

Use tempo to underscore the message of your lyric.

The appropriate tempo for your song is one that puts your listeners in sync with the song's emotional message. If your song is introspective or thoughtful, consider a slow tempo—70 to 90 BPM—a la Christina Aguilera's "Beautiful" (76 BPM). Sensual grooves also work at this tempo; 50 Cent's "In Da Club" at 90 BPM is a good example. To add emotional energy, try 112 to 130; most Country and Pop hits fall in this range. For a solid, body-moving dance track, try 132 to 140. If it's a passionate, all-stops-out rocker, try something faster; most of Nickelback, Foo Fighters, Seether, and Daughtry's songs are all well up in the 150 BPM range. For a high energy, fast moving Country feel, check out Dierks Bentley's "What Was I Thinkin'" at 165 BPM!

Here's something else to keep in mind when choosing a tempo. If your song has a busy, fast-paced lyric style, consider using one of the slower tempos, 94 to 100 BPM, to give your listeners enough time to hear what you're saying. Jason Mraz's "Remedy (I Won't Worry)" is a good example at 94 BPM. You can give these slower tempos plenty of momentum by using some of the rhythmic feels described in Shortcut 112.

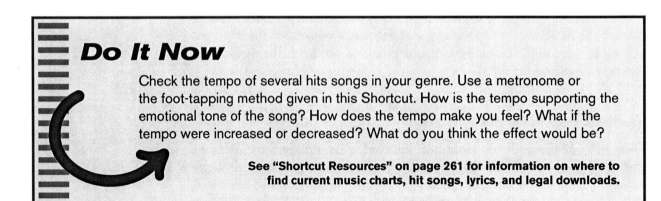

Do It Now

Check the tempo of several hits songs in your genre. Use a metronome or the foot-tapping method given in this Shortcut. How is the tempo supporting the emotional tone of the song? How does the tempo make you feel? What if the tempo were increased or decreased? What do you think the effect would be?

See "Shortcut Resources" on page 261 for information on where to find current music charts, hit songs, lyrics, and legal downloads.

Shortcut #112

Groove Basics: Learn the Grooves the Hit Songs Use

Duple and quadruple beat divisions add interest and momentum.

What is it that makes us feel like swaying and dancing when we listen to music? Why is it easier to jog with music than without it? If it's just the steady pulse of the song's tempo, why doesn't the regular click of a metronome at 120 BPM make us feel like dancing? *Because a metronome can't "groove."* It only keeps track of the steady, evenly-paced beats of a song. To get a groove going, you need to divide up those beats in interesting ways that would drive a metronome crazy!

Find out more about BPM and tempo in Shortcut III.

Finding the basic groove

In Shortcut 74, you learned how to count the underlying beats of a song in groups of four. (Most hit songs are based on this grouping.) In every group of four, the first beat of the group is emphasized; this is Beat 1. It's followed by three more steady beats that are also emphasized, but to a lesser degree. Together, these four beats are the ones the metronome counts. There's no groove here, just a steady pulse. As soon as these beats are divided in half, however, things get more interesting. If you add an "and" between each beat, you get a basic groove that looks like this:

1 *and* 2 *and* 3 *and* 4 *and.*

This is called an 8th-note groove or *duple* feel. It has eight subdivisions per measure; each of the four beats is divided into two. This groove forms the backbone of Folk styles such as Irish jigs and Polka music, as well as many Rock songs of the 1970s and '80s. A famous example of a song with a duple feel is "Every Breath You Take" by The Police with Sting's steady, pulsing bass line laying down the 8th-note groove. Today, you can hear the duple feel in Rock hits like "The Pretender" by the Foo Fighters and "It's Not My Time" by 3 Doors Down.

An 8th-note groove, or duple feel, divides each beat in half.

Divide the beat to add interest and momentum

When you divide a beat, you add more activity and a feeling of momentum. Test this for yourself, right now. Count to four at a slow, steady pace. Then count to four using the same pace, but add the "and" in between each beat. Try going back and forth—counting with and without the "and." You'll feel the subtle increase in energy and momentum when you use the duple feel.

More beat division

So, if you can add interest and momentum by dividing a beat in half, what would happen if you created more divisions within each beat? How about dividing each beat into four? Would it result in even more interest and momentum? You bet it would!

A 16th-note groove, or quadruple feel, divides each beat into four parts.

Just as you added the word "and" between each beat to create a duple feel, you can add more syllables between each beat to create another feel called a 16th-note groove or *quadruple* feel. The nonsense syllables *"e"* (pronounced like a long "e" vowel sound) and *"uh"* (pronounced just like it looks) are added to the "and." Here's how a measure of quadruple feel looks:

1 e and uh, 2 e and uh, 3 e and uh, 4 e and uh.

Each measure has sixteen subdivisions with each beat divided into four. *This is the feel that's featured in the majority of today's hit songs.* Among the Pop hits using this groove are Maroon 5's "Makes Me Wonder," KT Tunstall's "Black Horse and the Cherry Tree," and Ashlee Simpson's "Pieces of Me." Many Country hits are now based on this feel, including Toby Keith's "Love Me If You Can," Taylor Swift's "Should've Said No," and Trace Adkins' "You're Gonna Miss This." Almost all songs in the Hip-Hop and R&B/Soul genres rely on the quadruple feel; it's characteristic of the genre.

Why the quadruple feel is used

Adding *"e and uh"* between each beat can seem like a lot of syllables to cram in, especially if the tempo is fairly fast. There's a lot going on and that's exactly the point! By using this groove, a song can create plenty of activity and momentum, even at slower speeds. Melody lines can start on any of the syllables between beats, giving today's melodies a lot of interesting choices and fresh rhythmic feels. See Shortcut 113 for practice in counting and using duple and quadruple feels.

Which BPM and groove is it?

Groove is sometimes in the ear of the beholder. In today's Rock genre, there are times when the basic, emphasized beats of a song can be counted slowly with a lot of divisions between beats—a quadruple feel, or counted twice as fast with fewer divisions—a duple feel. In other words, Nickelback's "Rock Star" could be at 72 BPM or 144 BPM (exactly twice as fast). At 72 BPM count four divisions to each beat (1 *e and uh*), at 144 BPM count two divisions per beat (1 *and*). When it comes to writing your own songs, it's a matter of what feels right to you and which is easier for you to work with.

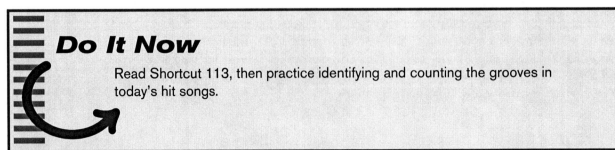

Do It Now

Read Shortcut 113, then practice identifying and counting the grooves in today's hit songs.

Shortcut #113

Get Your Song Into the Groove

Build on the underlying rhythmic feel of today's hits.

The previous Shortcut demonstrated how to find and count a groove, specifically duple and quadruple rhythms. However, that's only part of the story. To really understand how grooves work in today's hit songs, your body needs to feel it. This is one of those things—like riding a bicycle—you must *do* in order to really get a handle on it.

Listen, feel, and count along: Duple Rhythms

A straight-ahead duple feel is hard to find these days in any genre other than Rock. To hear it and get a feel for it, use the "1 and 2 and 3 and 4 and" pattern and count along with a song like "Radio Nowhere" by Bruce Springsteen or The Fray's "Over My Head (Cable Car)." Start by counting the four emphasized beats, then add the "and" in between. Read Shortcut 74 and 112 if you're not sure how to do this.

To understand a groove, listen to it, feel it, and count along.

For a duple feel with a contemporary, alternative edge, check out "So Happy" by Theory of a Deadman, or Seether's "Rise Above This." You'll hear the fast, steady chug-chugging of the "1 and 2 and 3 and 4 and" duple rhythm in the bass and low acoustic guitars.

Listen, feel, and count along: Quadruple Rhythms

Unlike the duple feel, the quadruple feel is *everywhere;* you'll find it in hit songs in every mainstream, commercial genre. Also, unlike the duple feel with its even, steady beat, many of today's songs "swing" the quadruple feel, giving it a body-swaying feel.

To count a quadruple feel, use the "1-e-and-uh, 2-e-and-uh, 3-e-and-uh, 4-e-and-uh" pattern. Start by counting the four emphasized beats (Beat 1, 2, 3, and 4), then fill in the rest of the pattern as you count along with some of these songs: "Truth Is" (Fantasia), "You're Beautiful" (James Blunt), "Love Me If You Can" (Toby Keith), "Makes Me Wonder" (Maroon 5), and "Dani California" (Red Hot Chili Peppers).

Included in the list above is at least one song from each mainstream commercial genre to show you that they *all* use the quadruple feel with more or less "swing" in it. If you're aiming for a hit song, consider using this wonderful, fluid groove. Listeners love it!

Finding a groove to write to

Once you begin counting along with the rhythmic feel of a hit song, you'll notice that the melody stays within the groove, using and emphasizing only those beats and beat divisions found in the underlying rhythm. Although the groove of your song will be interpreted in the production phase by the drums, bass, and guitars, it's important to write your song with a rhythmic feel in mind *so your melody can take full advantage of it!*

GUITAR: If you write your songs on guitar, learn a few hit songs that use the swing quadruple feel, like Mat Kearney's "Nothing Left to Lose" or James Blunt's "You're Beautiful." Play along with these songs until you can comfortably reproduce the rhythmic feel on guitar. Then write a song of your own using that groove.

KEYBOARD: Try using a drum loop to provide rhythmic feel; this will leave you free to chord along and not have to worry about playing a groove. You can find drum loops in music software programs (see "Shortcut Resources" on page 261 for suggestions). Many keyboards come with a built-in library of drum grooves. Before you buy a keyboard, audition these loops to see if you like them. Try counting along with these loops and grooves to see if they have the kind of quadruple feel you hear in today's hits.

Use a ghost song groove

You can use a ghost song to provide a groove. Learn to play the chords of the ghost song and play along to the track, or use a karaoke version of the song. When you can play along comfortably, turn down the volume level of the ghost song so you can still hear the beat and you can sing louder than the track. If you want, you can turn off the track and work on your song for a while. Then, whenever you think you might be losing the rhythmic feel, play the track again as a reminder.

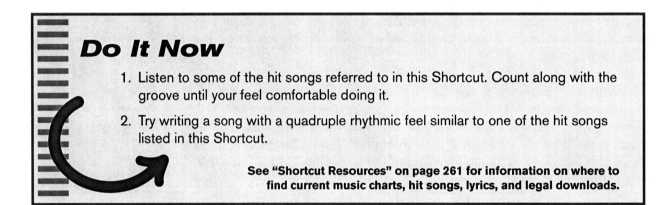

Do It Now

1. Listen to some of the hit songs referred to in this Shortcut. Count along with the groove until your feel comfortable doing it.

2. Try writing a song with a quadruple rhythmic feel similar to one of the hit songs listed in this Shortcut.

See "Shortcut Resources" on page 261 for information on where to find current music charts, hit songs, lyrics, and legal downloads.

PART SEVEN

Shortcuts to Hit Songs

Take a "whole song" approach.

Allow your song to go through stages

of completion, from raw material to first draft,

then the rewriting stage and, finally, finished song.

At each stage, assess what you want to accomplish

and decide how you will go about it …

Shortcut #114

Give Your Song a Chance to Develop

Give it time. Try different ideas. Shape it and craft it.

Imagine this scenario: Michelangelo is standing in his studio staring at a gigantic block of raw marble. He takes a couple of whacks at it with a chisel and hammer. Just then some guy named Lorenzo walks in. "Hey Mike," he says, "that's really ugly." Michelangelo turns to him, gives him a withering stare, and declares, "It's not done yet!"

It's easy to forget that a song can be "not done yet." When you expect a song to sound great right from the start, you don't allow it to go through a raw, development stage. Instead, the melody that comes to you first is the one you want to use, just as it is. Perhaps you rewrite the lyric a little, but you don't want to lose the magic, so you keep most of it. That's it. Then you play your song for a publisher or a live audience and their reaction is a little like Lorenzo's. Catastrophe!!! You veer wildly between emotions: "The world is full of idiots!" "I have no talent!" "They just don't recognize my genius!" "I'll never write another song!"

STOP! Your song … is just … not … done … yet.

Give yourself permission to go through a "roughing out" phase. Take what comes to you—like the raw block of marble—but don't confuse that with the finished piece. You are going spend time giving it focus, making sure it communicates what you want to say, and sharpening the melody so that it's memorable and underscores your lyric effectively. It's important to allow your song to go through this developmental stage. It may not sound great, it may not even sound good, but it's part of the process that gives it strength, originality, and allows it to find its own voice.

When you do that, then you're working like Michelangelo, shaping and crafting the stone until it becomes a luminous work of art. What makes you think you can skip that step? Michelangelo wouldn't dream of it!

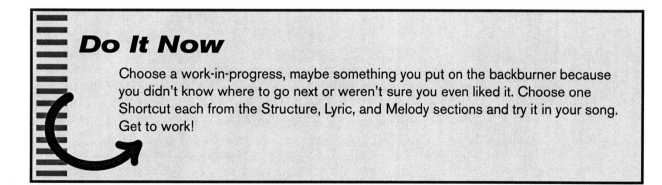

Do It Now

Choose a work-in-progress, maybe something you put on the backburner because you didn't know where to go next or weren't sure you even liked it. Choose one Shortcut each from the Structure, Lyric, and Melody sections and try it in your song. Get to work!

Shortcut #115

Give It the "Fresh Ears" Test

Record rough demos as you write.
Take a break, then come back to listen.

Here's a simple piece of songwriting advice that will save you hours of frustration: *Know when to walk away!*

Why you need to take breaks

As basic as it seems, knowing when to give yourself a break from your song, and how to return to it with "fresh ears" is a crucial songwriting skill. Here's why:

- When you work on a song too long, you lose touch with what appealed to you initially, what got you excited in the first place.

- Creativity requires a lot of energy. When you don't take breaks, your brain gets tired and creativity suffers.

- When you play the same verse or chorus over and over, you lose perspective. The melody and lyric become too familiar and you start changing things to maintain your interest. Big mistake!

There's a method to taking breaks

You'll need to decide for yourself how long you can work before you need a break. Notice when you start to get tired and when the ideas aren't coming. At that point, record a rough version of what you're working on. It can be just a quick vocal version of the melody and words onto your digital or cassette recorder. Be sure to keep time by clapping, tapping your foot or using a metronome. Don't trust that you'll just remember your song later—that's not the point. You're going to come back after your break and listen to what you recorded as if you're hearing it for the first time.

After you record your rough version, *walk away!* Take a 20-minute break. Run an errand, wash dishes, hike around the block. Don't think about the song. The idea is to forget about it for awhile. Give yourself long enough to get the song out of your head.

Take a break and come back with fresh ears.

When you've given yourself a real break from the song, go back and play your recording. Listen to it with fresh ears. Make notes on this first "fresh ears" pass. Does your melody sound too complicated or is it too predictable? Are the lyrics developing the situation in an organized way or are they too hard to follow? Is there enough contrast between sections to make the song structure clear? Try using some of the Shortcuts to help you address any problems you hear. By the time you finish doing that, you'll be ready for another break. Record what you have and … walk away!

Shortcut #116

The "Whole Song" Checklist

Use this list to polish your song to a brilliant shine.

Make certain that your song has the competitive strength it needs to muscle its way into a publisher's office and onto the radio. Use this checklist to give it a final "whole song" polish. The numbers that follow each question refer to Shortcuts where you can find more information.

Structure
1. Are you using a time-tested song structure? (24–26)
2. Are your sections clearly defined? (21, 22)
3. Are your transitions fresh and interesting? (32)

Lyrics
1. Do you have a single, clear theme or situation? (36–38, 69)
2. Do you have a strong title? Is it defined in your chorus? (39–43, 51)
3. Does your lyric develop over the length of the song? (52–55)
4. Are your "key lines" strong? (56)
5. Are you using fresh images, details, and action words so your listener can visualize what's happening? (57–62)

Melody
1. Have you given listeners enough melodic variety to keep them interested and enough repetition to be memorable? (78, 88)
2. Do you have melodic contrast between sections? (80, 81)
3. Are you building tension and releasing it effectively? (79)
4. Is your chorus melody a real ear-grabber? (82, 83)

Genre
1. Are you within the lyric and melodic style of your genre? (117)
2. Are your chords and groove in the genre you're targeting? (109, 112)

> *Use the lyric, melody, and structure Shortcuts to help you answer YES to all these questions.*

When you can answer "yes" to the questions on this checklist, you know you've got a song with plenty of commercial potential and listener appeal. Take it out and show it off!

Do It Now

If you have a song that you feel is close to being complete, run through this checklist and make sure you've given it everything it needs to be competitive.

Shortcut #117

Aim Your Song at a Specific Genre

Even up the odds by standing out at fitting in.

Like ice cream, songs come in different flavors: strawberry, chocolate, peach, and rocky road. And, like ice cream flavors, there are very real differences between the four mainstream music genres—Country, Pop, Rock, and R&B/Soul—and each one appeals to a different audience.

Throughout this book, I've suggested that you listen to hit songs *in a genre you're interested in.* Usually this will be the genre you like to listen to and I recommend you aim for that. You're going to be spending a lot of time with this music style, so make sure it's a "flavor" you enjoy.

Why write in a genre?

Listeners expect to hear the kind of music they came for!

When you tune into a radio station that plays Country music, you expect to hear a range of songs that share a certain sound. If you switch to a Jazz station, you expect to hear something that sounds different from the Country music station and you certainly will. Today's radio stations need to keep listeners happy if they want them to stick around. If listeners are expecting hit songs with a Country sound, that's what the station has to play.

If you write a Country song but throw in some Jazz chords, you might get airplay on a few eclectic NPR stations but mainstream, hit-driven Country radio will be very wary. Their listeners might be put off by a sound they aren't expecting to hear.

Get to know your genre

In this book, you have all the tools you need to explore the genre in which you want to write. Hit songwriters in every contemporary mainstream genre use the Shortcuts described in this book to reach their listeners. *How* they use them is what gives each genre its particular flavor. For instance, the R&B/Soul genre tends to feature plenty of melodic syncopation, much more than the Country genre. However, it's an important tool in *both* genres and you need to know *how* it's used in your particular genre.

Explore these elements in hit songs in your genre

To become familiar with the characteristics of your genre, listen to hit songs in that style and try to answer the questions on this list. (Check the Song List on page 265 for a list of songs in the four mainstream genres.)

➢ **What to look for in the lyrics**
What themes are featured?
What kind of language is used: direct, slangy, poetic?
Are there a lot of examples, concrete images, and details?
How are situations developed? Do we know a lot or a little?
What sorts of characters turn up in these songs, including the singer?

➢ **What to look for in the melody**
How much contrast is being used between sections?
What kind of contrast: Pace? Note range?
How is tension being built? How much tension is used?
How much repetition is used and where?
Is there a lot of syncopation or a little?
What beats do phrases start on? Is there a mix of phrase lengths?

➢ **What to look for in the structure**
What is the predominant song structure in your genre?
Are there other structures?

➢ **What to look for in the chords**
Do you hear the basic songwriter chords primarily?
What other kinds of chords are being played?
How much chord repetition do you hear?
How frequently are the chords changing?

➢ **What to look for in the groove**
Does this genre feature duple or quadruple grooves?
Do the tempos generally feel slow, medium, or fast?
Does the groove have a "swing" feel?

Important! Use enough genre characteristics to fit into a radio format.

The answers to these questions will open the door into your genre. No one wants to sound *exactly* like everyone else but you do want your song to incorporate enough of a genre's characteristic sound so that it will fit comfortably into a radio format.

Do It Now

1. If you don't know what genre you're interested in, use the Song List on page 265 to find songs you like in a specific genre. Or, check out the music charts and listen to songs on each of them until you find ones that interest you. See "Shortcut Resources" on page 261 to find out more about how to do that.

2. Go through several recent hits in your genre and answer the questions about lyrics, melody, structure, and chords listed in this Shortcut. Use this information when you're writing your own songs.

See "Shortcut Resources" on page 261 for information on where to find current music charts, hit songs, lyrics, and legal downloads.

Shortcut #118

Use a Ghost Song as a Genre Guide

Use a hit song to study the characteristics of your genre.

What genre are you writing in—Rock, Country, Pop, or R&B/Soul? These are the four main melodic genres. Maybe you're not sure yet. Perhaps you're thinking of writing in more than one of these genres. The best way to get to know a genre is to study hit songs in that style … up close and personal. And the best way to do that is to use hit songs as ghost songs to practice getting the feel of the lyric, melodic, chord, and rhythmic styles that create the characteristic sound of each genre, the sound that fans want to hear.

To choose a ghost song, listen to recent hit songs in the style you're interested in studying. Look for a song that has a clear structure and a strong chorus melody with a memorable hook. You're going to be spending time learning and working with this song so be sure to choose one you like.

 *The lyric and melody of the hit song are protected by copyright. This exercise is for practice only.*

If you don't find any songs you like among recent hits in a given genre—say, within the last five years—then consider looking at a different genre. In order to write songs that will get radio airplay in the current music market, you need to use several of the elements that characterize today's hits. Don't try to single-handedly change the sound of a genre to something you think is better; be creative but stay within the general sound!

Once you've chosen a ghost song, follow the steps in Shortcut 2 to use it as a guide for writing a new song. As you go through the steps, pay special attention to those elements that give your genre its characteristic sound. Shortcut 117 has a list of questions that will help you identify and define these characteristic elements.

Do It Now

Listen to recent hits songs in the genre you're interested in. Choose a song to use as a ghost song and write a new melody and lyric of your own. Pay special attention to the lyric, melodic, chord, and rhythmic styles that characterize this genre and set it apart from others.

See "Shortcut Resources" on page 261 for information on where to find current music charts, hit songs, lyrics, and legal downloads.

Shortcut #119

Let Your Song
Tell the Producer What to Do

The song takes the lead when it comes to production.

"The arrangement will give my chorus more punch!" "I can make that verse more interesting in the demo." "Background vocals will give me the feel I'm looking for." You'll get better results from your songwriting if you avoid this kind of thinking.

Of course demo production can add dimension and energy to a song; we hear it all the time in hit songs ... as well as those songs that tank. Production is no guarantee that your song will be a hit. The reason why production works so effectively in hit songs is this: *It is supporting what the song is doing already.* The big dynamic build, contrast between sections, and feeling of forward momentum are all put there by the songwriter. The producer uses that information to create a road map for the arrangement.

Production can add strength to your song by supporting what you write!

In the Dance and Rap genres where the arrangement is created first, complete with beats, riffs, and even chord progression, the songwriter's challenge is to make it sound *as if* the track is supporting the song! Writing a melody with dynamic changes and contrast between sections is a real challenge in these genres. Use variations in note range, pace, and phrasing to help you accomplish this. (See Shortcuts 79–88, 92, and 95.)

When both song and production are working together, they create an effect that's greater than either of them can achieve alone. Don't rely solely on production to fix problems with your song. If the demo has to do all the work or even fight the song to create dynamics and excitement, you'll have a tough time competing with those songs that have everything working together.

Do It Now

Check out a few hit songs. Notice how the production supports what the melody and lyrics are doing in terms of contrast and dynamic builds.

See "Shortcut Resources" on page 261 for information on where to find current music charts, hit songs, lyrics, and legal downloads.

Shortcut #120

Collaborate to Add Energy and Strength

Even a good songwriter can benefit from collaboration.

Every couple of months I check the hit songs in various radio formats. One of the things I find consistently is that many of the top hit songs are collaborations. In the Country format frequently *all* of the top ten songs are collaborations; the same goes for the Urban Contemporary (R&B/Soul) format. Rock is dominated by band and producer collaborations. Only the Hot AC (Pop) format, with its focus on singer-songwriters, lists more solo songwriters than collaborations.

Even if you have strengths as both a lyric and melody writer, you can gain a big advantage by working with a collaborator. It's no coincidence that most hit songs are collaborations.

Even if you're a good songwriter, a collaborator can add focus, fresh ideas, and energy.

- A collaborator gives you new ideas and input to react to.

- If you get married to a line that isn't working, a collaborator can point it out and keep the song moving forward. The collaborator is probably not as in love with the line as you are.

- Working with a collaborator gives you added motivation and a goal to meet.

- A collaborator contributes knowledge and experience.

- Chances are you're stronger in one area (lyrics or music) than another. A collaborator can add strength where you are weak.

Where to find collaborators

School music departments: The easiest way to find a collaborator is to use the resources that are already available to you. If you're in school or if there's a college or university in your area, check out the music department. Post a "Song Collaborator Wanted" notice on the bulletin board. Include the genre in which you're interested and a way to contact you.

Local music stores: Many music stores offer music lessons. They may have teachers and students who are interested in songwriting. Ask to speak to a teacher who gives guitar or piano lessons and tell him or her you are looking for a song collaborator.

Clubs and music venues: You can find potential collaborators at clubs in your area. Look for a performer or band whose style you like and introduce yourself. They'll probably tell you they write all their own material and don't need a collaborator, but don't let that stop you. Explain that you want to pitch the songs to publishers and mention that this could open up new writing avenues for them.

The Internet: You don't have to limit yourself to songwriters in your area; the Internet makes long distance collaboration easy. Do your research. Look for established Web sites with forums where songwriters meet to share songs, get feedback, and find collaborators. Spend some time getting to know the regular contributors. Listen to their songs, especially their collaborations. When you find someone you think would make a good collaborator, go ahead and contact him or her.

How to collaborate

There's no "right way" to collaborate; there are as many ways to write a song together as there are songwriters. Talk to your collaborator to see what's comfortable for each of you. Do you want to work together in the same room batting around ideas? Or will one of you provide a rough lyric then let the other work on it awhile and share the results?

Work in a way that feels comfortable and creative for both of you.

Discuss how you'll work as soon as you get started. Commit to a general timeline and keep to it. Be sure to keep your appointments to meet whether in person, on the phone, or online.

Here are a couple of things to keep in mind:

If you write lyrics ... Give your collaborator as much information as you can about what you hear in your head. If you hear a rhythm or melody along with your lyric, record a rough vocal version while clapping along to indicate the beat. Your collaborator may or may not use it but at least you'll communicate what you have in mind.

If you write melody ... Be sure your melody has a clear, well-defined song structure so the lyricist doesn't have to guess where the chorus or verses begin! You can indicate the verse and chorus by recording a vocal label if needed but it should be obvious from just listening to the melody.

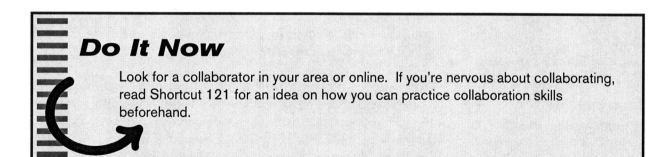

Do It Now

Look for a collaborator in your area or online. If you're nervous about collaborating, read Shortcut 121 for an idea on how you can practice collaboration skills beforehand.

Shortcut #121

Practice Collaborating
With a Ghost Song

Nervous about collaborating? Get some practice.

The thought of collaborating makes a lot of people uncomfortable. Nobody likes to let someone else see their unpolished ideas, their raw beginnings, or the emotions with the rough edges. A good way to get past this resistance is to practice collaborating. But how can you do that without a collaborator?

Use a ghost song to practice collaborating

When you write a new lyric to a ghost song melody, in essence you are collaborating with the songwriter who wrote that melody. It's as if a hit songwriter gave you a melody and said, "Here, write a lyric to this." A similar thing happens when you write a new melody to a ghost song chord progression or when you create a new melody to a ghost song lyric. In each case, there is pre-existing material with which you're expected to work, just as there would be with a collaborator. It's good practice!

➢ **Write lyrics to a ghost song melody**
   1. Choose a hit song in the genre you're interested in (see the Song List on page 265 for some suggestions). Make sure the song has a clearly defined structure and a melody that appeals to you. Remember, if a collaborator gives you a melody you don't like, you don't have to write that song with them. Politely decline and move on to another song.

   2. Follow the steps for writing a new lyric to a ghost song melody in Shortcut 73.

➢ **Write a melody to a ghost song lyric**
   1. If you're going to be creating a melody to an existing ghost song lyric, look for a hit song with a clearly defined structure and a lyric that is well written. If a collaborator gives you a lyric you feel is weak, you can either suggest a rewrite or move on to another song.

   2. Write out the ghost song lyric on a sheet of paper. Read through the chorus several times, speaking the words with honest, direct emotion. This will help you find the rhythm and pitch that *naturally* occur when the words are spoken. To get started on your chorus melody, exaggerate this natural rhythm and pitch. Look for places where the words suggest a repeated rhythm pattern in the melody. Use Shortcut 76 to find out more about how to turn an existing lyric into a melody.

(!) *The lyric and melody of the hit song are protected by copyright. This exercise is for practice only.*

Shortcut #122

Make Your Song Coverable: Melody
Make the artist sound good. Give radio what it needs.

If you're not going to record your song yourself, then getting your song recorded by a successful artist—getting a cover—is your goal. You want to be sure your song has a melody that will attract artists and appeal to radio. Before you record that final demo, listen carefully to your melody and make sure it has "artist friendly" and "radio's gonna love me" written all over it.

Check the note range of your melody

The note range of your melody refers to the distance between the lowest and highest notes of your song. It doesn't matter where they occur; the singer is going to have to hit both.

The key to a coverable song: Make your melody appealing to artists and radio!

You can count on most singers having a range of ten to eleven notes. This is their comfort zone. Many can go one or two notes beyond that for a moment, but if it's outside of their comfortable range, don't ask them to hold a high note with strength for several beats. Few singers like to max out their voices. They want to keep something in reserve, making the audience feel there's plenty more where those notes came from!

Some singers like Celine Dion, Josh Groban, and Mariah Carey have much larger ranges and, at times, you can take advantage of that in your melody. Be aware, however, that it may limit the singers to whom you can pitch your song.

Make the singer sound goooooooood!

If you're writing for a particular artist, study the songs he or she has already recorded. Write down the lowest note and highest note in each song. Look for areas of strength and weakness in the note range. Emphasize the former and play down the latter. Note anything about this artist's range that characterizes his or her unique sound.

Ask yourself what vocal tricks this artist likes to use: Voice breaks are a popular device among many singer-songwriters (a quick leap between chest and head voice), does this artist use that technique? If it's a male artist, does he like to use falsetto? Does the singer do well with fast-paced melodies or does he prefer to stretch out and soar? Tailor your melody to this artist's preferences.

Give your melody radio appeal

Many recording artists can write their own album cuts—the eight to ten songs that comprise most of a record. However, hit songs with plenty of radio appeal are a different matter. Artists are open to recording someone else's song if it will increase their chances of getting radio airplay.

Use the melody Shortcuts to help you write a coverable song.

Use the Shortcuts in this book to give your song the kind of melody radio likes to hear. Changes in dynamic levels keep audiences interested and involved (see Shortcut 79). A well-organized melody is easy to remember (Shortcut 95). Save something special for your chorus, whether it's a high note that's not used anywhere else in the song or an unexpected twist that leads to the payoff line (Shortcut 94). Pay special attention to your hook; make certain it's catchy and memorable (Shortcut 83).

These are qualities that appeal to radio audiences. If you've written a melody that sounds like it has the potential for radio airplay, you have a good chance of attracting an artist to your song.

Do It Now

1. Look for these melody techniques in hit songs in your genre.

2. Check through the melodies in your own songs to see if you can give them more artist and radio appeal with some rewriting.

See "Shortcut Resources" on page 261 for information on where to find current music charts, hit songs, lyrics, and legal downloads.

Shortcut #123

Make Your Song Coverable: Lyrics

Keep your lyric conversational and appropriate for the artist.

A little reworking of your lyric before you record your final demo may mean the difference between a song that languishes in your back catalogue and one that gets snapped up by a publisher who just knows she can get a successful artist to record it, in other words, get a *cover* of your song.

Use conversational language

A singer needs to sound believable. Like an actor, he has to convince the audience that every line just occurred to him and it comes straight from the heart. Daughtry doesn't want his listeners thinking, "Gee, what a clever line that was. Those songwriters are really good." So, even when you're using vivid imagery in your lyric, keep the surrounding words conversational and use a word order that sounds natural.

Keep your language appropriate for the singer

Choose vocabulary words and phrases that reflect the age, background, and education of the singer as he or she is portrayed in the song. Make sure your singer sounds *convincing*. If you're writing for the Teen Pop genre, avoid a literary word like "immeasurable" or a phrase like "You're a real kick in the pants." This is not contemporary-sounding language for this age group; it will sound false coming from a young teen. Listeners will immediately mistrust the singer and then you've lost the emotional link between the listeners and the singer that's so important to the success of your song.

Make sure the singer sounds believable. Use language that is natural and appropriate.

Don't fall back on cliché language that you *think* sounds right. Do your homework! In the case of Teen Pop, get on the Internet where these kids are blogging. Watch Disney Channel and Nickelodeon shows that appeal to young teens. Immerse yourself in the hit songs in this genre. The same advice holds true for the Country, Rock, and Pop genres. Use appropriate language. *If you don't know your audience well, do your research!*

Create a character the audience can relate to

In your song, give the singer the kind of interests, relationships, and age range the genre's audience can relate to. Of course you don't have to state all of this directly in your lyric; you can imply it. It doesn't take Sherlock Holmes to figure out a number of important things about the singer in the Brad Paisley's Country hit "Mud On the Tires": a. he has a steady job; b. he doesn't earn much money at his job; and c. he likes to be out in nature. The audience is told all of this indirectly via the images and style of language in the lyric. (How did Sherlock do it? a. The bank was willing to make a loan, b. he couldn't pay cash for the car; c. he knows how to use a trotline and what time the sun sets.)

Look at the character the artist or genre likes to project

Whether you're writing for a specific recording artist or aiming at a wider target like a genre, look at how the artists in that genre generally portray themselves. In the Hard Rock genre, for example, many artists project a very dark persona. If you're not comfortable with writing for that persona, you may want to reconsider working in this genre or be prepared to look for another approach this audience can trust and identify with.

In the Country genre, today's big stars like to portray themselves as honest and capable of strong feelings, but also ready to have a good time. You'll want to avoid writing a lyric that shows the singer in a bad light—no lying or cheating on the singer's part unless you've got an angle that might justify it. When Carrie Underwood sings about trashing her boyfriend's car, the songwriters make sure we understand she has a very good reason!

Tongue twisters and misheard lines

Stay away from tongue twisters!

1. Watch out for writing tongue twisters! Singers hate them, especially if they're going to sing your song on stage. A line like "She sees such sense …" is going to kill a singer! And it may also kill your chance for a cover.

2. Avoid clever twists that are only understandable when you see the word written down. For instance, a hook phrase might be "I'm making a You-Turn." Listeners who don't see this written down, will assume the lyric is using the more common "u-turn" and your clever twist will be lost.

3. Be careful about lyrics that can be misheard. There are many famous examples, so obviously it happens, even in hit songs: "rock the casbah" sounds like "rob the cat box," "kiss the sky" sounds like "kiss this guy." Of course, you can't avoid all of these—people are going to hear what they're going to hear—but try rewording lines like these to make them clearer.

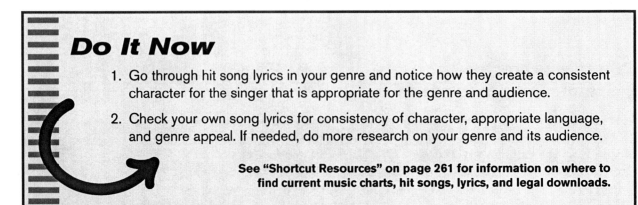

Do It Now

1. Go through hit song lyrics in your genre and notice how they create a consistent character for the singer that is appropriate for the genre and audience.

2. Check your own song lyrics for consistency of character, appropriate language, and genre appeal. If needed, do more research on your genre and its audience.

See "Shortcut Resources" on page 261 for information on where to find current music charts, hit songs, lyrics, and legal downloads.

Shortcut #124

Say "Goodbye" to Writer's Block

*Identify and solve the problem so you can
keep rolling forward.*

At one point in my career, I had to write three to four songs a week for a television series. Writer's block was simply not an option If I failed to turn in my songs on time, the show came to a swift and expensive stop. Early on, I learned an important lesson: *Writer's block is not about a lack of creativity; it's about identifying and solving a problem so you can get on with things.*

Problem 1: Getting started

There are few things more intimidating than starting a song. Maybe all you have is an idea or a theme and every time you think about getting to work on it, you feel overwhelmed. Try breaking down the initial process into a series of steps and do them one at a time.

To get past writer's block, solve the problem! Don't blame your creativity.

1. Start by finding a title you're interested in. If you don't have one already, use Shortcuts 40 through 43 to help you find one.

2. Find the questions suggested by the title. Then create the raw material for your lyric by making lists of related and contrasting images and phrases. See Shortcut 44 for more on the title questions and Shortcut 45 for creating the word lists.

3. Decide on a song structure and make a rough sketch of your lyric development, so you have an idea of what you want to say in each section. Check out Shortcuts 28 and 29 to help you with structure and Shortcut 47 to show you how to sketch out your song.

4. Rough out a chorus lyric. To get your melody started, use the pitch and rhythm of the spoken lyric. Shortcut 76 can walk you through this process. Read through the chorus and verse melody Shortcuts (Shortcuts 82 through 87) for more ideas on how to develop your melody.

Problem 2: Fear of failure

Not sure whether you're making the "right" choices? Hate all your ideas? Nothing seems to be working? Second-guessing yourself by constantly wondering if your song is any good? Try putting this song on hold for a little while. You're not wasting time; you'll be coming back armed to the teeth with confidence and new ideas!

Strive to be good—not perfect!

Check out Shortcut 2 in the "Quick Start Manual" at the beginning of this book. It will show you how to use an existing hit song as a foundation on which to practice building new songs of your own. Go through the process one or two times. Aim for a rough lyric and melody when working with a ghost song. You don't need to spend time polishing and reworking your lines. Take a few chances. Loosen up. Throw out what doesn't work and keep what does. Try the "sandbox" approach (see Shortcut 17). When you return to working on your own song, hold onto this attitude. "Audition" new ideas. Choose a Shortcut at random and apply it to your song just to see what will happen. If you don't like the result, back up and try something else.

Don't let your inner critic spoil the fun.

Sometimes your inner critic can be the problem, jumping in too soon, criticizing everything you do before it's had a chance to develop. Check out Shortcut 15 for games you can play that will give your creativity a chance to thrive.

Problem 3: Lack of clarity and focus

While you're writing, a great lyric line occurs to you that you just *have* to use. Be careful; it may be a line that doesn't belong in the song you're currently working on! By trying to force it into your lyric, you could be creating a problem you can't solve and, as a result, end up blocking further development of your song. Try giving your creativity some guidance—read Shortcut 70 to find out how.

In a similar way, an inspired melody line can lead you away from your core melodic rhythm patterns and into trouble. Go through your melody and identify the repeated melodic rhythm phrases. If your new melody line is unlike any of the others, it may belong in a different section of the song—the bridge, perhaps—or a different song altogether. Record it and put it aside until you determine where it belongs. Then return to your core ideas and keep working. See Shortcut 95 for more ideas on organizing your melodic rhythm patterns.

Whenever you feel blocked, go through the Shortcuts and look for ideas to audition. Choose a course of action and keep going. And remember to give your song (and yourself) permission to be a work-in-progress!

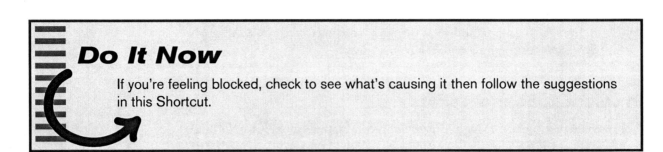

Do It Now

If you're feeling blocked, check to see what's causing it then follow the suggestions in this Shortcut.

Shortcut #125

Don't Learn to Take Rejection.
Get Better!

Strengthen your songs and make them competitive.

Fact of Life: You love your songs and you're only human. These two things guarantee that it's going to hurt when someone rejects your song.

So, am I going to tell you to toughen up and live with it? *No!* Instead of accepting the idea that rejection is going to make your life miserable, *make your songs better!*

When you know you've got the goods, rejection is a lot easier to handle. It can even be useful. Sure it will still bother you, but if your songs are competitive—well constructed, contemporary, and emotionally effective—then, like an athlete, you can lose a race but still know you've got what it takes to win the next one. It's that knowledge that will protect you from the dangers of rejection.

When you know you've written a competitive song, rejection loses a lot of its sting.

When is rejection harmful?

Rejection is harmful when it reinforces your own insecurities and mistaken beliefs. It does the greatest damage…

- If you're not sure whether you have talent.
- If you're guessing what the industry wants.
- If you think your song is perfect but no one else recognizes it.
- If you believe pitching your songs is like playing the lottery.
- If you're clinging to an outdated style because you believe it's your authentic voice.
- If you think what comes out of you spontaneously is a completed song that can't be changed.

In these instances, you may feel overwhelmed, confused, or take up a defensive posture. Don't let that happen. It doesn't help you grow as an artist or move forward with your career. Worse yet, it may cause you to keep your songs to yourself.

When can rejection be helpful?

Rejection can be a big help when it spurs you to work harder and move closer to your goal. For example …

- If it makes you ask the publisher or producer what they're looking for.
- If it sends you back to study the hits in your genre.
- If it encourages you to practice your rewriting skills.

- If it gives you direction for future songs.

- If it encourages you to go through the Shortcuts in this book to help you add strength to your song.

"If I wrote a hit song, I wouldn't need to deal with rejection."

Success is never a cure. Don't think that if you write a hit song it will make rejection easier to take. In fact, if you don't know how you wrote that hit, it can make rejection even more painful. All successful songwriters have to deal with rejection. It's *how* you deal with it that can help you carve out a successful career.

Do It Now

Use the Shortcuts in this book to help you write a song. Combine the melodic and lyric techniques of recent hit songs with a theme that has emotional resonance for you.

Shortcut #126

What About Songwriting Talent?

Talent can be a deceptive notion. Don't fall for it!

Talent is something we all wonder about. "Do I have it?" "Have I got enough?" "Has someone else got more than I do?" We make assumptions about our own talent. "If I had talent, this would be easier." "If I had more talent I would be further along in my career." Or: "I have talent; why don't publishers and record labels recognize it?"

What is talent?

Talent is something we all wish we had more of, but do we ever stop to think about what it really *is?* Talent simply refers to an innate ability to grasp or master something more quickly than others. Someone with a talent for languages, for example, can learn to speak a foreign language much faster than I can. It doesn't mean I can't learn a language; I just won't learn it as quickly.

When it comes to songwriting, to answer questions like "Do I have talent?" or "Have I got enough talent?" you first need to ask a different question: A talent for what? What talent or talents do you think you need to be a hit songwriter? A talent for writing words that flow well with a melody? A talent for writing words that express emotion? A talent for writing melodies that sound familiar yet have fresh twists? All of these are *skills*. You can learn them by studying song craft, particularly by analyzing good songs.

Talent is the ability to master a thing faster than other people can.

Yes, there are people who are born with the ability to soak up song craft like a sponge. Often they (and we) don't even realize that's what they're doing; they just seem to "get it." However, they often excel in a particular area of song craft, while other areas are just as difficult for them as for the rest of us. *Talent never solves all problems.*

Take the time you need to hone your skills and don't waste time thinking about how fast or how easily the other guy is writing. You have no idea what that other songwriter is dealing with, what pitfalls he or she will stumble into, or how much work it really took to write that hit song.

Is it talent or hard work?

A dozen inexperienced songwriters have pointed out to me that Sting woke up in the middle of the night and wrote "Every Breath You Take" in 30 minutes, pointing to this as a model of talent and inspiration. It only takes a moment of reflection to realize that, while Sting is certainly talented, that song actually took 30 minutes plus five albums and six years of constant recording and touring to write!

The only talent you really need to have is the ability to recognize emotional truth. That's the only thing you can't learn from studying song craft. I can't teach it to you and I don't believe anyone else can. If you have that one thing, you can learn the rest!

Do It Now

Look through the shortcuts in this book. Which ones have you started using instinctively on your own? Which ones do you feel you learned easily? These are the areas where you have innate talent. Choose a couple of Shortcuts that you think may be difficult for you. Focus on improving your skills in one of them. Spend extra time on that one. Do the "Do It Now" exercise a few times. Once you've done that, everyone else will think you have a special talent for it! (You don't have to tell them you worked at it.)

Shortcut Resources

I. Learn from current hit songs

➤ **Use the Song List on page 265**
The Song List consists of 36 songs arranged by genre—Pop, Rock, Country, and R&B/Soul. Buy a few of the songs you're interested in, read the Shortcuts, and get familiar with how these songs work. Updates to the Song List can be found at www.RobinFrederick.com.

➤ **Use radio airplay charts**
To keep up with current hit songs, consult the radio airplay charts. These charts reflect the amount of national radio airplay a song is receiving. Since hit songs get a lot of airplay, this is a quick and easy way to find them.

In radio, music genres are grouped into *formats*. Airplay charts are based on radio station formats rather than music genres. See the sidebar for a list of music genres and the radio formats that play them. You can find radio airplay charts here:

Nielsen BDSradio – www.bdsradio.com
(Under "Select format here" choose a format from the menu.) Currently you do not need to register or log in to see these charts. For more information on BDS Radio's services: 323-817-1508

Radio-Info – www.radio-info.com
(Under "Programming" click on "Formats & Charts." These are the same charts you'll find at BDSradio.com.) This web site is a good source of information about the world of radio airplay.

Yahoo! Music – www.music.yahoo.com
(Click on "Artists," select "Charts," then click on "Songs." Not sorted by format.)

➤ **Buy the hit songs you want to study**
When you find a hit song on the music charts you want to study or hear something on the radio that grabs your attention, go to a legal download site and buy it. Hit songs are also available on CD, either as complete albums or CD singles.

iTunes – www.apple.com/itunes
The iTunes player is a free software download. Hit songs are available for purchase through the iTunes player. (Supports both Mac and PC.)

Radio charts use "formats" instead of genres. Some of the common formats are:

Genre: Pop
Formats: AC & Hot AC
(Adult Contemporary)

Genre: Country
Format: Country

Genre: R&B/Soul
Formats: Urban
 Urban AC
 Hot R&B/Hip-Hop

Genre: Rock
Formats: Rock
 Alternative
 Modern Rock
 Triple A

Amazon.com – www.amazon.com
Amazon offers mp3 downloads of top selling albums and songs.

Rhapsody – http://mp3.rhapsody.com
Mp3 downloads can be purchased at mp3.rhapsody.com. Up to 25 full-length songs per month can be streamed for free. Monthly paid subscriptions allow unlimited streaming. (Web services are available for PC and Mac. Software application for PC only.)

Napster – www.napster.com
Songs are available for purchase as mp3 downloads. There's also an option to stream full length songs. (Web services support both PC and Mac. Software application for PC only.)

➤ **Find hit song lyrics**
While song lyrics are available online, most Web sites that carry them don't have publisher permission and do not pay for the use of the lyrics. However, there are sites that do offer lyrics legally.

> *Yahoo! Music* – http://music.yahoo.com/lyrics

> *AOL Music* – http://music.aol.com/lyrics

➤ **Find hit song chords**
The best way to learn song chords is to listen and learn the chords by ear. If the song is complicated or you can't figure out the chords, look for a "fake book" or sheet music with chords. Fake books, available online and at most large bookstores, tend to rely on older hits so, for the latest hit songs, try a Web site that offers sheet music downloads.

> *MusicNotes.com* - www.musicnotes.com

> *Sheet Music Plus* – www.sheetmusicplus.com

➤ **Use a chord finder**
If you need help figuring out how to play a chord on guitar or keyboard, here are some useful online resources.

Online:
> *Guitar* – www.chordbook.com (Click on "Guitar Chords.")

> *Keyboard* – www.gootar.com/piano

Books:
> *Guitar Chord Encyclopedia* – Steve Hall

> *The Keyboardist's Picture Chord Encyclopedia* – Leonard Vogler

➢ **Type in the chords**
   If you don't play an instrument, here are two resources that will create an arrangement and play it for you. All you have to do is type the chords.

   Band-in-a-Box® – www.pgmusic.com

   JamStudio – www.jamstudio.com

II. Get support for writing your original songs

➢ **Rhyming dictionaries and thesauruses**
   These tools can come in handy but, if overused, can add a stilted, unnatural feel to your lyric. It's a good idea to stick with conversational words and rhymes (see Shortcut 64).

   Online:
   RhymeZone.com - www.rhymezone.com
   An easy-to-use, online rhyming dictionary.

   WikiRhymer - www.wikirhymer.com
   Type in the word you want to rhyme and this free Web rhymer will give you hundreds of vowel rhymes. Look for conversational rhymes or words that suggest creative ideas.

   Thesaurus.com - www.thesaurus.com
   Search for synonyms for a word. Click on the results to explore more words.

   Books:
   The Complete Rhyming Dictionary – Clement Wood
      & Ronald Bogus
   This is the granddaddy of all rhyming dictionaries and still useful.

   The Essential Songwriter's Rhyming Dictionary –
      Kevin M. Mitchell
   A small-format book that features frequently used, conversational words.

   Roget's Thesaurus
   There are many editions of *Roget's Thesaurus*.
   Choose the one that works best for you.

➢ **Music instruction**
   Take a few lessons with a teacher to get started, then check out these books and DVDs.

   Keyboard:
   Mel Bay's You Can Teach Yourself Piano Chords
      – Per Danielsson (book and DVD)

   How to Play from a Fake Book (Keyboard Ed.) – Blake Neely
      (book)

Guitar:
> *Fender Presents: Getting Started on Acoustic Guitar*
– Keith Wyatt (DVD)

> *Hal Leonard Guitar Method, Complete Edition* –
Will Schmid & Greg Koch (CD)

➤ **Music software**
Whether you're creating a rough demo of a song idea or looking for a rhythm loop to keep a groove going while you write your song, you'll find a choice of music software programs to fit your needs and your budget. Take some time to explore what these software programs can do by visiting their Web sites and reading reviews. Many offer free downloadable demos.

Entry-level software:
> *Garageband® (Mac)* – www.apple.com/ilife/garageband

> *Acid® Music Studio* or *Acid Xpress (PC)* –
www.acidplanet.com

> *RealBand®* – www.pgmusic.com

Advanced software:
> *Reason®* – www.propellerheads.se

> *Logic®* – www.apple.com/logicstudio

> *Sonar™* – www.cakewalk.com

> *Pro Tools®* – www.digidesign.com

> *Digital Performer®* – www.motu.com/products/software

> *Cubase®* – www.steinberg.net/en/products/musicproduction.html

> *Ableton Live™* – www.ableton.com/live

> *FL Studio™* – www.flstudio.com

➤ **Strengthen your voice**
Even if you're not thinking of performing the songs you write, vocal ability can be helpful, enabling you to communicate your melody ideas to a collaborator or demo producer and make rough demos as you write.

> *Singing for the Stars* – Seth Riggs and John Carratello (Book & CD)

> *Voice Lessons to Go* – Ariella Vaccarino (Book & CD series)

Song List:
Recent Hits in the Four Mainstream Genres

These songs are available for purchase on CDs or at legal download sites.

TITLE	GENRE FORMAT	ARTIST (SONGWRITERS)	USED IN SHORTCUTS
Better as a Memory	Country Country	Kenny Chesney (Carusoe/Goodman)	21, 24, 28, 92
Bless the Broken Road	Country Country	Rascal Flats (Boyd/Hanna/Hummon)	36, 75, 88, 94, 96
In a Real Love	Country Country	Phil Vassar (Vassar/Wiseman)	36, 85, 93
Live Like You Were Dying	Country Country	Tim McGraw (Nichols/Wiseman)	25, 31, 36, 50, 54, 62
Love Me If You Can	Country Country	Toby Keith (Wallin/Wiseman)	48, 51, 79, 85, 112, 113
Mud On the Tires	Country Country	Brad Paisley (Du Bois/Paisley)	21, 48, 58, 61, 68, 83, 123
Somebody Like You	Country Country	Keith Urban (Shanks/Urban)	24, 28, 36, 64, 80, 85, 87
What Hurts the Most	Country Country	Rascal Flatts (Robson/Steele)	21, 26, 36, 49, 78, 83, 86, 108
What Was I Thinkin'	Country Country	Dierks Bentley (Beavers/Bentley/Ruttan)	84, 86, 96, 111
You're Gonna Miss This	Country Country	Trace Adkins (Gorley/Miller)	27, 48, 50, 87, 108, 112

Breakaway	Pop AC	Kelly Clarkson (Benenate/Gerrard/Lavigne)	27, 33, 36, 52, 74, 90
Complicated	Pop AC/Hot AC	Avril Lavigne (Alspach/Edwards/Fownes/Lavigne/Spock)	32, 49, 83, 95
Ever the Same	Pop AC	Rob Thomas (Rob Thomas)	33, 36, 60, 62, 65, 85, 87
First Time	Pop AC/Hot AC	Lifehouse (Cole/Wade)	28, 36, 75, 80, 93
How Far We've Come	Pop Hot AC	Matchbox Twenty (Cook/Doucette/Thomas/Yale)	21, 32, 36, 50, 92
It's Not Over	Pop AC/Hot AC	Daughtry (Daughtry/Wattenberg/Wilkerson/Young)	21, 50, 78, 83, 84, 94
Over My Head (Cable Car)	Pop AC/Hot AC	The Fray (King/Slade)	32, 83, 113
Pieces of Me	Pop AC	Ashlee Simpson (DioGuardi/Shanks/Simpson)	33, 80, 112

GENRE FORMAT	TITLE	ARTIST (SONGWRITERS)	USED IN SHORTCUTS
Remedy (I Won't Worry)	Pop AC/Hot AC	Jason Mraz *(Alspach/Edwards/Fownes/Mraz/Spock)*	31, 36, 79, 81, 111
Unwritten	Pop AC	Natasha Bedingfield *(Bedingfield/Brisebois/Rodrigues)*	8, 26, 36, 62, 64, 79, 86
Who Knew	Pop AC/Hot AC	P!nk *(Gottwald/Moore/Sandberg)*	28, 54, 80, 83, 85, 91, 96
You're Beautiful	Pop AC/Hot AC	James Blunt *(Blunt/Ghost/Skarbek)*	36, 79, 93, 105, 113

Be Without You	R&B/Soul Urban	Mary J. Blige *(Austin/Blige/Cox/Perry)*	92, 109
I Remember	R&B/Soul Urban	Keyshia Cole *(Cole/Curtis)*	25, 54
Irreplaceable	R&B/Soul Urban	Beyoncé *(Bjørklund/Eriksen/Hermansen/Knowles/Lind/Smith)*	27, 32, 49, 66, 91, 94
Like You'll Never See Me Again	R&B/Soul Urban	Alicia Keys *(Augello-Cook/Brothers)*	36, 38, 75, 80, 86, 93
Moving Mountains	R&B/Soul Urban	Usher *(Harrell/Nash/Stewart)*	36, 58
Take a Bow	R&B/Soul Urban	Rihanna *(Eriksen/Smith)*	32, 36, 54, 84
Truth Is	R&B/Soul Urban	Fantasia *(Cantrall/Isley, E./ Isley, M./Isley O./Isley, R./ Isley, R.B./Jasper/Karlin/Nkhereanye/Shack/Smith)*	26, 36, 48, 54, 62, 113

It's Not My Time	Rock Rock/Alternative	3 Doors Down *(Arnold, Harrell/Henderson/Roberts)*	32, 65, 112
Paralyzer	Rock Rock/Alternative	Finger Eleven *(Anderson/Anderson/Beddoe/Black/Jackett)*	26, 61, 80
Photograph	Rock Rock/Hot AC	Nickelback *(Adair/Kroeger/Peake/Turton)*	21, 36, 54, 105, 108
The Pretender	Rock Rock	Foo Fighters *(Grohl/Hawkins/Mendel/Shiflett)*	32, 48, 92, 112
Rise Above This	Rock Rock/Alternative	Seether *(Humphrey/Morgan/Stewart/Welgemoed)*	32, 36, 80, 92, 113
Someday	Rock Rock/Hot AC	Nickelback *(Kroeger/Peake/Turton/Vikedal)*	26, 32, 57, 83, 86
Vertigo	Rock Rock/Hot AC	U2 *(Clayton/Evans/Hewson/Mullen)*	27, 80, 93, 96

INDEX

middle eight, 44. *See also* bridge

momentum, 4, 152, 197–198, 229
  in groove, 235–236
  lyric development and, 115–116
  in melody, 162, 197–198
  pre-chorus and, 183
  in song structure, 54, 71
  transitions and, 54, 69–70
  weak beat emphasis and, 197–198, 235–236

"Moving Mountains" (Usher), 78, 124

Mraz, Jason, 68, 79, 170, 173, 234, 266

"Mud On the Tires" (Brad Paisley), 43, 86, 106, 123–124, 130, 253–254, 265

muse, 33–34

music instruction, 263

music software. *See* software, music

music trade publications. *See* trade publications

"My Happy Ending" (Avril Lavigne), 135, 143, 201

"My Heart Will Go On" (Celine Dion), 200

N

Napster, 262

"New Shoes" (Paolo Nutini), 79, 106, 124, 130

Nickelback, 44, 55, 69, 70, 79, 117, 122, 178, 184, 223, 228, 234, 236, 266

"No Scrubs" (TLC), 130

"Nothing Left to Lose" (Mat Kearney), 238

Nutini, Paolo, 79, 106, 124, 130

O

"Ode to Billie Joe" (Bobbie Gentry), 47

one-and-two-and-three-and-four-and, 190, 235, 237. *See also* duple feel

one-e-and-uh-two-e-and-uh-three-e-and-uh-four-e-and-uh, 236. *See also* quadruple feel

OneRepublic, 200

"1 2 3 4" (Feist), 160

"Ordinary People" (John Legend), 230

"Overjoyed" (Jars of Clay), 78

"Over My Head (Cable Car)" (The Fray), 70, 178, 237, 265

"Over the Rainbow" (Arlen, Harburg), 203–204

overthinking, 36

"Over You" (Daughtry), 71, 229

P

pace, 170, 173–174, 211

Paisley, Brad, 43, 106, 123, 130, 143, 160, 169, 178, 192, 253, 265

"Paralyzer" (Finger Eleven), 55, 130, 171, 266

pauses, 180, 191–192, 197–198
  elimination of, 197–198
  phrase-ology and, 161–162

payoff lines, 109–110, 120, 201–202, 208–209

persona, 144, 254

"Photograph" (Nickelback), 44, 79, 117, 228. 266

phrase-ology, 161–162, 211, 218

phrases, melodic, 161–162, 192–196, 201–202, 211
  phrase lengths, mixing, 175, 192–193
  starting points of, 194–196
  uses of, 162

"Pieces of Me" (Ashlee Simpson), 71, 171, 236, 265

P!nk, 60, 117, 171, 178, 181, 195, 206, 266

P.O.D., 78

poetic language, 120, 127–128, 152

Police, The, 168, 186, 188, 210, 235

Pop genre, 265–266
  chords and, 232
  chorus and, 43, 53, 175
  folk form and, 48

radio formats and, 261
tension and, 68
  See also specific songs and artists

Porter, Cole, 49, 135

post-bridge sections, 71

Powter, Daniel, 69, 105, 183

pre-chorus, 44, 54–56, 183–184, 209
  song form, 54–56
  See also lead-in lines

"Pretender, The" (Foo Fighters), 70, 106, 197, 235, 266

production, support and, 23, 46, 68, 247

progressions, chord. *See under* chords

Q

quadruple feel, 236, 237–238
  tempo and, 236

Quick Start Manual, 3–9

Quick Start Resources, 10

R

R&B/Soul genre, 266
  chords and, 228, 230–231
  note range and, 172
  quadruple feel and, 236
  radio formats and, 261
  syncopation and, 244
  tension and, 68
  See also specific songs and artists

radio, 3–4, 16, 197
  airplay charts, 3–4, 21, 261
  appeal and, 251–252
  station formats, 261

Radio & Records, 261

"Radio Nowhere" (Bruce Springsteen), 106, 124, 237

Rap genre, 144, 172, 247

Rascal Flatts, 44, 55, 78, 107, 162, 168, 183, 188, 202, 206, 229, 265

raw material, lyrics, 98–99, 102, 207

raw material, melody, 163–166, 179, 217
  rhythm and, 163–164

CPSIA information can be obtained at www.ICGtesting.com
Printed in the USA
236848LV00001B/20/P